Rhinegold Study Guides

A Student's Guide to A2 Music

for the **Edexcel** Specification
2006–2007

by

Paul Terry and David Bowman

Rhinegold Publishing Ltd
241 Shaftesbury Avenue
London WC2H 8TF
Telephone: 020 7333 1720
Fax: 020 7333 1765
www.rhinegold.co.uk

Rhinegold Study Guides
(music series editor: Paul Terry)

A Student's Guide to GCSE Music for the Edexcel Specification
Listening Tests for Students (Books 1 and 2): Edexcel GCSE Music Specification
A Student's Guide to AS Music for the Edexcel Specification
Listening Tests for Students (Books 1 and 2): Edexcel AS Music Specification
A Student's Guide to A2 Music for the Edexcel Specification
Listening Tests for Students (Books 1 and 2): Edexcel A2 Music Specification

Similar books have been produced for the AQA and OCR Music Specifications. Also available are:

A Student's Guide to GCSE Music for the WJEC Specification (separate English and Welsh language versions)
A Student's Guide to AS/A2 Music Technology for the Edexcel AS and A2 Specification
AS/A2 Listening Tests for Music Technology

The following books are designed to support all GCSE and GCE music courses:

A Student's Guide to Composing (Book 1 for GCSE and Book 2 for A-level Music)
A Student's Guide to Harmony and Counterpoint (for AS and A2 Music)

Other Rhinegold Study Guides

Students' Guides to AS and A2 Drama and Theatre Studies for the AQA and Edexcel Specifications
Students' Guides to AS and A2 Performance Studies for the OCR Specification
Students' Guides to AS and A2 Religious Studies for the AQA, Edexcel and OCR Specifications

Rhinegold Publishing also publishes Classical Music, Classroom Music, Early Music Today, Music Teacher,
Opera Now, Piano, Teaching Drama, The Singer, British and International Music Yearbook,
British Performing Arts Yearbook, Music Education Yearbook, Rhinegold Dictionary of Music in Sound.

First published 2001 in Great Britain by
Rhinegold Publishing Limited
241 Shaftesbury Avenue
London WC2H 8TF
Telephone: 020 7333 1720
Fax: 020 7333 1765
www.rhinegold.co.uk
Reprinted 2002, 2003, 2005, New Edition 2005, Reprinted 2006

You should always check the current requirements of the examination, since these may change.
Copies of the Edexcel Specification may be obtained from Edexcel Examinations at
Edexcel Publications, Adamsway, Mansfield, Notts. NG18 4FN
Telephone 01623 467467, Facsimile 01623 450481, Email publications@linneydirect.com
See also the Edexcel website at http://www.edexcel.org.uk/

A Student's Guide to A2 Music for the Edexcel Specification (2006–2007)
British Library Cataloguing in Publication Data.
A catalogue record for this book is available from the British Library.
ISBN 1-904226-87-6
Printed in Great Britain by WPG Group Ltd

La musique exprime ce qui ne peut être dit
et sur quoi il est impossible de rester silencieux.

Music expresses that which can not be said
and on which it is impossible to be silent.

Victor Hugo (1864)

Contents

The authors

Paul Terry was director of music at the City of London Freemen's School for 15 years. He currently works as a music editor, engraver and publisher. He has been a music examiner for 25 years and has worked as a consultant to various examination boards. Paul has served as a member of the Secondary Examinations Council and its successor the Schools Examinations and Assessment Council. He was chief examiner for the Oxford and Cambridge Schools Examinations Board (now part of OCR) and he was a chief examiner for London Examinations (now part of Edexcel).

Paul Terry's publications include three books on aural (all with CDs) for A-level music, and six *Student Guides* to AS and A2 Music, all written in collaboration with David Bowman (see below), and he has contributed to *Music Teacher* and *Classroom Music* magazines. He is also co-author with William Lloyd of *Music in Sequence, a complete guide to MIDI sequencing* (1991), *Classics in Sequence* (1992) and *Rock in Sequence* (1996), and also *Rehearse, Direct and Play: A Student's Guide to Group Music-Making* (1993), all published by Musonix/Music Sales.

David Bowman was for 20 years director of music at Ampleforth College and was a chief examiner for the University of London Schools Examination Board (now Edexcel) from 1982 to 1998. He now spends more time with his family, horses and dogs.

David Bowman's publications include the *London Anthology of Music* (University of London Schools Examinations Board, 1986), *Sound Matters* (co-authored with Bruce Cole, Schott, 1989), *Aural Matters, Aural Matters in Practice* and *Listening Matters* (all co-authored with Paul Terry, Schott, 1993, 1994 and 2003 respectively), *Analysis Matters* (Rhinegold, Volume 1 1997, Volume 2 1998), and six *Student Guides to AS and A2 Music* (co-authored with Paul Terry, Rhinegold, 2000 onwards). He has also written sections in a number of Rhinegold's *Student Guides to GCSE Music* and he has written numerous analytical articles for *Music Teacher*. David Bowman is a contributor to the *Collins Classical Music Encyclopedia* (2000) edited by Stanley Sadie and is author of the *Rhinegold Dictionary of Music in Sound*.

Acknowledgements

The authors would like to thank Dr Hugh Benham, Edexcel's Chair of Examiners in Music, for his expert advice so freely offered throughout the preparation of both the original edition and this new edition of the Student Guide. Nevertheless, if any errors have been made it is only right to state that these are the responsibility of the authors. We would also like to thank Dr Lucien Jenkins and Luke Harley of Rhinegold Publishing for so much help and encouragement in the preparation of the entire series of Rhinegold Study Guides.

Introduction

This book is intended to assist students preparing for the Edexcel A2 Music examination. Like other *Rhinegold Study Guides* it is intended to supplement, but not supplant, the work of teachers.

The full Advanced GCE in Music is made up of six units, three AS and three A2. This book deals only with the latter.

We have included many suggestions and tips which we hope will help you do well in performing and composing, but the main emphasis is on preparation for the paper in *Analysing music*. As part of this unit you will be extending your knowledge of **one** of the areas of study that you covered for AS *and* you will also be working on **one new** area of study.

The basic information for each of the areas of study is given in **A Student's Guide to AS Music for the Edexcel Specification** and we have not repeated those details here, so you will need to refer to the AS guide during your A2 studies.

A Student's Guide to AS Music for the Edexcel Specification (2001–2004) by Paul Terry and David Bowman. *Rhinegold Publishing Ltd.* ISBN: 0-946890-90-0.

In this book each of the chapters dealing with an area of study concentrates on the topics of 'continuity and change' and 'special focus' works that are prescribed for study in the A2 exam. The questions during the course of these chapters will help you check your understanding of the context, style and technical features of the music – they are not intended to be representative of actual exam questions. If you have difficulty with these, you will generally find the right answers by rereading the preceding pages. The sample questions in these chapters are more demanding and these should be worked under examination conditions. For examples of the questions that are likely to be encountered in the exam, you should be guided by the specimen and past papers published by Edexcel and by the Listening Tests published by Rhinegold (*see right*).

Listening Tests for Students for the Edexcel A2 Music Specification by Hugh Benham and Alistair Wightman, *Rhinegold Publishing Ltd.* Book 1 (ISBN: 1-904226-46-9) and Book 2 (ISBN 1-904226-67-1).

CDs with answer booklets are available for both volumes.

A glossary of technical terms is given at the end of the AS guide. If you need further help with terminology you encounter during the course, we recommend you consult **The Rhinegold Dictionary of Music in Sound**. This comprehensive resource not only gives detailed explanations of a wide range of musical concepts, but it also illustrates them using a large number of examples on a set of accompanying CDs.

The Rhinegold Dictionary of Music in Sound by David Bowman. *Rhinegold Publishing Ltd.* ISBN: 0-946890-87-0.

Planning is the secret of success. Initial ideas for composing are best formulated early in the course and plans for performing need to get under way as soon as possible. Preparation for the *Analysing music* unit needs to be completed in time to allow for revision and the working of complete papers in the weeks before the actual exam.

Remember that it will help enormously if you can perceive the many varied connections between the music you hear, the music you play and the music you compose. Understanding the context and structure of music will not only enhance your enjoyment when listening, but will also inform your performing and illuminate your composing. Composing, performing, listening and understanding are all related aspects of the study of music, and this integration of activities is fundamental to the Advanced GCE in Music.

A2 Music

There are three units: *Performing and composing*, *Specialist options* and *Analysing music*. The first two of these each account for 30% of the total A2 mark, while the third is weighted at 40%.

Performing and composing

There are two parts to the *Performing and composing* unit, both of which build on work you undertook for AS music:

+ an assessment of your performing during the course. For this you will need to keep a log of the pieces you have performed and then choose the best four for assessment (you must include at least one solo piece and at least one ensemble item). The work will be assessed by your teacher and the mark moderated by Edexcel (for moderation purposes a recording of one **solo** piece of performing during the course is required)

+ a timed test in compositional techniques, marked by an Edexcel examiner. For this part you will work in greater depth on **one** of the compositional techniques you studied for AS.

Specialist options

You must choose one of two different pathways through this unit, both of which are marked by an Edexcel examiner:

+ **either** you will have to write two compositions (together lasting at least six minutes) each based on a different topic from a given list; one of these must be on the same topic you chose for AS

+ **or** you will have to perform a 20-minute recital of music, which will be recorded for assessment purposes.

Analysing music

There are two separate papers for this unit, which are sat one after the other in the same three-hour exam session. Both are marked by Edexcel examiners:

+ a listening paper, consisting of three questions on music on a CD that you can play as many times as you wish within the 60 minutes allowed for the test; the music will be selected from a wide variety of styles

The *New Anthology of Music* is published by Peters Edition Ltd, ISBN: 1-901507-03-3 (CDs, ISBN: 1-901507-04-1), and is available from Edexcel publications (see page 2) or all good music retailers.

+ a two-hour written paper based on questions about **two** areas of study you have prepared from the *New Anthology of Music*, an unmarked copy of which you may use for reference in the exam.

The details of the specification are correct at the time of going to press, but you and your teachers should always check current requirements for the exam with Edexcel as these may change.

Key Skills

Key Skills are becoming increasingly important for success at work, entry into higher education and for making the most of everyday life. A2 Music offers a number of opportunities for you to develop your knowledge and understanding in five of the six Key Skills: Communication, Information Technology, Working with Others, Improving own Learning and Performance, and Problem Solving. You are therefore recommended to discuss with your teachers the ways in which the work you undertake for A2 Music might also be used as evidence for your acquisition and development of skills for these Key Skills units at Level 3.

Performing and composing

1. Performing during the course

This section accounts for 50% of the marks for the *Performing and composing* unit. Like the similar component in AS Music it offers an excellent opportunity for you to receive credit for the performing you do during the course. This needs careful planning and record-keeping, and you need to meet all of the following requirements:

✦ you must submit four *different* pieces for assessment; these must not include any items that you offered for AS Music nor, if you are opting for performing as your *Specialist option*, any piece that you present in your recital

✦ at least one of the four pieces must be a solo

✦ at least one of the four pieces must be an ensemble item

✦ performances must be completed in time for your submission to reach the examiner by 15 May in the exam year

✦ one solo item must be recorded for moderation purposes

✦ your teacher must have been present for at least three of the four performances.

To be sure of meeting all these requirements it is going to be essential to make your plans at the start of the A2 course and to discuss with your teacher the practicalities of the last two points above. Remember that there may be little time to arrange performances at the start of the summer term in the exam year.

You can include a performance in which you were the director or conductor of an ensemble, but you may submit only one such piece. In this part of the exam you are allowed to include performances that encompass improvisation if you wish.

The combined length of the four pieces you submit must be at least 7–8 minutes, but there is no maximum time limit. The difficulty of the music is taken into account in assessment and is expected to equate with grade 6 standard (your teacher will help explain what this means if you do not take graded exams). The mark scheme allows credit if the music is of a higher standard. Although the highest marks are not available if the pieces are below grade 6 in level of difficulty, you will probably get a much better mark if you choose music that is well within your capabilities rather than pieces that are so hard that they will cause you to struggle and perhaps even break down in performance. When choosing pieces remember that, while accuracy is expected, the majority of the marks at this level are awarded for your **interpretation** of the music.

The performances can be given in class to your fellow students, or they may include events such as lunchtime concerts, rock gigs, music festivals or concert tours – but remember that your teacher must be present for at least three of the performances you submit. You may include playing on any instrument or singing, but marks are awarded for quality and not variety, so there is no advantage in including music on instruments that you don't play well.

There must be an audience at the performances, even if it is only a couple of people, and for that reason you are not allowed to include performances given at music exams or auditions in which there is no audience in the normal sense of the word. However you can include exam and audition pieces if you perform them on some more open occasion.

Ensemble performances can be of many different kinds – piano duets, wind trios, string quartets, jazz bands, rock groups, choirs or orchestras. However a piece in which you are the one dominant performer throughout does not count as an ensemble. Thus in a piece for flute with piano accompaniment the flautist cannot submit the work as an ensemble item, although the accompanying pianist can. When choosing ensemble performances to include on your list, remember that the work will need to be assessed – this may be difficult if it is a piece in which you have played a very minor role in a large ensemble.

Some advice on solo performing is given later in this guide, as part of the section on the recital. A useful handbook which will give you many ideas for getting the best out of ensemble performing of all kinds is:

Rehearse, Direct and Play by William Lloyd and Paul Terry. *Musonix Publishing*, 1993. ISBN: 0-9517214-3-7, £4.95. Order from http://www.musonix.co.uk

Keeping a performance diary

You will need to keep your own diary of performances, which should include the following information:

✦ the precise title of the work you performed and the movement(s) performed if it was not complete

✦ the name of the composer

✦ a note of whether it was a solo or ensemble item

✦ the nature of the occasion (such as a lunchtime recital, a rock concert, an arts festival, etc)

✦ the role in which you participated (such as flute in wind trio, second trumpet in county youth orchestra of 80 players, bass guitar in rock group, one of 12 altos in choir of 60, etc)

✦ the date and whether it was an internal event at your centre or an external event that occurred elsewhere.

Remember that you will need a recording of one of the solo items which you submit, and a photocopy of your part in the piece.

By early May in your exam year you will have to select the four best pieces from your diary, in accordance with the requirements listed on the previous page, and transfer the details to a log form provided by Edexcel. When you do this be careful not to include the same piece more than once, and do not include any pieces that you offered for assessment in your AS Music examination or that your perform in your recital (if you have chosen this as your *Specialist option* for A2 Music).

2. Compositional techniques

This section accounts for the remaining 50% of the marks for the *Performing and composing* unit.

You have to continue and extend your study of the same techniques topic that you chose for AS Music. You will be required to sit a timed exam paper in which you will have to complete an exercise in your chosen technique. During the exam you will be allowed access to a musical instrument and/or music-technology equipment (but not to any written notes or other reference materials).

The exercise to be undertaken will be related to the coursework you did for AS Music, but it will be more demanding, not only because it must be completed as a timed test but also because you will be required to supply more music in your answer.

The table below shows the choice of topics. Remember that you must choose just **one** technique, and it must be one of those that you chose for AS. The table also summarises how the requirements at A2 differ from those you undertook for AS Music.

Compositional technique	AS coursework	A2 exam
A1 Baroque counterpoint Complete an upper part to a given figured bass	12–16 bars	18–24 bars
A2 Minimalism Complete a given opening to make a piece lasting about one minute	For keyboard	For three melody instruments
B1 Bach chorale Add three lower parts to a chorale	Harmonise the cadences only	Harmonise the whole passage
B2 32-bar popular song Realise the middle-eight and turnaround	Add a bass part from given chord symbols	Add chord symbols and a bass part
C1 Renaissance counterpoint Add a part to two given parts	8–10 bars	12–16 bars
C2 Serialism Extend a given opening	For solo instrument, about 12 bars in length	For two instruments, about 20 bars in length
D1 Extended instrumental techniques Develop one of two given openings to make a one-minute piece which exploits: vocal contrast, prepared piano, woodwind chords, glissandi or vocalising through the instrument	Exploit one of the listed techniques in your piece	Exploit two of the listed techniques in your piece
D2 Electro-acoustic music Record a given ostinato, then add material to make a piece lasting about one minute which exploits: envelope shaping, filtering, pitch shifting, sampled sounds, reversing or looping.	Add one track and employ one of the listed processes in your piece	Add one or two tracks and employ two of the listed processes in your piece

In the case of electro-acoustic music you are required to submit a recording as well as some form of notation (not necessarily a score). You will be allowed time to set up the equipment and to record the given ostinato outside the timed part of the examination.

Detailed help on compositional techniques A1, B1, B2 and C2, along with many tips and practice exercises, is given in **A Student's Guide to Harmony and Counterpoint** by Hugh Benham. *Rhinegold Publishing*. ISBN: 1-904226-31-0.

We have given some general guidance on the various options below. Your teacher will explain to you the specific techniques required, since these are very detailed and vary greatly between options, but in all cases it is important to listen to (and study, and preferably perform) examples of the music concerned. In addition, aim to practise working plenty of examples and, most important of all, try to learn from any mistakes you might make in those workings.

Baroque counterpoint

Useful books on this topic include **Bach: Chorale Harmonization and Instrumental Counterpoint** by Malcolm Boyd, published by *Kahn and Averill*, ISBN: 1-871082-72-2, and **A Practical Approach to Eighteenth-century Counterpoint** by Robert Gauldin, published by *Waveland Press* (USA), ISBN: 0-88133-853-2.

You will be required to complete an upper part to fit with a given figured bass in the style of Corelli, Handel or their contemporaries. The passage will be 18–24 bars in length. It is likely that the music will include modulations and you may be expected to find opportunities to use imitation and develop the given melodic material. In addition to the harmony you encountered when studying for AS music (first and second inversions, 7ths, 9–8 and 4–3 suspensions and accidentals) the passage may contain the following figuring: $\frac{6}{5}$, $\frac{4}{3}$, $\frac{4}{2}$ and 7–6. Remember that stylistically appropriate melodic decoration is important, that leading notes and 7ths must be correctly treated, and that you must check for consecutives. It will be useful to study (and perhaps play) some of Bach's two-part inventions, Corelli's violin sonatas and Handel's flute sonatas.

Minimalism

You will be required to complete a given opening to make a piece for three melody instruments lasting one minute. Be prepared to use both treble and bass clefs. If you use a MIDI workstation for the task remember that you must nevertheless write for acoustic instruments, taking into account their ranges, characteristics and practicalities in performance. As the required length is only one minute it will not be practical for ideas to unfold slowly, as often happens in this style. Try to study some of the early works of the 'New York minimalists' listed on page 19. Note how, when motifs are shifted out of phase with one another (as occurs in *NAM 12*) new patterns arise from the resulting combination, and notice the free use of unprepared dissonance in this style of music.

Bach chorales

Useful books for this topic include **Bach: Chorale Harmonization and Instrumental Counterpoint** by Malcolm Boyd, published by *Kahn and Averill*, ISBN: 1-871082-72-2 and the examples of Bach's own harmonisations in **Bach: 371 Harmonized Chorales**, edited by Riemenschneider, published by *Schirmer / Music Sales*.

You will be required to add three lower parts to a given chorale melody, in the style of Bach. Revise your AS work for this topic, since the correct harmonisation of cadences is essential to the style. Much of the rest of the harmony can often be established by working progressively backwards from the cadences. Examiners will be looking for strong bass lines, good spacing of parts, the use of quaver passing notes and suspensions. Check your work thoroughly for inappropriate use of second inversions and forbidden consecutives.

32-bar popular song

A useful general resource for this topic is **Songwriting: a complete guide to the craft** by Stephen Citron, *Hodder and Stoughton*, ISBN: 0-340-48872-7. Citron's recent study of **Stephen Sondheim and Andrew Lloyd Webber: The New Musical** is published by *Oxford University Press* (USA) ISBN: 0-19-509601-0. Most useful of all is to make a study of the harmony in some of the many AABA forms in albums of songs by Cole Porter, Irving Berlin, Jerome Kern, George Gershwin, Richard Rodgers, and in collections of jazz and pop standards.

You will be required to complete an AABA popular-song structure by writing a chord sequence **and** bass part for the 'middle eight' (the B section). Your chords should contrast with the given harmony of the A section and should introduce one or more passing modulations to keys such as IV, ii, iii or vi (more remote keys may be appropriate in some styles). You should end with a turnaround that prepares for the return of the A section in the tonic key. The bass part should include passing notes and appropriate licks and fills. The examiners are likely to be more impressed with a strong and stylish use of a wide harmonic vocabulary (including secondary dominants and other chromatic chords) rather than memorised stock chord progressions that are poorly suited to the context.

You will be required to add a part to two given parts, in a late 16th-century style. The passage will be 12–16 bars in length and may be either sacred or secular vocal polyphony. You need to remember that control of dissonance is a key feature (including 4ths with the bass), and that the sharpened leading-note will be required in most cadences. Remember to spend time trying to find natural points for imitative entries. Aim for correct underlay of the text, with stressed syllables usually falling on accented beats.

You will be provided with a note row, from which you must construct a piece for two instruments of about 20 bars in length. In addition to using the four basic versions of the row (which you should identify with the letters O, I, R and RI above the staves) you should look out for the opportunity to exploit patterns such as hexachords and trichords in the given material, and to use more advanced techniques such as rotation. Examiners will look for a musical result with melodic shape, idiomatic instrumental writing and a sense of style (note that at A2 the given material may determine the style, such as a specific dance or a jazz style).

As at AS you will be required to develop one of two given openings to make a one-minute piece, but at A2 your composition will have to use **two** of the techniques listed on page 9. You can employ both techniques in a work for a solo performer, or you could write for two or more performers and use the techniques in different parts. Whichever you choose, you must identify in the score which techniques you have employed. Your piece must be performable and you should also give a full explanation in the score of how the techniques are to be realised. The examiners will be looking to see how well your use of the techniques integrates with the musical intentions of the piece, so you should avoid writing music which is merely a study or experiment in the use of technical effects.

As at AS you will be required to record a given ostinato which you must loop or repeat to produce the basis of a one-minute piece. To this you must add one or two tracks which feature **two** of the processes listed on page 9. Your added material could be derived from the given ostinato, or it may be entirely new. It can be either electronic or acoustic, but if you use any pre-existing samples you must identify these and credit their source. The examiners will be looking for a good sense of balance, a clear stereo image and full use of the audible frequency range, as well as appropriate organisation of your musical ideas. For this topic your work should be submitted as a recording, but you should also include written documentation (a computer-printed score, graphic notation, track diagram, table or flow chart) that includes a description of the processes you have used.

What the examiners look for

Whichever topic you choose, examiners will award marks for:

✦ a clear and accurate presentation of your score (or recording)
✦ an outcome that is creative, musical and which responds to the demands of the question
✦ an awareness of style and a fluent use of technical procedures
✦ a coherent and controlled use of structure in your work.

Renaissance counterpoint

A useful reference book for this topic is **Modal Counterpoint, Renaissance Style** by Peter Schubert. *Oxford University Press.* ISBN: 0-19-510912-0.

Serialism

Useful books for this topic include **Serial Composition and Atonality** by George Perle. *University of California Press*, ISBN: 0-520-22921-5, and **Serial Composition** by Reginald Smith Brindle, *Oxford University Press*, ISBN: 0-19-311906-4.

Extended instrumental techniques

Useful works to study for this topic include *NAM 10, 11* and *40*. See also *Stripsody* by Cathy Berberian, an excerpt of which can be found in *Sound Matters* (Bowman and Cole), and *Eight Songs for A Mad King* by Peter Maxwell Davies. The latter includes a wide range of extended techniques for all its performers.

Electro-acoustic music

Specialist option A: Composition portfolio

You must choose one of two different pathways through the unit entitled *Specialist option*, depending on whether you want to focus on composing or performing. Turn to page 23 for the latter.

For Pathway A you have to write **two compositions**, based on two different topics from the following list. One of your topics must be **the same one that you chose for unit 2 in AS Music**.

✦ Variations
✦ Romantic miniatures
✦ Neo-classicism
✦ Post-modernism
✦ The popular song
✦ Club dance and hip hop
✦ Fusions
✦ Film and television
✦ Music theatre.

The score should be appropriate to the style of the music. It may be fully notated, a lead-sheet, a track sheet or an annotated diagram.

The two compositions together must last at least six minutes. You have to present both works as scores **and** in recorded format. You will also have to submit a short written description of each piece. Your work must reach the examiner by **15 May** in the exam year.

Planning

Start planning your compositions early in the course, as you will need plenty of time to develop initial ideas, make preliminary sketches and try these out in performance before you even start on the final scores and recordings.

You will first need to decide on the resources you are going to use. Be realistic in what you have time to achieve. While it may be tempting to write for an orchestra, band or large choir, this will require a lot of work and it may prove impossible to get the necessary resources together when needed. It is usually better to write for people who will be available to work with you during the whole composing process, such as the other students in your group or people with whom you regularly rehearse and perform.

You could write for just a solo instrument, especially if it is a harmony instrument such as the piano or guitar, but at this level it is good to be a little more ambitious, and two or three players will give you much more flexibilty and textural variety. Consider combinations such as piano duet (either two pianos, or two players on one piano), piano with solo instrument or voice, acoustic guitar and flute, as well as trios or quartets of various kinds.

As we recommended in the AS Guide, start by discussing with your performers how the characteristics of their instruments and/or voices can best be exploited. Try to identify the skills (and weaknesses) of each performer so that you can use their individual strengths in your composing. Discuss what sort of things are easy and what are difficult for each instrument or voice, and try some improvising both separately and together.

Research

Begin by investigating some of the existing music in your chosen topic area. You may find examples in the music you play as well as in the *New Anthology*, but you will also need to investigate what can be found in libraries and in music and recordings that you may be allowed to borrow from your teacher or music department. Aim to make a **detailed** study of several examples that differ in style, mood and resources, and make notes on:

✦ **Melody** – is there a melody line? If so, what makes it distinctive or memorable? What role does rhythm, particularly rests and repeated notes, play in its construction? Does it have a point of climax? Is the melody regularly phrased? Is it developed? Is it formed from smaller motifs and are these developed separately? How is the melodic material distributed around the various performing resources? Is there any contrapuntal interest?

✦ **Accompaniment** – is there a distinct accompaniment or do all the parts have equal melodic interest? Does the accompaniment possess musical interest of its own? Is there rhythmic variety in the accompaniment? Does it have a strong bass line? What role does the accompaniment have when there is less interest in the main melody? What role is played by repeated notes and rests in the accompaniment?

✦ **Structure** – how is the music given shape? How much repetition is there? Is it varied repetition? How much contrast? Do areas of contrast sound as if they are part of the same piece? Why? Are changes of key used to provide areas of contrast? How are these established? Are there distinct sections in the piece? If so, how are they linked? How does the piece begin? How does it end?

✦ **Texture** – how are different textures used to provide variety? How are the voices and/or instruments exploited? How do changes in texture contribute to climaxes in the music? What use is made of different tone colours within various textures?

In addition, make a note of any useful **techniques** that relate to your chosen topic and try to identify any potential problem areas that you could encounter in your own composition. You will soon begin to accumulate a store of information that will be enormously helpful in planning your own work.

While it is possible to start a composition at bar 1 and gradually work through to the end, you will find your task easier if you first plan out the structure and main events, leaving the detail to be sketched in later. This also makes it easy, if you get stuck, to leave the current section and try out some ideas for later in the piece.

Musical style

Compositions may be in any style that is appropriate to the topic you choose, but you will want to show the best you can do, so it is probably best to opt for a format that will allow you to use a variety of textures and techniques. If you adopt a style that is exceptionally repetitive or very slow-moving it may be advisable to write a relatively long work so that you can achieve some variety and a sense of development in your composing.

Whichever topic you choose, note that you are **not** expected to write in the style of a specific composer. For instance, if you decide to compose a romantic miniature you are not required to write in the style of Chopin or Schumann – you might decide on a modern interpretation of this genre. Similarly, variations are not expected to be realised in the style of Bach or Mozart – you may want to write jazz variations or an electro-acoustic piece in a modern cross-over style that uses a ground bass formed from a tape loop.

The topics simply provide you with broad guidelines, which you should interpret imaginatively, and we have suggested some ideas to help you with this later in the chapter. However your two compositions should be in different styles – you should not, for example, write two similar songs for a musical and submit one as a popular song and the other as music theatre.

Information technology

You may find it useful to use a MIDI workstation to develop your compositions, but unless your work is intended only for electronic realisation (as may be the case with club dance and some types of film music) reread the advice on pages 13–14 of the AS Guide, paying particular attention to the notes about computer-generated scores. Don't become so engrossed with the technology that you neglect the composition, and remember that music technology will not give you feedback on the practicality (or enjoyability) of your music that you can expect from live performers.

Developing the brief

Painters often begin with a number of preliminary pencil or charcoal sketches, sometimes followed by some drafts in watercolour, before starting work on the final canvas. A similar procedure can work well for composing. Improvising, either alone or in a group, can be a good start. Each student could contribute a variation to a given theme, or all could arrange a given passage for the ensemble each intends to use in their own compositions.

More specific exercises may involve your trying several alternative sketches for key features of your piece – such as different layouts for the opening, a central climax, or a complex contrapuntal section. You may want to experiment with different voicings in the scoring, or provide alternative treatments for a passage that is technically difficult. Once drafted in rough, ideas for short sections can be tested at the piano or MIDI workstation, and then trialled in performance workshop sessions. Record these for later playback and analysis, noting if some sections seem to flag, fail to cohere, are unplayable, or do not achieve the effect you desire.

Reread pages 16–17 of the AS Guide, noting the following points:

+ Aim to **balance unity and diversity** in your work. Too much repetition will lead to a lack of variety, but too much new material will prevent the piece hanging together. Use your research to suggest ways in which ideas can be transformed, adapted and developed, so there is a sense of moving forward during the work and a sense of completion when it ends. Pay particular attention to ends of phrases and sections, where the music can easily lose its impetus. Explore your musical ideas in depth, exploiting the potential of individual motifs, not just manipulating complete tunes, and experiment with unusual changes of key and more complex types of structure. Watch out carefully for unwanted predictability, such as too many four-bar phrases in succession or rondo/chorus structures in which it is all too obvious where the theme will come round yet again.

✦ Remember that **variety of texture is essential** for success. All parts should be musically interesting and ideally all should play a leading role at some point in the piece. Use instruments or voices in different parts of their ranges, and remember that rests are more valuable than notes in providing changes in texture. Check that you have contrasts in dynamics and articulation, and ensure that accompanying parts are rhythmically interesting. Remember that long melodies can often be split into shorter motifs that can be assigned to different parts within the texture, and that a counter-melody or some short contrapuntal motifs can add interest to the repetition of a section. Plan points of tension and areas of relaxation carefully, using changes in texture, dynamics and articulation to heighten their contrast.

✦ Plan your schedule to allow time for testing in performance and subsequent refinement of ideas, before embarking on the final recording and neat copy of the score. Unsatisfactory sections may need to be replaced, and the work as a whole polished. Sometimes a work can get totally stuck, and if this happens you may need time to start afresh on something new.

Presentation

Reread pages 14–15 of the AS Guide and use the composition checklist on page 15 to ensure that you haven't missed anything. If you submit a lead-sheet or chord chart instead of a score, note that it must contain **all** significant cues and performing directions. Similarly, track sheets must include **full** details of the processing you used. For each of the two compositions you will have to submit a score (which may be a lead-sheet or track list if appropriate to the musical style), a recording and a structured commentary which will require answers to the following questions:

✦ How does your composition relate to the chosen topic?
✦ What musical resources have you used?
✦ What is the form or structure of the piece?
✦ What improvements were made in the process of composition?

Use the commentary to make your intentions clear to the examiner. It is not necessary to explain how you discovered the dominant 7th, or how you mislaid your computer disk and had to start again. Nor should you write a programme note about the piece. However you should draw the examiner's attention to any points about the piece that you feel are important and identify any material you have used that is not original (such as lyrics, samples, or someone else's theme on which you have written variations).

Composition topics

Variations

Listed below are just a few of the more accessible works that use variation form. Aim to make a *thorough* study of about five works, selected from different periods.

Variations for solo instruments

Bach's *Passacaglia in C minor* for organ, *Goldberg* variations and Chaconne from the *Partita in D minor* for unaccompanied violin. Mozart's Piano sonata in A, K331 (first movement) – his complete piano variations are also available. Haydn's *Variations in F minor*, Beethoven's *33 Variations on a Waltz by Diabelli* and Schubert's *Impromptu in B♭* (Op. 142 No. 3). Chopin's *Variations brillantes* (Op. 12), Mendelssohn's *Variations sérieuses* (Op. 54) and Brahms' *Variations and Fugue on a theme by Handel* (Op. 24). Ives' *Variations on 'America'* and Webern's *Variations* (Op. 27). Also look out for CDs of 19th-century virtuoso piano music, such as **The Earl Wild Collection** (*Vanguard* OVC 4033) which includes a number of works based on variation technique.

Excerpts from Bach's Chaconne in D minor, Brahms' *Variations on a Theme of Handel* and other works in variation form can be found in *The Rhinegold Dictionary of Music in Sound*. The third movement of Webern's Variations appears in *Sound Matters* (Bowman and Cole).

Variations for small ensembles

Pachelbel's *Kanon* (a canon over a ground bass), Purcell's *Chacony in G minor* (for strings) and various ground-bass arias (see *left*). Mozart's Duo for Violin and Viola in B♭, K.424 (last movement), his piano trios in G, K.496 (last movement) and K.564 (second movement) and Clarinet Quintet, K.581 (last movement). Haydn's *Emperor* quartet (second movement). Beethoven's *Harp* quartet (last movement) and his Piano trio in B♭, Op. 11 (third movement). Schubert's *Death and the Maiden* quartet (second movement) and *Trout* quintet (fourth movement). Mendelssohn's *Variations concertantes* for cello and piano. Stravinsky's Octet (second movement).

Ground-bass arias by Purcell can be found in *NAM 36*, *Aural Matters* (Bowman and Terry), *Sound Matters* (Bowman and Cole) and *The Rhinegold Dictionary of Music in Sound* (A75).

The slow movement (theme and variations) of Haydn's String Quartet in B♭, Op.9 No.5, can be found in *Sound Matters* (Bowman and Cole). Excerpts from the variations in Haydn's *Emperor* quartet can be found in *The Rhinegold Dictionary of Music in Sound*.

Orchestral variations

The second movements of Haydn's symphonies Nos. 94 (*Surprise*) and 103 (*Drumroll*). Mozart's piano concertos in B♭ (second movement) K.450, and in G (third movement) K.453. Brahms' *Variations on a theme by J Haydn* (also for piano duet) and the last movement of his symphony No. 4 in E minor (a passacaglia). Tchaikovsky's *Variations on a Rococco Theme* (for cello and orchestra). Reger's *Variations and Fugue on a Theme of Mozart* (based on K.331 above). Richard Strauss's *Don Quixote*. Elgar's *Enigma* variations. Schoenberg's *Variations for Orchestra*. Dohnányi's *Variations on a Nursery Tune* (for piano and orchestra). Vaughan Williams' *Five Variants of Dives and Lazarus*. Britten's *A Young Person's Guide to the Orchestra* (subtitled *Variations and Fugue on a Theme of Purcell*). Walton's *Variations on a Theme of Hindemith*. Lloyd Webber's *Variations* (compare with Rachmaninov's *Rhapsody on a Theme of Paganini*).

When you study (and hopefully perform) some of these pieces, note how the theme is constructed and harmonised, as well as how the entire work is structured. Many sets of variations build up tension by using increasingly complex figuration as they proceed. Some provide contrast with a slow and/or minor-key variation before an exciting finale (which may be less clearly asssociated with the theme). Some end with a short coda which refreshingly refers back to the theme in its original form.

Notice how most themes are simple and based on strong chord patterns – these usually offer the greatest potential for exploitation in the ensuing variations. Make detailed notes on the types of variation used and the differing moods that these can create. The methods employed may include any of the following (often two or more of these techniques will be used simultaneously):

✦ elaborating the melody with many types of decoration
✦ redistributing the notes of the melody between different hands (in piano music) or between different instruments
✦ changing the harmony and/or tonality
✦ altering the rhythm, metre or tempo (or a combination of these)
✦ fragmenting the theme
✦ developing a new theme from the fragments
✦ reusing the harmony but creating a new melody above it
✦ treating the theme contrapuntally by using imitation or adding a counter-melody.

If you decide to adopt a theme-and-variations structure, consider whether you want to write your own theme, or use an existing one. Composition will be more straightforward if the theme has a clear melodic outline and strong harmonic structure. You could instead use a freer variation structure (such as a fantasia on a theme) or a tighter one (such as a ground bass or chaconne), although the latter can be a much harder format within which to work.

Double themes and variations were frequently used by Haydn. For example, in the slow movement of his *Drumroll* symphony a theme in C minor is followed by one in C major, and this pair of themes is then varied in each of the following sections. Explore ways in which you can vary the often predictable variation plan. The slow movement of Stravinsky's Octet repeats the first variation as a sort of rondo after some of the later variations, and ends with a repeat of the theme, giving the form $A–A^1–A^2–A^1–A^3–A^4–A^1–A$.

Aim to include a range of variation techniques, not just different embellishments of the melody line, and if you are working in a tonal idiom, plan how you will achieve variety of key – it is all too easy for sets of variations to get stuck in one key with little or no modulation. Beethoven avoided this as early as 1802 in his *Six Variations* (Op. 34). The theme is in F major and the variations fall in thirds through D, B♭, G, E♭, C minor and back to F major.

Decide whether your variations are going to proceed in discrete sections or if you are going to link them into a through-composed format, like the free variations on a double theme which form the foundation of Richard Strauss's tone poem, *Don Quixote*. This work is of a type known as 'character variations' – each variation portrays one of the fantastical adventures of the hapless old knight. Similarly, each of Elgar's *Enigma* variations portrays the character of one of the composer's friends. Perhaps there might be an idea here for a set of variations characterising your own friends or emotions, or perhaps reflecting various favourite places you have visited.

Finally, remember that variation technique pervades many types of music – it is fundamental in serial music, jazz improvisation, the Indian *rāg* and in the simultaneous variation of gamelan music.

Romantic miniatures

A 'romantic miniature' could be a song, a dance form such as a waltz or short ballet movement, an entirely abstract piece (eg a prelude, intermezzo or impromptu) or a 'character piece' that aims to suggest a specific idea, such as a mood, person or place. You could write a piece in the form of a study for your instrument, but studies often concentrate on just one technique, which may make it difficult for you to show a range of skills in composing.

NAM 23 consists of three miniatures from *Kinderscenen* by Schumann. See also *NAM 24* (Debussy) and *NAM 39* (Fauré). Romantic miniatures in the *Rhinegold Dictionary of Music in Sound* include works by Chopin, Mendelssohn's *Venetian Gondola Song*, an excerpt from Liszt's *La Lugubre Gondola I*, a waltz from Grieg's *New Lyric Pieces*, the Trepak from Tchaikovsky's *The Nutcracker* and extracts from *Préludes* by Debussy and from Saint-Saëns' *Carnival of the Animals*.

Romantic miniatures can be found in many instrumental teaching books and in collections of graded exam pieces. Some of the well-known collections for piano include Schubert's *Moments musicaux*, Mendelssohn's *Songs without Words*, Chopin's preludes, nocturnes, waltzes and mazurkas, Grieg's *Lyric Pieces* and *Poetic Tone Pictures*, and the various cycles of short piano pieces by Schumann, such as *Papillons*, *Carnaval*, the *Davidsbündler* dances, the *Album for the Young* and *Kinderscenen*. In addition, there are many attractive works in this genre by minor composers such as Burgmüller, Fibich, Gurlitt, Karganoff, John Field and others.

The character piece proved enduringly popular, so there are many examples from later 19th-century composers such as Tchaikovsky, Borodin, Cui, Dvořák and Smetana. Remember that you are not necessarily expected to compose in a romantic style. Debussy's *Préludes*, Kabalevsky's *24 Pieces for Children*, or Bartók's shorter piano pieces (such as those in *For Children* and *Mikrokosmos*) will reveal how 20th-century composers reinterpreted this genre.

If you are writing for solo instrument with piano or small ensemble, look out for some of the popular arrangements and encore pieces such as Elgar's *Salut d'amour*, *Chanson de matin* and *Chanson de nuit*, Raff's *Cavatina*, Massenet's *Méditation* from *Thaïs*, Monti's *Czardas* and Dvořák's *Humoresque*. If you want to work on a more ambitious scale, look at movements from Grieg's *Holberg* and *Peer Gynt* suites, Dag Wiren's *Serenade for Strings*, movements from Saint-Saëns' *Carnival of the Animals* and the individual dances in Tchaikovsky's ballet scores, such as the 'characteristic dances' from *The Nutcracker*. Singers should remember that German *Lieder* and 19th-century French *chansons* are essentially types of romantic miniature, as are such popular art songs as Tchaikovsky's 'None but the lonely heart' and Dvořák's 'Songs my mother taught me'.

From this wealth of material you should be able to deduce that the romantic miniature is short, focused on a single musical idea and usually memorably melodic, all ingredients that make for easy listening. Note the forms used, which are often quite basic (binary, rounded binary or ternary) perhaps with a short introduction and coda. It may be difficult to sustain your own piece for three minutes or more with such simple forms, so look carefully at what happens in longer works. You could, if necessary, write a matching pair of movements, perhaps both based on the same theme.

Notice that while some works in this genre have abstract titles, such as prelude or 'album leaf', others specify the style of the piece (march, waltz, song without words) and still others (such as those in *NAM 23*) suggest very specific images. You can use whatever is appropriate to your own work, but try to make the title relevant to the musical content.

Although melody is important, you should notice that harmony is often quite luxurient. Try to analyse why. You should spot that chromatic chords such as secondary dominants and diminished 7ths are often used, and tertiary modulations (shifts to a key a 3rd away, such as G to E♭) are employed to give an exotic effect. Notice how dissonances are created by lingering on non-harmonic notes and by using long appoggiaturas, often with resolutions that are so brief that they seem almost to be an after-thought.

Neo-classicism

Three movements from Stravinsky's *Pulcinella* suite are printed in *NAM 7* – try to listen to the rest of the suite or the original ballet score. Stravinsky arranged some of these movements for violin and piano in his *Suite Italienne* (also available for cello and piano) – this version would be particularly useful for study. Other well-known neo-classical works by Stravinsky include *The Soldier's Tale*, the concerto for piano and winds, Symphony in C, *Oedipus Rex* (modelled on the baroque oratorio) and *The Rake's Progress*.

The *Bransle Simple* from Stravinksy's neo-classic ballet *Agon*, is included in *Sound Matters* (Bowman and Cole) No.42.

The Rhinegold Dictionary of Music in Sound includes an extract from Ravel's *Le Tombeau de Couperin* (C33) – compare it with the extract of a Forlane by Couperin (C32) in the same publication.

Works by other composers include Prokofiev's *Classical* symphony (try to hear at least the third movement, which is a modern gavotte), Hindemith's *Ludus Tonalis* for piano, and Satie's *Sonatine bureau-cratique* (a satiric paraphrase of a classical piece by Clementi). The clear textures of neo-classicism can be found in the work of a number of other early 20th-century composers, including Bartók (Dance suite for orchestra), Poulenc (see *NAM 19*) and Shostakovich (*NAM 25*).

Your own piece could take the form of a sonatina, a contrapuntal form such as a trio sonata or fugue, or perhaps some linked dance movements, using pre-1800 dance forms interpreted in a bitonal idiom. While it is possible to base your work on existing music, this technique was quite rare among the neo-classicists – the only other work by Stravinsky which does so is *The Fairy's Kiss*, in which he reworked compositions by Tchaikovsky.

Post-modernism

A good starting point for research is the early work of the 'New York minimalists': *In C* (Terry Riley), *Music in Similar Motion*, *Music in Fifths* and *Another Look at Harmony* (Philip Glass), *Phase Patterns* and *Drumming* (Steve Reich). An excerpt from Reich's *Clapping Music* is included in the *Rhinegold Dictionary of Music in Sound* (C89) and his *New York Counterpoint* is in *NAM* (No. 12).

Other post-modernist music in the *Rhinegold Dictionary of Music in Sound* includes extracts from the music of Giles Swayne (C91), Sylvie Bodorová (C96) and James MacMillan (C97).

Look out for larger-scale works such as Stockhausen's *Stimmung*, and *Harmonium* (1981) and *Harmonielehre* (1985), both by John Adams. Certain post-modernist pieces became immensely popular in the closing years of the 20th century, particularly Jonathan Dove's comic opera, *Flight* (1998), Henryk Górecki's third symphony, *Short Ride in a Fast Machine* by John Adams, and the works of Arvo Pärt and John Tavener (both influenced by the mystical style of Eastern Orthodox church music). Tavener's *The Lamb* is in *NAM* (No. 32) and an excerpt from his much earlier *Ultimos Ritos* can be found in the old London Anthology, No. 119. Look out also for his cello concerto (called *The Protecting Veil*) and *Song for Athene*.

Because musical change tends to occur over a long time span in minimalist music, you will need to consider how you can show a range of skills if you choose this style – it may be necessary to write a piece rather longer than the minimum requirement. In addition to art music (choral works, instrumental pieces, etc.) you could choose other formats in which a contemporary musical style is appropriate – educational pieces that might incorporate parts for children, music intended for a sound installation (eg music for a science exhibition or a virtual-reality experience) or a suite of music for a computer-games program (splash-screen music, mood music to underline fear, safety, excitement and aggression, location music for different levels of the game, and so forth). If you are tempted by this last category, remember the need for consistency (a 'brand image') across separate items, be sure to include some more extended pieces as well as shorter looped tracks, try to avoid items that are purely sound effects, and concentrate **on the music** as CD-ROMs, artwork or videos are not required. However you can submit your work on tape, CD or minidisk, accompanying it with explanatory diagrams or a flow chart.

The popular song

You could write a song with accompaniment for piano or guitar, or a more elaborate setting that includes backing vocals, rock group, jazz band or even orchestral parts. Any style is acceptable (including folk, jazz, soul, reggae, as well as contemporary styles) but remember that you will need to show a good range of skills within a single composition, so try to avoid types of music in which there is much repetition and little variety. Your song will be expected to feature a vocal line (the lyrics of which will not be assessed). You are permitted to submit your work as a lead-sheet, but the accompaniment must be fully worked out on the recording. Aim for a strong bass line, and remember that you will be expected to show imagination in your choice of chords and modulations, and in the musical detail you assign to backing instruments. Aim for an interesting structure, perhaps with varied treatment of verses and choruses, a middle section in a more remote key, and additional sections such as an intro, an instrumental bridge and a coda. Consider how these might be unified through the use of a hook line or common chord pattern. Pay attention to stylish licks and fills, and aim for some variety when writing drum patterns.

There are many songs for you to study in the popular music and jazz section of the *New Anthology*, and in the jazz and pop section of *Sound Matters* (Bowman and Cole). However most pop music is published in easy arrangements for voice and piano/guitar, and this format does not form a good model for study as too much important detail is missing. Instead look out for the detailed transcriptions that are published in the *Rock Scores* series by Music Sales and in the *Off the Record* series from IMP, as well as collections such as *Beatles: The Complete Scores* (Music Sales).

There are also detailed scores of 17 classic hits from the 1950s to the 1990s, with hints on sequencing, in *Rock in Sequence* (Lloyd and Terry), published by Music Sales.

Club dance and hip hop

At first sight this topic may appear rather confusing: hip hop developed in 1970s New York as a cultural movement of the urban ghetto, in which music (and specifically rap) is only one element. Club dance music, on the other hand, can encompass a broad range of music that may include anything from 'golden oldy' tracks by Abba and Queen, through house, techno, trance, garage, jungle and Nu-NRG to eclectic mixes by that night's DJ. In Britain, hip hop became popular in the early 1980s, quickly being adopted by the strong club scene. This commercial, dance-orientated style (which has been disparagingly called trip-hop) tends to avoid the violent subject matter and frank language sometimes found in rap itself.

However the intention here is to give you the opportunity to submit modern dance music and not to limit you to one particular style. It is likely that your work will include tightly sequenced rhythms, carefully set at the appropriate speed (bpm) for the intended dance style, and it may well include samples of pre-recorded material. You may choose to include a vocal part, either sung or rapped, or you may prefer to write a purely instrumental dance track.

Research will need to be mainly by ear from existing recordings, since this type of music is not normally notated, although magazines and web sites on hip hop may be useful. You may wish to produce a score of your own piece but this is not necessarily expected – a good-quality recording plus a fully annotated track diagram showing the processes used will be fine. Note that it is essential to identify all samples used in your recording.

Your composition should show variety in its use of textures and drum patterns, so you should be sure to adopt a style in which this is possible. Work at this level should be ambitious in structure, with a variety of well-balanced tracks and an imaginative use of sampled sounds, perhaps modified by various effects processes, in order to achieve a rich mix of stylish material.

Fusions

Here again there is the opportunity to work in any one of a huge range of styles, the essential requirement being that the music draws on different cultural traditions, combining elements from both to produce a distinctive style of its own. Originally the term fusion was applied to the rock-influenced jazz style adopted by Miles Davis in the late 1960s, and taken up by groups such as Weather Report. Other types of fusion popular at this time included folk-rock, the latin-based rock of Carlos Santana, the art-rock interpretations of classical music by Emerson, Lake and Palmer, and the vocal jazz arrangements of Bach performed by the Swingle Singers.

Recent decades have witnessed a still greater range of fusion styles, including bhangra, salsa and celtic rock. Indeed, many multi-cultural pop styles can be seen as a type of fusion, arising from the influence of western pop music on local cultural traditions. In addition there has been further exploration of the ground between pop- and art-music styles in the work of cross-over artists such as Steve Martland and John Casken. It might also be useful to explore some earlier examples of the use of popular styles in art music, such as Debussy's *Golliwogg's Cakewalk*, Satie's *Parade*, Walton's *Façade*, Stravinsky's *Ragtime* for 11 instruments and the use of popular idioms in the music of Maxwell Davies.

Casken's *Piper's Linn* and Martland's *The World is in Heaven* appear in *Sound Matters* (Bowman and Cole). Martland's *Principia* and folk-rock from Steeleye Span can be found in *Aural Matters* (Bowman and Terry). Both these books also include examples of world music that may be useful for this topic. *The Rhinegold Dictionary of Music in Sound* includes excerpts from Debussy's *Golliwogg's Cakewalk* and the *Popular Song* from Walton's *Façade*.

Your work may be in any appropriate form, but it should exploit the idea of fusion and draw on appropriate elements from the different styles and idioms involved.

Film and television

The *New Anthology* provides one of the most useful sources of research material for this topic. There are also a number of books and websites about film music composition. Themes from many famous films are available as sheet music, but such publications are usually simplified arrangements for piano, and thus omit many important details, and they seldom include more than the main title theme so they are unlikely to be very helpful. However it would be useful to look out for scores and CDs of the following works, which are all based on film music: Prokofiev's *Suite from Lieutenant Kijé*, Walton's *Henry V Suite*, Copland's *Our Town Suite* and Vaughan Williams' Symphony No. 7 (based on his music for the film *Scott of the Antartic*).

Your own music could be for an existing film or video, an imaginary one, or perhaps one that is being made by other students at your school or college. You may submit your work as a recording dubbed on video if you wish, but this is not required – a clear account of the image that the music is intended to underscore is sufficient.

The subject could be historical (possibly giving the opportunity for some pastiche of an old musical style), a travelogue such as a video of a school foreign trip (perhaps including local musical styles to give a sense of location to the various scenes), a cartoon, a sports sequence or an extended commercial. Try to choose a topic with some dramatic content as this is likely to give you the opportunity for some interesting and vivid contrasts in your music.

It is acceptable to submit several short extracts for this topic – perhaps a title theme, a piece of illustrative music, various link passages (eg bridges that are designed to change mood) and a sequence for the final credits. Try to maintain a consistent style in such a submission and, if appropriate, link the sections thematically. Aim to convey a clear sense of mood, paying attention to the way music is used in the visual media to heighten and release emotional tension, as well as to create atmosphere. This will need careful attention to scoring.

Music theatre

For exam purposes this topic covers any type of music that involves a staged element in its presentation and so includes opera, operetta, ballet, musicals and rock opera, as well as the type of small-scale, semi-staged work in which the instrumentalists frequently take a dramatic role and which is often specifically described as music theatre. This last category includes works such as Stravinsky's *The Soldier's Tale*, Schoenberg's *Pierrot Lunaire* (which is often staged), Britten's church parables, such as *Curlew River*, and Peter Maxwell Davies' *Eight Songs for a Mad King* and *Vesalii icones*.

One of the songs from *Pierrot Lunaire* is in *NAM* (No. 40) and an extract from another is in *The Rhinegold Dictionary of Sound*. An excerpt from *Vesalii Icones* can be found in *Sound Matters* (Bowman and Cole).

Your own composition could be a short section of a musical or other music-theatre work, perhaps including a vocal introduction, a solo or duet, and ending with a dance number or a finale in which you could combine several voices and a chorus. It is not essential to score the accompaniment for full orchestra – you could confine yourself to a piano reduction (as used in rehearsals) or you could write for just a small ensemble of accompanying instruments. You could instead choose to write purely instrumental music designed for a dramatic work, such as an overture, music for a contemporary dance production, or incidental music for a play.

Choose a subject that will give you the opportunity to show a dramatic quality in your music, and a sense of theatre. A slow, dreamy ballad might be part of the submission, but it would be best to include some points of tension and conflict as well.

Specialist option B: Recital

If you choose pathway B for the specialist option, you will have to perform a solo recital instead of submitting the composition folio described on pages 12–15.

described on pages 12–15.

Requirements

You will need to plan a program that lasts at least 20 minutes. The minimum size of audience is two (your teacher and one other person) but you may feel that performing to such a small group seems more like an exam than a recital. Some people find that a class concert presented to a group of friends and fellow students is more natural, and provides a good focus for the preparatory work involved, but the occasion can be on any scale, including a lunch-time or evening concert at your school or college, or a gig at a public venue. Note, though, the requirements that your teacher must be present and that the recital must be recorded, so you need to discuss the proposed occasion with your teacher.

Any music that you play which is intended to be accompanied must be performed with accompaniment. This can be provided by a keyboard instrument, a group of other performers, or by a tape or electronic backing. It is important that you should feature clearly in a solo capacity in any ensemble pieces you choose to include, such as jazz improvisations or rock numbers. Remember that the examiners need to hear and assess only your part, and not the playing of other musicians.

If you are at all unsure if a particular piece would be regarded as a solo, check with your A level teacher, since Edexcel provides guidance on this matter.

You can include just selected movements from longer works if you wish, and if there are long sections in which only the accompaniment plays (as may occur in a concerto) these can be curtailed. But in other respects the music must be complete – you should not omit sections that you find too difficult.

You may use more than one instrument in your recital. For example trumpeters may wish to include a piece for cornet or flugelhorn, or perhaps a baroque piece for trumpet in D. Similarly a recorder player may wish to include works for both descant and treble instruments, and percussionists should certainly plan to show their skills on a range of both pitched and unpitched instruments.

Note that there are no marks for diversity. For example, if you are primarily a singer who can also manage a bit of piano playing, there is nothing to be gained by including an easy piano piece – it would be better to concentrate on achieving a high standard in your vocal repertoire. If you do play a second instrument to the same standard as your main study, the music for that instrument should be chosen with regard to achieving a coherent overall program.

Difficulty level

The technical difficulty of the music you choose also needs careful consideration. Easy pieces played musically are much more likely to be successful than difficult pieces marred by hesitations and breakdowns. In order to be able to achieve the highest marks the pieces need to be of grade 6 standard or higher (if you do not take graded exams your teacher will help explain what this means). If the majority of works are at grade 7 standard (or higher) your mark will be scaled up accordingly. There is no need to struggle to reach a high difficulty level (and risk a potential disaster if it proves too hard) since you will be given credit for what you can do with the music you offer, but you should be capable of presenting a recital in which all of the pieces are at least of grade 5 standard if you choose this option. If the pieces are below grade 6 in standard, or if the recital is less than 20 minutes in length, your mark will be scaled down.

Whatever your technical standard it is better to choose music that you can perform with confidence than to attempt a difficult work which stretches your technique to its limit. Works that are too demanding will leave no leeway for the inevitable nervousness that *will* arise under the conditions of a live assessment. The anxiety and tension they generate will be communicated to the listener, and will inevitably impede your musical interpretation.

Choice of music

The minimum 20 minutes length for the recital can include time for applause and any brief spoken introductions you choose to make. Audiences greatly appreciate the latter – it provides a moment of human contact rather than just seeing you sneak on and off without apparent awareness of others in the room. However keep to a short announcement of the work and perhaps a word or two about your reaction to the piece – such as why you enjoy performing it. Avoid a lecture about its date and form, and try to be positive – if you sound miserable and scared, your audience will be, too.

Choose pieces that you enjoy playing and that allow you to show a range of skills. Note that you must not include any items you offered for AS Music, or that you performed during the course as part of the *Performing and composing* unit. A surprising number of pieces, whether single-movement classical works or pop songs, are only about three minutes in length, so make sure that you have enough repertoire to last at least 20 minutes.

A programme with some variety is likely to serve you best. Your audience (and that includes your examiner) are likely to be more impressed by items which vary in style, mood and speed than a succession of all-too-similar slow movements. Try to start with something that grabs the attention, but that is not necessarily too difficult, such as a baroque allegro, or a lively electric-guitar solo. Alternate slow pieces with more lively items, and try to end with something destined to get the audience still wanting more – a humorous modern work or a hard-rock number.

Also remember to pace yourself carefully. Don't start with the most challenging work – if it goes wrong, your nerves may be shattered for the following items. Plan some items for the middle where you can relax a bit, such as an expressive slow movement or a lazy blues. This is especially important if you are a wind player or singer as you will need the opportunity to recover your breath and/or lip. Note that the recital can consist of a single long work, such as a concerto or song cycle, since this will by its very nature include the necessary variety for both performer and audience.

Preparation, performance and assessment

Reread the advice on pages 10–11 of the AS Guide, noting the importance of performing the complete programme in advance to someone who can give you some dispassionate feedback. Adequate rehearsal with the accompanist (if applicable) is vital, and a run-through in the final venue is essential.

You are required to provide programme notes on a form supplied by Edexcel. Mention the characteristics of each piece and how you intend to convey them, and also give reasons for your choice and order of items. After the event you can, if you wish, add a comment about the extent to which your intentions were realised in the recital. Note that the examiner will require photocopies of your solo part(s) as well as a recording of the event and programme notes.

Analysing music

There are two parts to this unit:

✦ a one-hour listening test that accounts for just under 40% of the marks for this unit, followed immediately in the exam by …

✦ a two-hour written paper that accounts for just over 60% of the marks for this unit.

1. Listening test

The test is presented on CD and you will be given your own copy of this CD which you are allowed to play as many times as you wish in the 60 minutes allowed. Each extract is recorded only once, so you will need to be familiar with the controls of your CD player in order to locate and repeat individual tracks efficiently; you will also need to pace yourself carefully so that you have time to answer all three questions in the test.

1. You will hear **three** different passages of music for which no notation is given. For each passage you will have to give a context for the music by answering questions on matters such as its style (eg baroque, minimalist, jazz, etc), its genre (eg anthem, opera, 12-bar blues, etc) and any prominent elements (eg atonality, irregular metre, etc). You will be asked to suggest a date of composition and to name a person (composer or performer) likely to be associated with the music.

   Context

2. You will hear **two** excerpts of music for which no notation is given. You will have to answer questions on the similarities and differences between the two excerpts in matters such as instrumentation, shared material, technique, style and so forth. The two extracts may be from different parts of the same piece or they may be from two different pieces by the same composer or band, that are related in style. Note that there may well be more differences than similarities, and that you may also be asked to identify the type(s) of music, and how they are related.

   Comparison

3. You will hear **one** excerpt of music for which a two-stave skeleton score will be provided. There will be three questions on pitch and rhythm, of which you must answer two:

   General test of aural perception

   (a) three short rhythms or melodies will be printed, and you must locate where in the score each of these is heard
   (b) you will be asked to notate the rhythm of a specific short passage heard on the CD
   (c) you will be asked to notate the pitches of a specific short melody heard on the CD (the rhythm will be given).

   In addition you will have to answer two further questions:

   (d) you will have to identify four specific keys, key relationships, chords or chord progressions in the music
   (e) you will have to write a short commentary on important features of the music that you can hear in the recording (and that are not obvious from the score or covered in the preceding questions) and place the extract in context.

I, II, IV, V (root position or first inversion)
III and VI (root position only)
VII in first inversion
V^7 in root position or any inversion
Ic, II^7b, diminished 7th
augmented 6th, Neapolitan 6th.

Bass part played by bassoon.
Opening phrase repeated octave higher.
Second section develops the opening motif.
Ascending chromatic scale in third section,
followed by oboe and flute in dialogue.
Dominant pedal prepares for the recap.
Flute imitates clarinet near the end.
Homophonic texture in the coda.

Listening Tests for Students (Edexcel A2 Music Specification) by Hugh Benham and Alistair Wightman, *Rhinegold Publishing Ltd.* Book 1, ISBN: 1-904226-46-9. Book 2, ISBN: 1-904226-67-1.

Listening Matters by David Bowman and Paul Terry. *Schott and Co Ltd.* ISBN: 1-902 455-08-8.

Aural Matters by David Bowman and Paul Terry. *Schott and Co Ltd.* ISBN: 0-946535-22-1.

Aural Matters in Practice by David Bowman and Paul Terry. *Schott and Co Ltd.* ISBN: 0-946535-23-X.

Sound Matters by David Bowman and Bruce Cole. *Schott and Co. Ltd.* ISBN: 0-946535-14-0.

The Rhinegold Dictionary of Music in Sound by David Bowman. *Rhinegold Publishing.* ISBN: 0-946890-87-0. This includes a chapter on 'Style, genre and historical context'.

In 3(d) questions on tonality will require you to identify specific keys, and they may involve recognising the following simple key relationships: dominant, subdominant, relative minor/major, and tonic major/minor (eg a change from C major to C minor, or vice versa). Questions on chords may involve identifying any of the chords listed left. Questions on chord progressions might include recognising the standard types of cadence, the circle of 5ths, and patterns such as V–I, I–V, IV–I, I–IV and V–VI.

In question 3(e) you will be asked to mention significant features of the music that are not immediately obvious from the skeleton score and that have not been identified in the other questions on this extract. You can answer in note form or continuous prose. You are likely to get one mark for each accurate point, so if eight marks are available you should aim to make eight points about the music. If you refer to specific events in the music you should give their location. For instance you should write 'imitation between flute and clarinet near the end' – not just the single word 'imitation'. An example of a successful type of answer is shown *left*.

If you include a general point about the impact of the music, make sure it is justified with evidence. For instance, you might state that 'a jolly mood is created by the major tonality, frequent cadences and lively articulation'. Just saying that it sounds happy, without giving reasons, will not be rewarded with a mark.

None of the music extracts in the listening test are linked to any particular area of study, so you are likely to encounter music which will be unfamiliar. In order to gain confidence in answering questions on identification it will be essential to listen to a wide range of music and to practise recognising its main features.

Beware of jumping to conclusions too quickly. For example the presence of a harpsichord in orchestral music might seem an obvious clue that the music is baroque – but if the orchestra also includes horns then the extract might actually be early classical, perhaps from the period 1750–80, when the harpsichord was still in common use. You need to listen for further evidence – if the phrase lengths run mainly in clear four-bar periods and the textures often consist of a melody with subordinate accompaniment, early classical would seem likely. But if the texture is more contrapuntal, and the parts are formed from short motifs that are spun out into long melodic lines, then late baroque might seem more probable. Similarly, remember that although church music might be sung by an unaccompanied choir, not all unaccompanied choral music is church music – it could be a madrigal or an excerpt from an opera, for instance. Get into the habit of tuning into a radio station such as Classic FM and trying to identify what you hear.

Your teacher will help you with practice materials (some are listed *left*), and you could also make your own listening tests by devising questions on a short extract from a piece that you play and could perform for the rest of the group to use as an aural test. You can also develop your own skills in dictation by writing down the rhythm and pitch of short melodic fragments you know by heart, and then checking the results by playing them on an instrument.

2. Written paper

For this part of the unit you must prepare **two** of the following areas of study:

- ✦ Music for large ensemble
- ✦ 20th-century art music
- ✦ Music for small ensemble
- ✦ Keyboard music
- ✦ Sacred vocal music
- ✦ Secular vocal music
- ✦ Music for film and television
- ✦ Popular music and jazz
- ✦ World music

One of your choices **must be an area of study that you offered for AS Music**. For A2 you will extend your earlier work by:

a) studying a prescribed 'special focus' work (or works) from the area of study, **and**

b) investigating a topic of continuity and change that relates to the area of study as a whole.

Your other area of study must be one that you did **not** offer for AS Music. For this area of study you are required only to prepare a prescribed 'special focus' work (or works). You do not have to learn about the other works in the area of study.

The music for each of these areas of study is provided in the *New Anthology of Music* (referred to as *NAM* in the rest of this book) with recordings on a companion set of four CDs. You are expected to use an **unmarked** copy of the anthology in the exam.

In the examination you will have to answer five questions, four from Section A and one from Section B, as follows:

Section A

There will be three questions on each of the 'special focus' works. You must answer **two** questions on the prescribed work(s) from the Area of Study that you also offered for AS Music **and two** questions on the prescribed work(s) from the new Area of Study that you have chosen for A2 Music.

> The rest of this book is based on the Special Focus Works and Topics set for examination in 2006 and 2007.
> It is expected that different works and different topics will be set in later years.

Section B

There will be two questions on each Area of Study. You must choose to answer **one**, which must be on the Area of Study that you started for AS Music and have extended for A2.

There is no division of works into list A and list B, as there is for AS Music. For A2 you need to study all of the works that relate to the prescribed topic of continuity and change. However remember that you only study **one** such topic – the one set for the Area of Study that you began at AS and that will appear in Section B of the paper. For the other Area of Study, the one that you start specially for A2, the only requirement is to study the prescribed 'special focus' work(s).

Preparation

Reread pages 21–23 of the AS Guide, noting the importance of focusing your studies on the music itself, not on peripheral matters such as learning biographies of composers or quotations of what other people have said about the pieces.

It is important that you have a clear understanding of technical terms relating to the music you study. Terminology is not an end in itself – it is merely a convenient way of explaining to other musicians precisely what you mean in as few words as possible. But remember that if you use technical terms incorrectly it will confuse rather than elucidate. We haven't included a glossary of terms in this guide, but you should refer to the glossary in the AS Guide if you encounter any term about which you are unsure. The most important thing is to be certain you know how the term relates to the sounds you hear – if you need further help, look up the word in the *Rhinegold Dictionary of Music in Sound*, play the example(s) on its associated CDs and check the notation in its set of scores.

For A2 it becomes increasingly necessary to listen to an extensive range of music, not only to prepare for the listening test but also to help you amplify your answers in the written paper. Try to make use of the holidays for this enjoyable task, remembering to listen for pleasure as well as for understanding.

The rest of this Guide consists of chapters on each Area of Study. These cover the information you are likely to need to know for the exam and sometimes include suggestions for additional listening and reading. During the course of each chapter there are a number of questions headed 'Private study' that are designed to help you check your understanding – these are not necessarily the type of question that you will encounter in the exam and in most cases the answers should be clear by carefully rereading the preceding paragraphs or the related section in the AS Guide. However at the end of each main section you will find a set of 'Sample questions' to give you some exam practice, particularly in your final weeks of revision. Some notes on how to revise effectively are given on pages 24–25 of the AS Guide.

Remember that your revision plan needs to include rereading the introductory information on your Areas of Study given in the AS Guide, as well as a thorough reappraisal of your AS notes for the Area of Study that you are carrying through from AS to A2.

Exam technique

In Section A you will have to answer four questions – two on each of your 'special focus' works. Each of these four questions attracts 10 marks (out of a total of 60) and your answer can be written in continuous prose, or note form, or as a set of bullet points. A good rule of thumb is to reckon that there will be one mark for each valid point that you make. A 'valid point' is one that helps answer the question directly. Just stating a fact about the music will not gain a mark if it is irrelevant.

In this book we often use expressions such as 'motif x', 'the second subject' or 'the third episode' when explaining music. If you do this in an exam answer, remember that it is *essential* to show the examiner exactly what you mean – for instance, 'the second subject (in the violin part of bars 15^4–26^3).

Support your points by making frequent references to the music, usually by means of bar numbers (eg 'a modulation to the dominant is confirmed by a perfect cadence in bars 13–14'). Be precise, adding the name of the part and/or the beat number(s) if necessary to avoid ambiguity. A widely understood method is to use small suffix numerals for beat numbers: for example, bar 4^3 means bar 4, beat 3. Be aware that giving detailed and relevant references to substantial points in this way can often gain you extra marks.

Make sure you answer the correct number of questions (four in Section A and one in Section B). Pace yourself carefully so that you are not rushed towards the end of the paper and that you have a few minutes to check your answers at the end of the exam. Choose your questions with care. Don't just dive in as soon as you happen to recognise the general gist of a question – first consider if you have enough knowledge to provide a really full answer.

For each of the four questions in Section A you are going to need to make 10 valid points in under 20 minutes. Although you have to answer only one question in Section B, it attracts 20 marks and must be written in continuous prose, as a short essay. It would therefore be wise to allow yourself 40 minutes to complete this question.

Essay writing

Developing a good clear style in writing prose will not only help your exam technique but will also prove useful in later life if you are required to write reports, evaluations or proposals. This takes practice, so it is important that you write essay answers (including some timed examples) during the course, as you work your way through your chosen specified topic.

The assessment will include your skill in written communication (which can gain you extra credit if it is good, and not just lose you marks if it is weak). If this is an area you find difficult, remember that one of the most useful tips listed below is to keep to short sentences. Make a point and then follow it up with an example (see the first essay on the next page). It will also help to make a brief plan of the essay, so you get an overview of all the points you wish to make, and can then arrange them in a logical order. Having to change tack in mid-essay in order to go back to some point you had previously forgotten can make your reasoning difficult to follow.

Nine tips for a good essay

+ Make sure that you understand the requirements of the question.

+ Plan the structure by making a note of the main areas to cover. It can be useful to devote one paragraph to each of these areas.

+ Begin by immediately addressing the question – don't waste time trying to 'set the scene' with background information.

+ Keep to the point. If you run out of ideas, it is better to examine the score carefully to see what you may have missed rather than to start introducing irrelevant facts.

+ Try to support each one of your arguments with evidence from the music itself, given in the form of references to specific bar numbers.

+ Avoid repetition. You don't get extra marks for making the same point twice, even if you clothe it in different language.

+ You should normally stick to factual information – if a personal opinion is required remember that it (like all your arguments) should be supported by reference to specific examples in *NAM*.

+ Avoid long sentences whenever possible.

+ Aim for handwriting that is legible and unambiguous.

Many of the Section B questions require you to make a specific evaluation of the works you have studied – such questions often begin 'Compare and contrast …' or 'To what extent does … '. The examiners will be looking for a balanced argument in your answer: 'In these respects there are similarities … but in these respects there are differences …'. Check that all your points relate to the question posed, since there is no credit for irrelevant information.

The ticks in these two examples show the type of points that are likely to be given credit, but they do not represent an official markscheme. In practice, the examiners will have agreed on a detailed markscheme for each question after an initial evaluation of a large number of answers.

As you can see from the example below, it is possible to cover a large number of points in a short essay if you are concise and stay focused on the question. When you look at this, and the essay on the next page, **remember that there is no one way of tackling a question – these are merely examples of different styles and neither represents a mythical 'right answer'.**

13a. *Compare the structures of the Sarabandes by Bach and Debussy*

Bach's Sarabande is in binary form, ✔ *typical of most baroque dances. The two sections are defined by their tonality.* ✔ *The first ends in the dominant at bar 12.* ✔ *The second is longer* ✔ *and modulates more widely* ✔ *before returning to the tonic at bar 29.* ✔ *At this point there is a modified restatement of the opening material.* ✔ *This is known as rounded* ✔ *binary form.*

The movement is based on a continuous development of the opening material. ✔ *For example, the sequence beginning in bar 5* ✔ *is derived from the motif in bar 1* ✔ *and the second section begins with a transposition of bars 1-2.* ✔

Debussy's Sarabande is also in two sections of unequal length, ✔ *separated by a double bar-line in bar 22, although the sections are not repeated.* ✔ *It also returns to the opening material in the second section (at bars 42).* ✔ *But whereas Bach's Sarabande is monothematic, Debussy uses a variety of independent themes.* ✔ *There are two in the first section (bars 1 and 9),* ✔ *the first of which is repeated at bar 15.* ✔ *He uses a new theme for the second section (bar 23)* ✔ *and another new theme at bar 50.* ✔ *Unlike Bach, he ends the movement with a coda, starting at bar 63.* ✔

While Bach uses tonality to define the sections of his form, Debussy's melodies are modal and his harmonies are complex, using key more as a means of colour than as a way to define structure. ✔

This is a first-rate answer which directly addresses the question by means of a valid point in every sentence. The structure is clear: the first half is devoted to Bach's Sarabande, the second to Debussy's, and comparisons are clarified in constructions such as 'Debussy's Sarabande also …', 'But whereas Bach …', and 'Unlike Bach …'.

The short sentences are unambiguous and almost every point is backed-up with references to specific bar numbers in the music. The use of technical language is secure, and the concluding paragraph is perceptive, showing an understanding that it is tonality which defines structure in Bach's Sarabande, but not in Debussy's.

Now, can you see why the following answer is less successful than the first? It is the same length, but relevant points appear far less frequently and there are no references to specific bars in the music.

13a. _Compare the structures of the Sarabandes by Bach and Debussy_

The sarabande is one of the dances of the Baroque suite. Bach's partita, which is really a suite, was published in 1728 and is in D major. Debussy's sarabande was written in 1894 and is a more modern version of the old dance.

Both works are lovely pieces, but Bach's music sounds more lively because it is often played on the harpsichord while Debussy's music is more dreamy because it is played on the piano.

Debussy uses thicker chords than Bach, to make his piece more interesting, and he uses more themes ✔ with several laid back tunes that pop up as the piece goes on.

Not everyone appreciated Debussy's music. Someone said 'he doesn't like the piano much'. That seems an unfair criticism.

Bach uses binary form ✔ but Debussy doesn't. He uses some other form. Another difference is that Debussy uses several different themes in his Sarabande. It is hard to work out the form because he doesn't write in clear keys for different sections like Bach ✔ does, but it looks like he has two sections and the second is longer, like Bach's. ✔

Debussy wrote a lot of other pieces, with titles like 'La Mer' and 'The Girl with the Flaxen Hair'. These were all composed after Bach had died so they are romantic pieces.

Neither sarabande would be very good music for dancing to, because they are both too slow.

There is nothing inaccurate in the first two paragraphs, but neither tells us anything about structure. The first is 'scene setting' narrative while the second consists mainly of subjective opinion.

Not until the third paragraph is there an attempt to tackle the question. The slang terms in the colloquial expression 'laid back tunes that pop up as the piece goes on' are not appropriate to this style of writing – it would be better to support the good first point by giving some examples (by bar number) from the score. The fourth paragraph throws in a memorised but unattributed quotation (it is actually from Debussy's piano teacher) which doesn't contribute to answering this question about structure.

The fifth paragraph is much more successful, with several valid observations (although the point about Debussy using more themes has already been made). The sixth introduces some irrelevant information, while the conclusion is unrelated to the question and misses the point that neither Sarabande was written for dancing.

Of course in reality most answers tend to fall between these two extremes, but hopefully these made-up examples will help you to develop your own written style in a clear and focused way.

Note that it is not necessary to copy out the question at the start. Some people find it helps to keep the wording in focus, but just writing the question number is sufficient.

Music for large ensemble

Special Focus Work for 2006 and 2007

NAM 4   CD1 Track 4
Vienna Philharmonic Orchestra
Conducted by Georg Solti

Wagner, Prelude to Tristan und Isolde

Before starting on this section you should work through (or revis
the information about the context and structure of this music give
on pages 33–34 of the AS Guide. Make sure that you understan
all of the terminology used on those pages.

Sounds and symbols

You will also need to understand how transposing and C-cl
instruments are notated in the score. Look at bar 83 of the sco
and learn the following points about Wagner's instrumentation:

Fl. 1,2,3	Three flutes, sounding as notated.
Ob. 1,2	Two oboes, sounding as notated.
C.A.	Cor anglais, sounding a perfect 5th below printed pitch.
Cl. 1,2	Two clarinets in A, sounding a minor 3rd below printed pitch.
B.Cl. (A)	Bass clarinet in A, notated in the bass clef and sounding a minor 3rd below printed pitch
Bsn. 1,2,3	Three bassoons, sounding as notated. The first and second bassoons here use the tenor clef. This indicates that middle C is on the second stave line down. From this, you can work out that the first and second bassoons are playing D♯ and B in bar 83.
Hn. 1,2 (F)	Two horns in F, sounding a perfect 5th below printed pitch when in the treble clef (when in the bass clef, as at bar 17, they sound a perfect 4th above printed pitch).
Hn. 3,4 (E)	Two horns in E, sounding a minor 6th below printed pitch.
Tpt. 1,2 (F)	Two trumpets in F, sounding a perfect 4th *above* printed pitch.
Tbn. 1,2,3	Three trombones. In bar 83, trombones 1 and 2 are using the tenor clef and play E♭ and C♭ – these are enharmonically the same pitches as those played by bassoons 1 and 2.
Tba	Tuba
Timp.	Timpani (kettledrums) – four different pitches are used in this extract.
Vln. I and II	Violins, divided into two groups (first and second) and sounding as notated.
Vla.	Violas. Sounded as notated, but written in the alto clef, in which middle C is the middle line of the stave. So in bar 83 violas are playing the same notes as trombones 1 and 2.
Vc.	Violoncellos (cellos). Here using the tenor clef and so playing the same E♭ as trombone 1.
Db.	Double basses, sounding an octave lower than notated.

Traditionally Italian served as a 'common language' for use in music scores throughout western Europe. However, Wagner was one of many 19th-century composers who sought to assert their national identity by increasingly using their own language for directions in scores.

Here are some other terms and signs you will see in the scor (foreign language terms are Italian unless otherwise indicated).

The German tempo direction in bar 1, *Langsam und schmachtenc* means slowly and languishing.

The figure '2.' (horns, bar 10) means that only the second horn i to play, while '1.' (flutes, bar 12) indicates that only the first flauti is required. At bar 15, 'a 2' means that both flautists are to play.

Look at the viola part in bars 16–18. The instruction *pizz.* (*pizzicatc* means pluck the strings while *arco* means bow the strings. In bar 22–23, *Sul G* directs the violinists to use the warm tone of thei lowest string (G) for these notes. In the cello part of bar 25, *zart* i German for 'tender'. In bar 29, *ten.* is short for *tenuto* ('held') an indicates that the note is to be sustained for its full length.

In the cello part of bar 36, *get.* is short for *geteilt* – this German wor indicates that the cello section must divide, with half the cellist taking the notes with upward stems and the remainder taking th notes with downward stems. Compare this with the viola part i bar 77. Here there is no instruction to divide, so all viola players will play both notes together as two-note chords. Playing two notes simultaneously on adjacent strings is known as 'double-stopping'.

The three strokes through the stem of each double-stop indicates the use of *tremolo* (confirmed by the abbreviation *trem.*) – in this case it is a bowed *tremolo*, which is produced by very short, fast up-and-down movements of the bow to create a succession of rapidly repeating pitches, so generating an exciting, rustling effect.

A different type of string *tremolo* can be seen in the violin and viola parts at bar 94 of *NAM 5*. This involves very fast finger movements, rather than bow movements, to create a rapid oscillation between two different pitches.

In bars 38–39, the German word *belebt* means 'animated' (at bar 43, *belebend* similarly indicates 'animating'). In the timpani part from bar 74 onwards, the abbreviation 'tr' (trill) followed by a wavy line instructs the timpanist to play a two-handed roll on each note.

At bar 84, the complex German phrase *Allmählich im Zeitmaß etwas zurückhaltend* could be translated as 'Gradually returning to the opening tempo – somewhat holding back'.

1. The title and Wagner's expressive intentions

Wagner's opera *Tristan und Isolde* is based on a story about a medieval knight called Tristan who is sent to bring Isolde from Ireland to Cornwall where King Mark awaits her as his bride. But Tristan and Isolde fall in love and betray King Mark's trust with disastrous consequences for all three of them. To all intents and purposes the Prelude is an overture which flows straight into the first scene of the opera (the curtain begins to rise in bar 106). This explains why it begins in A minor, but ends inconclusively with an imperfect cadence in C minor.

Wagner's expressive intentions are clear in the programme notes he wrote for a performance of the prelude that took place in a concert hall long before the first complete theatrical performance of the opera. In his purple prose Wagner says that the Prelude rises from 'insatiable longing … through anxious sighs … to the mightiest onset … of love's endless rapture … [before] the heart sinks back to languish in longing'.

These moods are represented by **leitmotifs,** thematic melodic or harmonic fragments that combine and mutate to make longer melodies. Thus 'insatiable longing' is represented by the rising chromatic motif marked *y* in Example 1 (*overleaf*), and by the famous 'Tristan chord' heard on the first beat of bar 2. Slightly modified versions of both motif and chord are repeated in an ascending **sequence** (bars 2–11) until, in an extended form, motif *x* strains upwards for Wagner's 'anxious sigh' – represented by the terrific **appoggiatura** in bar 17 (B sounding against an F major triad). The 'mightiest onset of love's endless rapture' is represented by rapturous sequences that reach the climactic return of the Tristan chord heard on the first beat of bars 81–83. The heart 'sinking back to languish in longing' begins with the strings' fiery descent from this unresolved discord (bar 83), continues with a varied recapitulation ('sinking *back*') of the first eight bars of the Prelude, and ends with the languishing cello/bass melody of the last six bars.

For an explanation of how some of the main leitmotifs relate to ideas in the opera itself, see page 34 of the AS Guide.

2. Motifs and leitmotifs

Leitmotif is a term that instantly comes to mind when Wagner is mentioned. It is, however, not very useful in discussions about this Prelude because, until the curtain rises, we do not have text or

Ex. 1

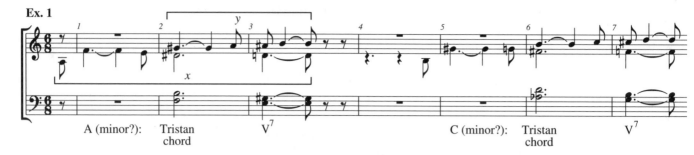

A (minor?): Tristan chord V^7 C (minor?): Tristan chord V^7

visual images with which they can be associated. The important thing to remember is that short motifs, such as those marked *x* and *y* above, can be joined to form longer melodies or contrapuntally combined to form textures of interwoven motifs. Remember too that harmonic fragments – even a single memorable chord – can function as leitmotifs.

Look at Example 1: motif *x* (which starts on the cellos and ends on the cor anglais) begins with a rising 6th followed by a chromatic descent from F to D. Motif *y* is an **inversion** of this descent – it is a four-note figure that *rises* in semitones from G♯ to B – and the two motifs combine to form two-part counterpoint. The close relationship between these two ideas is even more obvious in Example 2 (*left*), which shows the cello part of bars 8–10 printed on a treble stave. The last four pitches of motif *x* are a melodic inversion of motif *y* (B♭ is the enharmonic equivalent of A♯). We have called this *y¹* to show that this is the first manipulation of motif *y*. So motif *x* contains within itself an inversion of motif *y*.

Ex. 2

You might notice that *y¹* above is the same as the pitches of *y* played backwards: there are examples of this retrograde technique in the Prelude but it is highly unlikely that you will be required to identify them in the exam!

While the Tristan chord is justly famous, equally interesting is the fact that Wagner does not resolve the dominant 7th which follows it (E⁷ in bar 3). The listener is simply left to imagine chord I in the silence that then ensues. Indeed, Wagner avoids simple triads completely until bar 17 – and then, as we shall see, it is chord VI of A minor, and not chord I, that emerges from beneath a long appoggiatura. This process of hinting at a tonic, rather than defining it through functional cadences, is crucial to Wagner's concept of unending melody, explained on the next page.

Don't worry if you find it mind-boggling that so much should be concentrated into so little – worse is to come! Earlier we mentioned that a short harmonic progression or even a single chord could act like a leitmotif. There can be no more famous example than the first two chords of the Prelude. The first of these is a chromatic discord that has since become known as the **Tristan chord**. It is a type of chromatic discord called an **augmented 6th chord** (the interval of an augmented 6th can be seen in bar 2 of Example 1 *above*, between F and D♯. Wagner adds further tension to this with a long appoggiatura on G♯, that only resolves onto A (the 3rd of the chord) at the very end of the bar. Like most augmented 6th chords, the Tristan chord itself resolves onto dominant harmony – except that chord V⁷ in bar 3 is decorated with a chromatic **accented passing note** (A♯).

In bars 4–7 this two-chord harmonic leitmotif is transposed up a minor 3rd so that it ends on chord V⁷ of C (major or minor – Wagner swaps from one to the other as though they were the same). In bars 8–11, a longer and more intense version ends on V⁷ of E (major or minor). All three phrases end on unresolved dominant 7th chords and it is this lack of resolution of discords which is chiefly responsible for the sense of intense and unfulfilled longing that pervades the whole Prelude.

In bars 12–13 the last two bars of the previous phrase are repeated an octave higher, and this phrase is followed by a double echo of the last two melody notes (bars 14–15). Later we shall see that this process of **fragmentation** is one of Wagner's most important compositional techniques. In bar 16 chord V⁷ of A minor supports a transposed version of motif *y* (played in octaves by the violins). Example 3 shows how it begins with a very dissonant appoggiatura (E♯), continues with dissonant passing notes (G and G♯) and ends on the 3rd of chord V^7 (G♯). Now, at last, the terrific tonal tension that has accumulated through dissonant melodic lines and unresolved dominant 7ths should surely be released by resolution to the tonic chord of A minor? No, this is not Wagner's scheme at all. Instead of the leading note (G♯) resolving up to the tonic, the melody leaps to the most climactic appoggiatura we have yet heard – B above a chord of F major (chord VI). So, instead of the expected perfect cadence (V^7–I), we hear an interrupted cadence (V^7–VI) that acts as a springboard for the next set of motifs.

A third melodic leitmotif (*z* in Example 4 *below*) begins as the appoggiatura in bar 17 resolves to the 3rd of chord VI. Although the melodic line passes from violins to cellos there is no sense of discontinuity. This is one of the many techniques that Wagner uses to create what he called 'unending melody'.

This new leitmotif can be divided into two parts, which we will call *a* and *b*. Unit *a* is a rising three-note figure, encompassing the interval of a 3rd with a characteristic dotted rhythm. Unit *b* is a falling two-note figure, starting on a strong beat and encompassing intervals as large as a 7th and as small as a 2nd.

Whereas the individuality of motifs *x* and *y* is determined by pitch, the character of motif *z* derives as much from rhythm as it does from pitch.

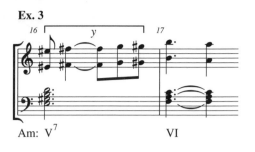

Ex. 3

Am: V^7　　　　　VI

3.　Unending melody

In the exam, if you want to refer to specific parts of the music using letters in the way we have done here, remember that you must show the examiner exactly what you mean by 'a' or 'b'.

Ex. 4

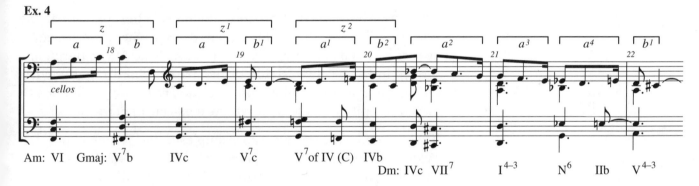

Am: VI　Gmaj: V^7b　　IVc　　　V^7c　　$V^7$of IV (C)　IVb
　　　　　　　　　　　　　　　　　　　　Dm: IVc　VII^7　　I^{4-3}　　N^6　　IIb　　V^{4-3}

Motif *z* is repeated in free **sequence** a 3rd higher (z^1), with the rhythm of its *b* unit reversed, and its falling interval contracted from a 7th to a 2nd. A third version of the leitmotif (z^2) is a tone higher still – its first note is tied on from the last note of b^1 – thus disguising the sequence – and the falling interval of *b* becomes a 5th (b^2 in bar 20). Wagner could easily have written straightforward sequences here, but instead he chose to manipulate his leitmotif so that the resulting melody sounds less mechanical. This use of varied sequence is another characteristic of his unending melody.

From bar 20, units *a* and *b* take on lives their own: a^2 is an **inversion** of *a* (and its first note is lengthened and syncopated), a^3 is a straightforward inversion of *a*, while in a^4 the pitch of the third note of the inversion is altered. Example 4 ends with a **repetition** of unit b^1. This technique of extracting small melodic units from a longer melody, and then developing these independently, is known as **fragmentation**. It is one of the chief means by which Wagner unifies his unending melodies.

N6 in bar 21 above is a neapolitan 6th – a chord that will be explained on page 37.

1. How does the clarinet part relate to the oboe part in bar 15?

2. What is the meaning of 'Sul G' in bar 23 (first violins)?

3. Explain 'a 2' in the bassoon part at bar 28.

4. Name the chord played by the four horns in bar 29 (you will first need to transpose all the parts to sounding pitch).

5. Find the following in the cello melody of bars 25–32 (you will need to refer to Example 4 on page 35 as well as the score):

   a) a sequence
   b) a transposition of unit a
   c) a transposed inversion of unit b^1
   d) transposition of unit b
   e) a new version of leitmotif z and a repetition of it

If you have answered these questions correctly and have understood the work we did on the first two leitmotifs (x and y) you should be able to tackle the melodies in the rest of the Prelude.

4. Harmony

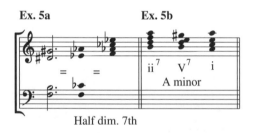

Ex. 5a   **Ex. 5b**

ii^7 V^7 i

A minor

Half dim. 7th

In Example 5a we have rewritten the Tristan chord enharmonically to show how it is the chord that jazz musicians know as a **half diminished 7th** – a diminished triad (F, A♭, C♭) plus a minor 7th (E♭) above the root. Notated this way it is the same as chord II^7 in a minor key (often used as an approach chord to a perfect cadence) as shown in Example 5b (given in the key of A minor for clarity).

And this is how the Tristan chord functions in the approach to the greatest climax of the Prelude (bars 81–83) where the harmony swings between II^7 and V^7 of E♭ minor in each bar. When the climax arrives in bar 83 this version of the Tristan chord rapidly fades, changes to the original notation and resolves to V^7 of A minor as a varied recapitulation of the first few bars gets under way.

There are other, less dramatic, examples of the Tristan chord, but Wagner uses the chord of the **augmented 6th** in a way that suggests that he regarded the two chords as interchangeable. In bars 36–41 a **harmonic sequence** features various versions of this chord resolving onto V^7 (with chromatic appoggiaturas, shown shaded *below*) or V$^{♭9}$. (The antiphonal woodwind repeats of each string phrase are omitted for clarity in the following example):

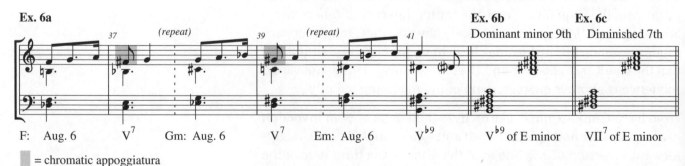

Ex. 6a   37   *(repeat)*   39   *(repeat)*   41   **Ex. 6b**   **Ex. 6c**

    Dominant minor 9th   Diminished 7th

F: Aug. 6   V^7 Gm: Aug. 6   V^7 Em: Aug. 6   V$^{♭9}$ V$^{♭9}$ of E minor   VII^7 of E minor

▨ = chromatic appoggiatura

Notice how the harmonic sequence is broken at bar 41 because, instead of resolving to V^7 of A minor there is an **irregular resolution** to the **complete dominant minor 9th** of E minor. This pungent discord (shown in both clefs in Example 6b) consists of chord V^7 plus a minor 9th (C) above the root (B).

If we omit the root from a complete dominant minor 9th chord we are left with a **diminished 7th chord**. It consists of four notes, each three semitones apart (see Example 6c). You can see this chord in context in Example 4, where it is marked VII^7 in the second half of bar 20. Like V^7, it most commonly resolves to chord I.

Another favourite chord of the romantic period is the **secondary dominant** – a chromatic chord that resolves to one of the triads of a major or minor key *without* bringing about a modulation. The chord marked * in Example 7 is G^7 (chord V^7d in C major) – but, despite the F♮, there is no sense of modulation to C major, since F♯ is quickly restored and the music clearly cadences in G major. The G^7 marked * is the dominant 7th of a *chord* (IVb in this case) rather than a *key*. You can see this secondary dominant used in context in the second half of bar 19 in Example 4 (on page 35).

Ex. 7

Example 4 also shows another colourful chromatic chord – the **neapolitan 6th** (marked N^6 in bar 21). It is a major triad on the flattened supertonic (a chord of E♭ in the key of D) and is generally used in first inversion, particularly as the approach to chord V in a cadence, as is the case here. The neapolitan 6th often appeared as chromatic spice in otherwise fairly diatonic 18th-century music. In the 19th century it was less favoured than the other chromatic chords we have discussed. Be that as it may, you should by now be able to spot another example in bar 61 and perhaps be able to compare the chords that surround it with those in Example 4.

The name 'neapolitan' refers to the city of Naples in Italy, where this chord became popular among early 18th-century composers. It is called a '6th' because, like all chords in first inversion, there is an interval of a 6th between the bass note and the root of the chord (G→E♭ in this case).

Finally we ought to notice how Wagner uses ordinary chords in an extraordinary way. Example 4 begins with a chord of F followed by the apparently unrelated chord of D^7. Yet they effect a modulation from A minor (remember that the F major chord is part of an interrupted cadence in this key) to G major. The answer lies in Wagner's systematic use of two fairly common techniques:

Binding notes are pitches that are common to two adjacent chords. All but two of the chords in Example 4 are linked in this way. Sometimes they are literally bound by a tie (e.g. the Ds in bar 19), sometimes the common pitches appear as repeated notes in the same part (e.g. the third and fourth cello notes) and sometimes they appear in different parts (e.g. the first cello note is repeated at the start of bar 18 by the second bassoon).

Conjunct voice leading refers to stepwise movement in any instrumental part. In Example 4 the bass is entirely conjunct until the cadence. Look at any of the other instrumental parts in the full score and you will find that they too are almost entirely conjunct.

Compare Wagner's conjunct bass part in passages such as this (and in bars 16–24) with the frequent leaps in Bach's functional bass part seen in *NAM 1*.

These two elements are characteristic of Wagner's mature chromatic idiom and they allow him to roam through the whole spectrum of keys while still avoiding atonality (though there are some pretty close shaves in this Prelude!). In Example 4 they play vital roles in the tonal change from A minor to G major at the beginning, where A and C are common pitches to the F major triad and the following dominant 7th, and where the bass part moves smoothly up a semitone). They are equally important in the unusual modulation from G major to D minor (where the **pivot chord** is a minor version of chord Ic in the first key and chord IVc in the second key).

5. Contrapuntal textures

Although Example 4 shows one of Wagner's most **homophonic** passages (witness the block chords in the accompaniment), even here there is contrapuntal tension between the cello melody and the bass (played by bass clarinet). The two parts have independent rhythmic lives, the treble often moving when the bass is sustained (and vice versa), and often in **contrary motion**. This combination of extremely chromatic harmony with contrapuntal textures is at the heart of Wagner's style.

The complex appearance of the score often disguises basically simple textures, based on up to three contrapuntal strands, each doubled at the same pitch and/or in octaves. Take a look at bars 80–82, where there are three contrapuntal parts:

+ Upper woodwind (who repeat motif z)

+ Horns, doubled by cellos then violas
  (who repeat the first four notes of motif x)

+ Trumpets (who repeat motif y)

These parts are supported by:

+ Double basses with third bassoon, tuba then third trombone, who underpin this contrapuntal display with the roots of the Tristan chord and V^9 of E♭ minor

+ Tenor trombones, who provide a harmonic filling to this well-upholstered contrapuntal texture.

6. Structure

We have already seen that, with the exception of bars 1–17, Wagner does his best to disguise the cadences that in earlier styles define phrases, complete sections and overall tonal structures. However, despite the seemingly unstoppable surge of his endless melody, there is a structure that is chiefly manifested through the varied repetitions of substantial passages, cadences, and tonal centres (acknowledged by the composer himself through his changes of key signatures). With music as complex and romantic as this there can be no one correct analysis, any more than one of the statements 'this glass is half full' and 'this glass is half empty' can be regarded as a true observation that makes the other false. So what follows is just one possible description of the form of the Prelude.

There are three themes, each made out of one or more of the three motifs: x, y and z. They appear as follows:

Theme 1 (bars 0–17) begins and ends in A minor, concluding with a massive interrupted cadence. It is fragmented into five phrases by lengthy silences (which are omitted in later recapitulations).

Theme 2 (bars 17^4–24, cellos then violins) starts in A minor but then modulates rapidly through D minor and B major to reach the first perfect cadence in the tonic (A major) in bar 24.

Theme 3 (bars 24^6–32^2, cellos later doubled by violins) begins in E major and ends on the tonic note (A) without a cadence.

Out of these three themes, Wagner builds the structure that we outlined on page 33 of the AS Study Guide, and which we will now explore in more detail here:

Exposition (bars 1–24): A minor/major

Themes 1 and 2 as above.

Middle section (bars 24^6–65): Shifting tonality centred on A.

A ternary structure. Section A begins with theme 3 (see *right*) and ends with a repeat of bars 17^4–21 (the beginning of theme 2, now on wind). Section B (bars 36^4–44) starts with antiphonal development of motif *z* from theme 2 and ends on a root-position chord of A major. Section A^1 (bars 45–65) is a re-working of section A. The dominant pedal on E in bars 63–70 links this section to the next.

Theme 3 is the eight-bar cello melody in bars 24^6–32^4. It is made out of motifs from theme 2, played in reverse order.

First recapitulation (bars 66–83): A minor/major modulating to E♭ minor

The start of this section is signalled by two statements of motif *y*, both at their original pitch (oboes and cor anglais). The second statement initiates a compressed recapitulation of the exposition in which the rests are omitted and some of the motives telescoped (woodwind, bars 68–74). Meanwhile the strings continue to develop motif *z* until, at bar 74, they repeat the first four bars of theme 2. The section ends (bars 77–83) with the contrapuntal combination of all three themes and the climactic Tristan chord.

Second recapitulation (bars 83–111): A minor modulating to C minor

The start of this section is really in bar 82, since it overlaps with the end of the previous section. It begins with motif *x* played *ff* on horns, trombones, violas and cellos, and it continues with motif *y* on oboes (bars 83–84). But instead of the long silences of the exposition, the violins link the phrases of theme 1 with motif *z* (bars 84–85 and 87–88). The route to the interrupted cadence (bars 93^4–94) involves a compressed restatement of the antiphonal treatment of motif *z* that was first heard in bars 36^4–40. As in the exposition, theme 2 (beginning in the cellos on the fourth beat of bar 94) overlaps the resolution of the appoggiatura, but motif *z* is divided between cellos and oboe, and the end of the phrase is modified so that it leads to an imperfect cadence in C minor in bars 99–100. In this key woodwind instruments make a vain attempt to start another recapitulation (bars 100^6–106) but the dominant pedal played by the timpanist recalls them to the foreign key of C minor. Finally the unaccompanied cello/bass melody starting in bar 107 links together the minor 6th at the start of motif *x* with the Tristan chord at its original pitch, but notated in C minor (E♭=D♯ and A♭=G♯) as the curtain rises.

Private study

1. What is a cor anglais?

2. Give the meaning of 'a 3' in the flute part at bar 73 and explain how the violas should play bars 77–83.

3. Write out the music on page 83 of the *New Anthology* on two staves, using only treble and bass clefs and notating all parts at their correct sounding pitch.

4. On the first beat of bar 97, how does the *sounding pitch* of the bass clarinet note (E♮) relate to the sounding pitch of the D♭ played by the double basses?

5. a) Name the three other pitches required to form the chord of a diminished 7th on B.

    b) Which of the following chords is the secondary dominant of chord II in C major: A^7, B^7, F^7 or G^7?

? Sample questions

In the exam there will be three questions on this work, from which you must choose to answer **two**.

1. What role does counterpoint play in the Prelude to *Tristan und Isolde*?

2. Comment on the orchestral timbres and textures used by Wagner between bar 80 and the end of the Prelude.

3. Explain what is meant by chromatic harmony, using examples from the Prelude to *Tristan und Isolde*.

Continuity and change in harmony and tonality

For examination in summer 2006 and 2007

You do not need to study this topic unless *Music for large ensemble* is the Area of Study that you undertook for AS Music and which you are now extending for A2.

Before starting work on this topic you need a thorough understanding of the material on *Music for large ensemble* in the AS Guide (pages 26–39). Remember that for A2 the topic draws on works from across the **entire** Area of Study, not just those in one of the two lists, A or B.

Introduction

It is important to be aware that tonality refers to the relationship between keys in music – it is nothing to do with the tone of musical sounds. *NAM 1* and *NAM 2* were written in the 18th century, at a time when harmony was primarily functional. This means that certain chords (particularly the dominant and tonic) had the specific function of defining keys through the use of cadences.

NAM 3, *NAM 4* and *NAM 5* were composed in the 19th century, at a time when the clear-cut relationships of functional tonality were becoming increasingly obscured by the ambiguities and exotic colours of chromatic harmony. In the 20th century there were many different approaches to harmony and tonality, from the use of highly dissonant chords and atonality (music that avoids the use of keys) to works that draw on harmonic ideas from the modal systems of folk and very old music, or on ideas from the blues or other types of world music. *NAM 6* is typical of this trend – it is strongly influenced by the modal styles of medieval and renaissance music, and contains little in the way of functional harmony.

Bach

Bach's harmony in the first movement of his *Brandenburg* Concerto No. 4 is almost entirely **functional**. The first ritornello (bars 1–83) begins in the **tonic key** of G major (bars 1–14), visits the **related keys** of D major (the dominant, bars 15–35) and C major (the subdominant, bars 40–43) and ends with a long passage in the tonic.

NAM 1 CD1 Track 1
Northern Sinfonia of England
Directed by George Malcolm

These keys are themselves functional since they trace the **primary triads** (I, IV and V) of G major. In this long opening section, functional harmony defines these keys by:

✦ **Root-position** tonic and dominant chords that form a set of **perfect cadences** in G major (bars 1–13 and 57–69) and D major (bars 23–35), with the **dominant 7th** treated as a **consonant chord** that requires no preparation.

✦ The careful preparation and resolution of **suspensions** of chords other than the dominant. In bar 44 the E in the first recorder part forms a dissonant 7th against F♯ in the bass, but it is prepared as a consonant part of chord II in the previous bar and it resolves to the 3rd of chord III (D) in bar 44. Similar suspensions occur on the first beat of the following three bars.

✦ **Diatonic harmonic sequences** that emphasise tonality by using every available diatonic chord. For instance, from the second quaver of bar 43 to the first quaver of bar 47 the return to the tonic key of G major is secured by the progression:

$$\text{IV–II–VII}^7 \quad \text{III–I–VI}^7 \quad \text{II–VII–V}^7 \quad \text{I–VI–IV}^7$$

✦ The use of segments of a **diatonic circle of 5ths** – a type of sequence in which the bass theoretically falls in 5ths, but in practice usually traces a repeating bass pattern of an ascending 4th coupled with a descending 5th (as in bars 79–80).

✦ The use of **diatonic root-position and first-inversion chords**. The only exception in this ritornello is the chromatic sequence in bars 69–72, which consists of secondary dominants resolving to root-position diatonic chords in an ascending pattern (see *right*). There is no modulation in these bars. What we hear are the chords IV, V and VI of G major, with each coloured by a prefatory chromatic chord. Such secondary dominants are by far the most common chromatic chords used by Bach.

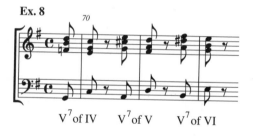

Ex. 8

$\text{V}^7\text{of IV}$ $\text{V}^7\text{of V}$ $\text{V}^7\text{of VI}$

✦ The use of a **pivot chord** (a single chord that is common to two keys) to create simple, smooth modulations. For example, the chord of E minor in bar 14 is both chord VI of the previous key (G major) and chord II of the new key (D major).

In the quotation on page 29 of the AS Guide, Haydn explained how his relative isolation obliged him 'to become original'. But if we are to appreciate his original harmony and tonality we ought first to look at passages which are *typical* of early classical music. In the first movement of Symphony No. 26 these are distinguished by:

Haydn

NAM 2   CD1 Track 2
Academy of Ancient Music
Directed by Christopher Hogwood

✦ Simple **tonic–dominant harmony** using all inversions of chords I and V^7 (for instance, bars 17–25 is a passage in F major in which no other type of chord is heard).

✦ Conventional 'sighing' **appoggiaturas** such as those that embellish chord Vb in bars 10 and 12

✦ **Feminine cadences** in which the dominant 7th is held over the tonic note with the resolution happening on the weak beat, as in bars 24–25 (note that there are two minim beats per bar in the very fast tempo specified by Haydn).

+ The **modulating circle of 5ths**, which is traced by the first note of each bar in the passage from bar 57 to bar 65. In order to avoid dropping below the range of the cellos and basses Haydn has to break back up a 7th in every other bar, thus emphasising the two-bar phrases of a melodic and **harmonic sequence**.

+ The **dominant pedal** in bars 65–68, above which chords V^7 and Ic alternate.

Most instrumental works from this period, including symphonies, do not use music to 'describe' things. They are works of 'absolute music' (or 'abstract music') that don't normally refer to anything beyond themselves. One aspect of Haydn's originality is the way in which he used this symphony as a vehicle for reflection on the crucifixion of Christ by using associated plainchant melodies as a cantus firmus in the oboe parts (as explained in the AS Guide). These passages differ from conventional early classical style in:

+ The **dissonant intervals** formed between the treble and bass in the opening bars – the key of D minor is obvious but without a harpsichord part (which Haydn would himself have improvised) the exact chords he intended are unclear.

+ The dissonant harmony of, for instance, bars 26–29, where the perfectly ordinary **tonic pedal** (second oboe) becomes a **double pedal** (F and A in the first violin) into which lower strings in parallel 6ths crash to form stunning discords.

+ Unexpected **diminished 7th chords.** After four bars of quiet tonic–dominant harmony in A minor in bars 65–68, suddenly chords VII^7b and Ib burst in to harmonise an augmented version of the melody that previously had been simply harmonised with chords I and Vb (bars 9–12).

+ The conventional tonal structure for a sonata-form movement is suddenly disrupted by the juxtaposition of the **tonic minor** (bars 80–99) with the **tonic major** (bars 100–133). Haydn obviously intended to suggest the eventual triumph of the cross, but this expressive use of tonality was unusual within a single movement in the early-classical style (or earlier).

Berlioz

NAM 3   CD1 Track 3
London Symphony Orchestra
Conducted by Colin Davis

There are some early romantic composers, such as Mendelssohn or Schumann, whose use of harmony and tonality can be seen to fit into a clear evolutionary progression stretching from Bach to Wagner. Berlioz is *not* one of them. Part of the reason is that this maverick French composer was so revolutionary that the English failed to understand his work until nearly a century after his death. Another part of the explanation is that in *NAM 3*, as in many of his works, Berlioz had particular expressive intentions that could only be realised in innovative and unusual ways.

For instance, in the third movement of *Harold in Italy* (*NAM 3*), Berlioz's use of harmony and tonality is determined by the rustic, folk-like images he sought to convey. These permeate almost every aspect of the music. The first section (bars 1–31) is an example of exceptional economy in harmonic and tonal resources. The key is C major throughout and the music consists of:

- A **double pedal** on the tonic and dominant. This bare 5th is intended to represent the drone pipes of an Italian bagpipe. In bars 14–20 it might seem that the dominant drone malfunctions – but a single **tonic pedal** is left.

- A folky oboe melody in C major (doubled an octave higher on piccolo) which, in combination with the first-viola part, forms chords I and V (or V^7) for 22 of the 31 bars of this *saltarello*.

- The somewhat flat 7th, so characteristic of bagpipes, is palely reflected by a real B♭ in bars 15 and 17. This encourages Berlioz to venture into subdominant harmony with chord IVc in bars 14, 16 and 18. In between he uses $V^7$of IV, which by now you should recognise as a **secondary dominant**. It is still the most frequently-used chromatic chord at this time and there are many more examples for you to find in the rest of the movement.

In the main body of the movement (bars 32–135) features that are typical of romantic harmony include:

- **Chromatic colour** offered by chords 'borrowed' from the tonic minor. For instance, the **half-diminished 7th** chord in bar 44 (D–F–A♭–C) is borrowed from C minor (where it is ii^7d) but here it colours the surrounding C major tonality.

- **Chromatic ornaments**, such as the A♭ above the chord of $G^{(7)}$ in bar 78 (this ornament is a **chromatic upper auxiliary**).

- The **irregular resolution** of one dissonant or chromatic chord to another. The passage in bars 170–176 is in C major and begins with ii^7d which, in bar 173, resolves regularly to V^7b (the 7th of the chord in the bass moves down a step to a consonant B). Next comes an irregular resolution of V^7b to 'V^7d of IV' (the leading note in the first chord falling a semitone instead of rising to the tonic). This secondary dominant ('V^7d of IV' in bar 174) then resolves irregularly to another secondary dominant ('$V^7$of II' in bar 175) which then *does* resolve regularly to chord II in bar 176. While these irregularly-resolved chromatic discords may seem complicated, they are actually common enough in both Bach and Haydn – and are two-a-penny in Wagner!

Among the many harmonic idioms that are peculiar to Berlioz are:

- Following the ancient device of a 4–3 suspension in bars 39–40 not with an expected tonic chord but with a diminished 7th (VII^7c of A minor) – and then proceeding directly to an inverted perfect cadence in C in bars 41–42. Harmony is being used for its pleasing colour rather than because it makes logical tonal sense within a pre-conceived tonal structure.

- The chromatic harmony of bars 53–57, which is incapable of functional analysis.

- The overall tonal scheme (or lack of it) in which C major persists throughout (apart from occasional forays into indirectly related keys, such as D minor in bars 97–111). Like chromatic harmony, tonality is being used for colouristic effect rather than to help build a satisfying musical structure.

Wagner

We have already studied the Prelude to *Tristan und Isolde* in some detail, so now might be a good time to go back and revise that part of the chapter (particularly pages 36–37) and then attempt an exam-style question on the work we have covered so far:

Sample question

Don't forget that there are essay-writing tips on pages 29–31 of this guide.

Compare and contrast Haydn's use of harmony in his Symphony No. 26 in D minor with Wagner's use of harmony in the Prelude to *Tristan und Isolde*.

Debussy

Debussy's indebtedness to Wagner is apparent as soon as we compare the opening chords of the *Prélude à L'Après-midi d'un faune* with those of Wagner's Prelude to *Tristan und Isolde*.

NAM 5   CD1 Track 5
Concertgebouw Orchestra
Conducted by Bernard Haitink

Ex. 9

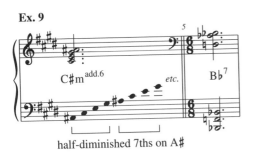

half-diminished 7ths on A♯

Debussy's first chord, heard in bar 4, is a half-diminished 7th and is followed by a dominant 7th on B♭ (see Example 9). The two chords are totally unrelated, excepting only that they share a common bass note (A♯=B♭).

Wagner's first chord, the Tristan chord heard in bar 2, is also a half-diminished 7th (disguised by enharmonic notation, as shown on page 36) and it, too, resolves onto a dominant 7th.

But there the similarity ends. Whereas Wagner's E^7 begins, however obliquely, to outline A minor as a principal tonal centre, Debussy's B♭^{7} is used purely for its colour and exotic effect in relation to the preceding chord. When this progression is repeated in bars 7–10, any suggestion that B♭^{7} is going to define the key of E♭ is negated by the repeated use of E♮ (notated as B) in the first horn part. The next chord occurs in bar 11 and is D$^{\sharp 7}$ (a triad of D major plus C♯). This is also tonally unrelated to B♭^{7}, but again a common pitch (D) is present, and it is this pitch which links D$^{\sharp 7}$ to another new dominant 7th (G^7/D). Because none of these chords suggest a key we have had to use chord names rather than Roman numerals in this description.

In fact, we have to wait until bar 13 before the key suggested by the key signature (E major) is confirmed by a decorated perfect cadence (easily detectable in the string parts). But the cadence is weakened by an added 6th in the horn part (C♯, notated as G♯). In the next bar A♯ and E♯ destroy this fragile sense of an E major tonal centre. Even in the closing bars, a perfect cadence in E (bars 105–106) leads in bar 108 to the same half-diminished 7th heard at the start of the Prelude. But now it resolves, not to a tonally-unrelated dominant 7th, but to an unambiguous tonic chord of E major.

In similar passages sustained bass parts, sustained major triads and decorated perfect cadences suggest *tonal areas* rather than definite key centres, for instance:

◆ The tonic key of E major is suggested by I–V harmony in bars 21–23 (E^{+6} in bars 21–22 and B^9 in bar 23)

◆ The A♭ in bars 51–54 (bassoons and double basses) and the recurring D♭ in bars 55–65 (double basses) suggest the unrelated key of D♭ major (an impression confirmed by the perfect cadences in bars 54–55 and 73–74)

- The inverted dominant pedal in bars 79–82 (second violins) together with the E major triad in the harp part strongly assert the tonic key, despite the chromatic flute part and the clashing bass part in bars 81–82

- The pedal E in bars 94–99 (horns and cellos) anchors the tonality to the tonic despite the chromatic and dissonant chords in the upper parts.

Elsewhere, Debussy uses chords for their colour, not for their function, so it is not surprising that tonality is often ambiguous. It is for reasons such as these that Stravinsky hailed the *Prélude à L'Après-midi d'un faune* as the first masterpiece of the modern era.

Tippett

The principal sources of Tippett's harmonic and tonal style in the *Concerto for Double String Orchestra* are the modal styles of the medieval and renaissance periods, and the lively, pungent discords employed by a number of early 20th-century composers, including Stravinsky. Let's consider each of these in turn.

NAM 6	CD1 Track 6
Academy of St Martin-in-the-Fields Conducted by Neville Marriner	

Sing the first orchestra's melody in bars 1–4 in free rhythm with each note roughly equal in length and you will discover it sounds like a fragment of medieval plainsong. You might also discover that it uses all five pitches of a pentatonic scale (A, B, D, E, G). So, although it sounds modal, we do not have enough information to identify a particular mode (like major and minor scales, modes all have seven pitches). But look at both of the melodies in bar 5 and you will discover the missing notes (C and F) of the **aeolian mode.**

The **aeolian mode** uses the same pattern of pitches as the natural minor scale: A, B, C, D, E, F and G.

Now look at the second orchestra's four-bar melody starting in the first bar. Notice that, like most plainsong melodies its range does not exceed an octave and that it includes all of the notes of the aeolian mode transposed up a tone (B, C♯, D, E, F♯, G, A and B). In plainsong, a single chromatic alteration of the mode is common, particularly to avoid outlining a tritone (e.g. between F and B). In terms of the aeolian mode on B, the two C♮s are chromatic notes needed to avoid outlining a tritone from the low G to C♯ (bars 2–3) and a tritone from C♯ to the high G (bar 4).

When combined, these two versions of the aeolian mode fight with each other to produce a seemingly random assortment of harmonic intervals. But there are only two discords (the 9th on the first quaver of bar 2 and the 7th on the second quaver of bar 3) and they both resolve correctly by falling a step to a consonant interval. In this and other aspects of his two-part counterpoint, Tippett was following the practice of the Tudor composers he so admired – but the **bimodality** of the first four bars (and other more complex passages) owes nothing to the past.

In such neoclassical works as *Pulcinella* (*NAM 7*), Stravinsky cultivated a 'deliberate wrong note' style, sometimes known as **pandiatonicism**, that was another important influence on Tippett. In bars 85–89 of the first movement from the *Concerto for Double String Orchestra*, there is a terrifically exciting passage in C♯ major. If you find it difficult to think in this key (in which every degree is sharpened) just forget the accidentals and imagine it to be C major. Sing or play the melodic strands and you will find they all make

Pandiatonic refers to music based on the free use of unresolved dissonances from the diatonic scale. These often appear in the form of added notes (e.g. the note D added to a C major triad, making C^{+2}).

Bar 51[1]	D	= V of G major
Bars 51[2]–52[1]	F	= ♭VII of G major
Bars 52[2]–53[1]	B♭	= ♭III of G major
Bars 53[2]–56	C	= IV of G major
Bar 57	G	= I of G major

perfectly good tonal sense, whether they descend conjunctly from the dominant to the tonic (e.g. second orchesta, violin 1, bars 85–88[1]) or leap about the notes of the tonic chord (e.g. cellos, bar 86). Add them together and it becomes apparent that the counterpoint in bars 85–86 strongly suggests chord Ib (even though there's an added 2nd in bar 85 and an added 4th bar 86).

A perfect cadence is formed between a spicy version of chord V in bar 87 and an astringent version of chord I in the next bar. But when we look at the intervals between the parts, on every quaver we find the same random collection of concords and discords as that in the first four bars – and this time they don't resolve 'correctly'. So, every note in these four bars is diatonic, and standard chord progressions can be detected. But the chords are infested with 'wrong notes' that ginger-up these conventional progressions. This is what is meant by pandiatonicism.

Now let's examine the second subject (bars 39–67) of this sonata-form movement where we will find more important features of Tippett's harmonic and tonal style. The passage revolves around G major, a tone below the tonic of the whole movement.

The most tonal passage in the whole movement occurs in bars 39–50. Essentially it is **an extended perfect cadence in G major**. In bars 39–42 chord I is implied by a melody that starts and ends on G and includes all but one of the degrees of a scale of G major (and no other pitches). In bars 43–45, alternating parallel root-position triads of D and C major (violins) over root-position arpeggios of D (violas, cellos and basses) make chord V[7] of G major (with an added 9th and 11th). The perfect cadence is completed when this chord resolves to the tonic in bar 46. Finally, bars 39–42 are repeated an octave lower to form bars 47–50, with the melody again implying chord I. The only modal touch is F♮ (bar 46) which, in this context, suggests a descending mixolydian scale (G–G on the 'white notes').

In bars 51–57, bass arpeggios outline a progression of root-position chords, shown *left*. All three primary triads of G are present (I, IV and V) but this functional harmony is coloured by modal-sounding chords on the flat 3rd and 7th degrees. This underlying harmonic progression is decorated with alternating root-position triads that are similar to those in bar 43. Here they sound very modal because of the flat 7ths they add to the arpeggios. None of these decorative chords turns the basic triads into dominant 7ths because none of them resolves. Listen out for Tippett's Tudor-like **false relations** (such as F♯/F♮ in bar 51) and notice the **lydian 4th** (F♯) in bar 56. The main tonal centre of the second subject (G major/minor) returns in bars 57–59, then alternating roots similar to those already discussed lead back to G again (bar 65) but the descending scale is cunningly bent towards E minor at the start of the development.

The development (bars 68–128) contains many passages of harmonic conflict where tonality disappears. The best example starts in bars 113–117 with cellos and basses outlining chords of A♭, C and E. No big deal – 3rd-related chords occurs in Wagner. But notice that Tippett wilfully sustains the A♭ of the first chord so that it grinds against the G♮ of the second chord (likewise the C of the second chord clashes with the B of the third chord). Now listen to the violin parts – can you spot the patterns based on a decorated **whole-tone scale**, starting at bar 113? In bars 113–117 this scale (that lacks clearly-defined tonality) clashes violently with the three major chords we have already discussed. But in bars 118–122 Tippett introduces an **augmented triad** (C–E–G♯) which surges upwards with a repetition of the decorated whole-tone scale. The augmented triad is the only type of triad that can be constructed from the pitches of a whole-tone scale. It is just as tonally ambiguous and its dissonant effect clamours for resolution. This comes when the ascending whole-tone patterns 'morph' into an ascending melodic minor scale of the tonic key (bars 126–128) leading to the recapitulation of the first subject, which starts at bar 129. Despite the best efforts of the lower strings of the second orchestra there can be no doubt about the aeolian tonality, now that the violins of the second orchestra supply all degrees of this mode. As in classical sonata-form movements, the second subject (bars 165–193) is now in the same key (A major) as the first subject.

The structure of the whole movement is defined by modes as well as by major keys – but both often contrast with passages in which a sense of tonality seems to disappear. Continuity is evident in a sonata-form structure that even Haydn might have recognised – but he would have been surprised to find that tonic–dominant polarity (or minor–relative major polarity in *NAM 2*) had been replaced with tonal centres a tone apart (A and G). Be that as it may, we are now in a position where we can discern this overarching tonal structure, summarised in the box on the opposite page.

Private study

1. a) Explain what is meant by functional harmony.
    b) The first example of functional harmony in *NAM 5* occurs in bar 13. What is it?

2. Show how the chord of G major in bar 39 of *NAM 1* functions as a pivot chord.

3. In *NAM 2*, how does the key of bars 100–133 relate to the tonality of the rest of the movement?

4. What is a double pedal? Give an example from *NAM 3*.

5. Wagner's work was described in his own time as 'music of the future'. How novel was his use of harmony in *NAM 4* compared with that in earlier works in this Area of Study?

Sample questions

In the exam there will be two questions on this topic, from which you must choose to answer **one**.

(a) Contrast Bach's approach to tonality in *NAM 1* with Tippett's approach to tonality in *NAM 6*.

(b) What similarities and differences do you notice between the harmonic resources used in *NAM 3* and *NAM 2*?

(c) By comparing *NAM 5* with *NAM 4*, show how Debussy's use of harmony and tonality was influenced by Wagner.

20th-century art music

There are *two* Special Focus works, *NAM 9* and *NAM 12*, both of which must be studied if you are taking the exam in 2006 or 2007.

Special Focus Work 1 for 2006 and 2007

NAM 9   CD1 Track 11
Coull Quartet

Shostakovich, String Quartet No. 8 (first movement)

Before starting on this section you should work through (or revise) the information about the context and structure of this music given on pages 47–48 of the AS Guide. Make sure that you understand all of the terminology used on those pages.

Context   If *NAM 9* is the only music by Dmitri Shostakovich that you have so far encountered, it may come as a surprise to learn that his long and varied output includes nationalist operas with almost 'sing-along' tunes, rousing marches, much film music (his score for the 1955 film *The Gadfly* includes one of the most famous and beautiful melodies ever written for film), and even a jolly suite for jazz orchestra, reflecting popular music styles of the 1930s.

Shostakovich's eighth string quartet is clearly at the opposite end of the scale from such works. Its intense and gloomy nature reflects the increasing introspection that colours much of the music that the composer wrote in the later years of his life.

The circumstances of its composition, along with an explanation of the DSCH motif, are outlined in the AS Guide. In addition to the personal stamp of DSCH, Shostakovich included many quotations from music that had a particular meaning for him throughout all five movements of the quartet. However, to this day musicologists debate exactly what these might signify.

The received wisdom is that the work was written 'in memory of the victims of fascism and war' (the dedication printed in the original edition of the score) and was composed by Shostakovich in 1960 as a response to seeing the aftermath of the wartime bombing of Dresden. However, Shostakovich had visited Dresden ten years earlier, when the devastation was much more obvious, and he had not been motivated to write any such 'war requiem' then. In 1960 he was not even staying in Dresden – he was convalescing some kilometres away in the town of Gohrisch. The story that he saw Dresden in ruins and wrote the quartet in three days is appealing, but it is equally likely that he had been formulating the work as the next in his long series of quartets long before going to Germany.

Shostakovich later wrote to a friend: 'One could write on the frontispiece: "Dedicated to the author of this quartet".'

The dedication to the 'victims of fascism and war' may not be as clear-cut as it seems – the words have the type of double meaning that many Russians became used to under communism. Dissidents had long referred to the communists as 'fascists' and they would have understood that Shostakovich's 'victims of fascism' did not necessarily refer exclusively to those persecuted by the Nazis. It is likely that the composer saw himself as one of those victims, and intended the eighth quartet to be his final work. 'When I die,' he wrote to his friend Isaak Glickmann, 'it's hardly likely that someone will write a quartet to my memory. So I decided to write it myself.'

The clearest evidence that Shostakovich saw his eighth quartet as his own memorial comes in the wealth of quotations it contains from works connected with death and suicide, to which the composer often links his own DSCH motif with poignantly autobiographical significance. Shostakovich's son has confirmed that his father's thoughts were turning towards suicide in 1960 – a crisis perhaps brought on because Shostakovich was being forced to join the communist party that he loathed, and doubtless exacerbated by the recent diagnosis of an incurable inflammation of the spinal cord, which had already led to paralysis of his right hand.

We will probably never know if Shostakovich intended this work to have an autobiographical subtext. The composer had long since learned that it was better to remain quiet about any extra-musical meaning in his music and he left few clues. However, these days many people find it difficult to escape the conclusion that Shostakovich saw his eighth quartet as a requiem for his own life under the Great Terror and its aftermath, even though he was prudent enough to give it a wider context.

Shostakovich's DSCH motto is shown in Example 1. A **motto theme** is a motif or a melody which is used to help give unity to a multi-movement work. The idea had been used by a number of composers from the 19th century onwards, and generally they ensured that the motto can easily be recognised by the listener, even when it is transposed or modified to suit different contexts.

Although you will often see DSCH described as a motto, his use of the technique in this work is altogether more subtle. The pitches of DSCH come from the four notes of a C minor scale bracketed in Example 2. Using scale numbers, we could describe these as 2317, as shown in Example 3.

DSCH (from here on we will call it 2317) first appears in the cello part at the very start of *NAM 9*. The cello is answered by the viola, also playing 2317, but transposed up a 5th to the key of G minor. You shouldn't have too much difficulty in spotting the many other appearances of 2317 in the first movement, providing that you can recognise the pattern in different keys and don't get confused by the alto C clef used in the viola part.

However, in bar 67 the first violin rises through a new version of the four pitches – 7123 (= HCDS in C minor). In the next two bars the second violin introduces the variant 1732 (= CHSD in C minor). Even more subtle is the viola part in bars 95–98, where we hear 3217 (SDCH) in A minor, as shown in Example 4.

Many other permutations of these four pitches, some fragmentary and some transposed, occur throughout the entire quartet. So, DSCH is not merely a motto but a compositional resource of immense power that Shostakovich can re-order in a myriad of ways, of which DSCH is just one variant, albeit the most prominent. By changing the order of 7123 Shostakovich is able to make his musical signature act as both a launch pad for new ideas and as a pervasive unifying device in a way that would be too obviously repetitive for a motto theme alone. It is a technique that gives the work an extraordinary unity.

The potential for alternative interpretations of this work is vividly illustrated by a series of 'hammer-blows' in the fourth movement: some commentators suggest they reflect the exploding shells raining down on Dresden – but the composer's son thought they were a chilling reminder of the secret police banging on his father's door in the middle of the night.

It is unlikely that you would need to go into detail on matters such as these in an exam answer. However, appreciating the circumstances under which this work was written should help explain its often pessimistic character.

DSCH

Ex. 1

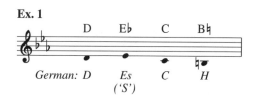

Ex. 2

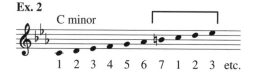

Ex. 3

Ex. 4

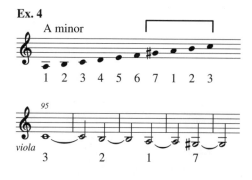

Form

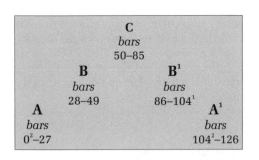

The first movement of the quartet is in **arch form**, which we can represent as ABCB¹A¹. In other words, the last two sections are modified repeats of the first two sections, with their order reversed, as shown *left*. When using bar numbers, notice that the movement begins with an anacrusis (an up-beat), so bar number 1 starts with the second note of the opening cello solo (E♭). Although the time signature is shown as $\frac{4}{4}$, Shostakovich's metronome mark ($\downarrow$=63) suggests a minim beat. So, when we have added superscript figures to bar numbers in the following account, they refer to the first or second *minim* beat in the bar.

Section A

The movement opens with **imitative** treatment of the DSCH motif, heard first in the cello (C minor), answered by the viola (G minor), restated by the second violin (C minor) and answered by the first violin (F minor). Although the harmony is dissonant, this choice of keys (I, IV and V in C minor) reveals how Shostakovich's style is often essentially tonal. However, the harmony in these opening bars allows for no simple cadences to define this tonality and offer points of repose – new dissonances always move the music on.

DSCH returns to the viola (marked 'solo') in bars 8–10 and then a clearer sense of C minor emerges as the viola sustains G as a dominant pedal, above and below which the three other parts play DSCH in octaves. But the G becomes the 3rd of a totally unexpected E minor triad in bar 13. The effect is disorientating, and so are the **parallel chords** in the lower string parts that follow it (E, E♭, D and E♭ again) – all below a sustained B♮ in the first violin. Yet, despite this non-functional progression, the key of C minor is immediately regained by the return of the DSCH motif in the solo for second violin starting at bar 15², where it is decorated with an **échappée** (the 'escape note' marked * in Example 5):

Ex. 5

C minor is also underlined by the resolution of the first violin's leading note (acting as an inverted pedal throughout bars 13–16¹) to the tonic and its descent through the tonic triad of C minor to another inverted pedal (E♭ in bars 17–19).

In fact this passage is a skilful fusion of the DSCH motif with a quotation from the opening bars of Shostakovich's first symphony:

Ex. 6

In the quartet the passage above is transposed down a semitone, the first four trumpet notes are superimposed on the DSCH motif, and the beginning of the original bassoon part is represented by the escape note in our previous example. It is also no accident that the falling minor 3rds and rising semitones correspond with the first two intervals of the DSCH motif. Shostakovich wrote his first symphony in 1926 when he was 19. It was brilliantly successful, but in a completely different style to his later works. It is as though the informed listener to the quartet is being invited to compare the devil-may-care attitude of the young man with the death-obsessed personality of the mature composer.

After another passage of ambiguous tonality (bars 19–22), C minor is affirmed in bars 23–27, supporting a clear statement of DSCH in the first violin part. The section ends with its first (and only) defintive perfect cadence (V^{9-8}–I) in bars 25–27.

Section B starts in bar 28 and is pinned to C minor by a **double pedal** (on I and V) lasting more than 17 bars, and by the return of the DSCH motif at its original pitch starting in the cello at bar 46. Above the very static accompaniment of the drone, the first violin introduces a chromatic phrase that falls then rises, ending with a triadic figure that Shostakovich modifies in a variety of ways in this section (see Example 7).

The section ends with a new permutation of pitches 2317 in the first violin part of bars 44–46 (marked *x* in Example 8 *below*). It includes the falling 3rd (E♭–C) of DSCH but D is replaced by D♭. The B♮ at the end of this variant is also the first note of 7123, which is used as a **countermelody** against the original DSCH motif in the cello (also shown *below*). The two together form inverted perfect cadences in C minor that mark the end of this second section.

Section B

Ex. 7

Ex. 8

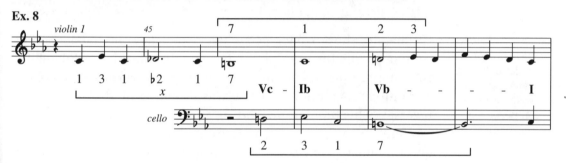

Section C begins at bar 50 (marked 'a tempo') with a first violin motif (Example 9) that, while seemingly new, emphasises the rising and falling semitones of DSCH. The second violin extends this motif to three bars (bars 52–54) by repeating the falling semitone, after which Example 9 is treated as a free rhythmic ostinato with changing pitch contours. The two-part counterpoint in bars 67–70 reveals Shostakovich's skill in manipulating his basic melodic material. Example 10 shows how one of the variants of the ostinato figure in violin 2 ends with the first two notes of the 1732 variant of DSCH (extended by sequential repetition of the falling semitone). Meanwhile violin 1 provides a countermelody consisting of 7123 and its retrograde (3217), linked by the common note 3 (E♭):

Section C

Ex. 9

Ex. 10

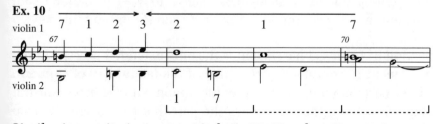

Similar ingenuity is apparent in bars 75–78, where two statements of the rhythmic ostinato in violin 2 are joined by a tie but the pitches derive from 2137 in D♭ minor (E♭–D♭–F♭–C♮). Notice how often D♭

– the flattened supertonic we discussed earlier – adds chromatic colour to variants of the second violin ostinato. All of this motivic manipulation is supported by a tonic pedal (briefly interrupted by a dominant pedal) which locks the chromatic variants of this rhythmic ostinato to the tonic key of C minor.

But the most striking feature of section C is the first violin melody which starts in bar 63. It begins with an E♮ that, with the lower parts, forms a chord of C major, but this ray of light is subverted by a descent that lingers on B♭, thus emphasising the tritone B♭–E♮ before continuing to G. This melody, along with the 3217 variant of DSCH, derives from a climactic melody in the first movement of Shostakovich's fifth symphony:

Ex. 11

trumpets **ff** *(with insistent side-drum rhythm)*   3   2   1   7

To understand this musical reference we must go back to January 1936, when Russia's president Stalin walked out halfway through a performance of Shostakovich's hitherto very successful opera, *Lady Macbeth of Mtsensk*. Within days *Pravda*, the state-controlled newspaper, publicised this offical displeasure by carrying a damning review of the work. The opera was banned, the premiere of Shostakovich's fourth symphony was summarily cancelled, and further denouncements of the composer appeared in the press.

Shostakovich knew the fate of other artists who had incurred the displeasure of the Satlinist state and for some time he was convinced that he would be arrested and imprisoned. Although this never happened, according to friends, the composer kept a packed suitcase ready for the night when the secret police would call.

Ultimately Shostakovich felt obliged to curry official favour by composing his fifth symphony (cringingly sub-titled 'A Soviet artist's reply to just criticism') for the 20th anniversary of the 1917 communist revolution – but he was shattered by this unexpected reversal of his reputation. And so it seems likely that by including a reference to the fifth symphony in his eighth quartet (and by quoting music from *Lady Macbeth* itself in the last movement of the quartet), he was underlining the dreadful personal impact of the shameful 'Lady Macbeth affair' in a quartet that is now widely regarded as uniquely autobiographical.

Returning now to section C, the end of this central part of the first movement is defined by a variant of the treble and bass parts of the cadence that concluded section A, with violin 1 stating DSCH in **augmentation** starting at bar 79. For the first three bars the texture is **homorhythmic** (all parts have the same rhythm) but the inner parts distort the harmony so that in bar 80 what had been chord Ib in bar 24 becomes the unrelated chord of E♭ minor. And the major version of chord IV (F major) in bar 81 only makes the minor 9th (A♭) and minor 7th (viola, F♭) in chord V (bar 82) seem even more threatening. But the dissonances resolve to V^7–I in bars 83^2–85, thus ending the section with a perfect cadence in the tonic key.

By now you may have noticed that each of the first three sections has ended with a clear reference to DSCH at its original pitch, followed by a perfect cadence in C minor.

Section B^1

Section B^1 begins at bar 86 and is the only extended passage in the movement to completely break free of the fateful key of C minor. Violin parts moving in 3rds provide a moment of greater warmth and below them the cello plays the part that had originally been allocated to violin 1 back in bar 28. Although the cello part is chromatic, the accompaniment clearly starts in A minor before giving way to F♯ minor with a prominent flattened supertonic (G♮).

C major briefly emerges at bar 95, but the first violin's statement of 3217 in C major (bars 96–99[1]) is undermined by the viola's 3217 in A minor in parallel 3rds. The cello E♭ in bar 97 impinges on both keys and leads to the chromatic bass line of bars 99–104.

In bars 104–114[1] the music of bars 11[2]–21[1] returns, leading to a final appearance of DSCH at its original pitch (violin 2, bars 118[2]–121). As at the conclusion of three of the previous four sections, this is the signal for a perfect cadence in the tonic. This occurs in bars 120–122[2], which are a repeat of the cadence at the end of section C (bars 82–84[1]) with violin parts swapped round. In bars 122–123 the second violin briefly refers to the motif from the central section (Example 9, page 51). A repeat of this motif is cut short by the sustained G♯ in bar 125. This is an **enharmonic** spelling of A♭ and it forms a link between the keys of C minor (first movement) and G♯ minor (second movement). The word *attacca* in the final bar indicates that the next movement should follow without a break.

Section A[1]

Notice how the staggered opening of this section in bar 104 (cello D, then second violin D, then the first violin's high D) and the viola's sustained G that continues from the previous bar, allows this final section to emerge gradually out of the end of the previous section.

You may feel that Shostakovich's preoccupation with ideas derived from 7123 seems a rather mechanical approach to composition. However, these pitches have great personal significance for the composer, especially because of their use in some of his most significant earlier compositions. We don't know in detail how Shostakovich worked, but many composers will say that the unity of a piece such as this comes less from mathematical juggling of pitches than from a largely subconscious process of working with enormous intensity on a carefully chosen set of very limited resources.

Private study

1. Explain precisely how the letters DSCH relate to the first four cello notes of the entire work.

2. What are the only two pitches played by the viola between bars 50 and 78?

3. Compare bars 87–92 with bars 28–33.

4. (a) What effect do you feel the long pedal notes have on the character of the music?

    (b) What do you notice about the tessitura of the string parts?

5. What examples would you choose from *NAM 9* to show that Shostakovich often reveals a traditional view of tonality?

Reich, New York Counterpoint (second movement)

Before starting on this section you should work through (or revise) the information about the context and structure of this music given on pages 50–51 of the AS Guide. Make sure that you understand all of the terminology used on those pages.

We concluded our study of *NAM 9* with the point that it is a work concerned with the exploitation of a very limited set of musical resources. This provides a clear link to *NAM 12*, the minimalist style of which is also dependent upon the manipulation of very limited resources. But the results sound very different. Why is this?

Special Focus Work 2 for 2006 and 2007	
NAM 12	CD1 Track 16
Roger Heaton	

Firstly, Steve Reich's movement is entirely **diatonic** – it contains not a single note outside of its notated key of B major. In contrast, Shostakovich's quartet movement, while centred on a rather gloomy C minor, is often chromatic, frequently subverts the sense of key, and is occasionally atonal.

Secondly, Reich employs a fast speed with syncopated and often conflicting rhythms to help portray the lively atmosphere of New York life. In contrast, Shostakovich suppresses rhythmic interest in favour of a very static style, often involving semibreves and long-held pedal points, in order to convey a deeply reflective mood. His slow-moving textures allow string players to engage audiences with their beauty of tone, shapely vibrato and so forth, on these long notes, while Reich's lively rhythms allow the clarinettist to create an exciting effect with lively, jazz-like articulation.

Thirdly, whereas Shostakovich was writing for the rather rarified audience of string quartet music, and so included many subtleties that take time and concentration to comprehend, Reich's music is designed more for a sensual than an intellectual impact. Part of the result of this is that you may find the following paragraphs rather less heavy-going than the first part of the chapter!

Context *New York Counterpoint* was commissioned by The Fromm Music Foundation (one of America's most important patrons of new music) for the clarinettist Richard Stolzman. Written in 1985, it is part of Reich's series of 'counterpoint' works that each explore the idea of a soloist playing live against a backing tape they recorded earlier. This started with *Vermont Counterpoint* (for flute) in 1982 and continued with *Electric Counterpoint* (for electric guitar), written for Pat Metheny in 1987.

Reich established his reputation in the late 1960s and early 1970s as one of several composers who rejected the complex technical and intellectual styles of much mid 20th-century music in favour of the diatonic simplicity and hypnotically repetitive rhythms of the style we now call **minimalism**. Many of these early works use very simple patterns that are subjected to systematic processes of gradual transformation – hence the alternative names of **process music** and **systems music**. As the patterns repeat and morph, they interact to form slowly-changing textures and harmonies.

Although Reich's style has become more complex and multi-layered over the years, the repetition of short patterns continues to play an important part in his work. He has also retained a lively interest in the possibilities of music technology, writing many works that combine pre-recorded and live performance, as well as pieces such as the *Sextet for percussion, piano and synthesisers*.

In *New York Counterpoint* Reich returned to some of the procedures he had used in his earlier works, as he explained in a programme note: 'The use of interlocking repeated melodic patterns played by multiples of the same instrument can be found in my earliest works, *Piano Phase* (for two pianos or two marimbas) and *Violin Phase* (for four violins) both from 1967. In the nature of the patterns, their combination harmonically, and in the faster rate of change, the piece reflects my recent works, particularly *Sextet* (1985)'.

NAM 12 is the second of three movements (fast, slow, fast) in *New York Counterpoint*. Although nominally it is the 'slow' movement, the use of predominantly semiquaver patterns gives the rhythm a much greater sense of urgency than, say, the reflective slow movement of *NAM 9*.

Reich uses the key signature of B major in the score, but since the clarinet is a transposing instrument the music will sound a tone lower when played on the standard clarinet in B♭ (and the bass clarinet parts will sound a 9th lower – that is, an octave plus a tone. Since all the parts transpose in a similar way, it is simpler if from here on we refer only to what you see in the score of *NAM 12*, rather than to the actual sounds you hear on the recording.

Although the music is entirely diatonic, it doesn't use the cadences of classical functional harmony to define key. And although it uses the key signature of B major, the principal focus of the movement often centres upon E. We could therefore say that it uses the scale shown in Example 12. This is known as the **lydian mode** – which you can find in a simpler form by playing the 'white notes' on a keyboard from F up to F an octave higher. It is the same as the scale of F major, except that its fourth degree is raised a semitone from B♭ to B♮, as shown in Example 13. The raised fourth degree of the lydian mode is marked * in both examples.

The modal quality of the work is enhanced by the fact that the melodic parts are restricted to the notes of a **hexatonic** (six-note) scale – the note D♯ occurs only in the pulsating **homorhythmic** textures that punctuate the music to provide a harder edge. Even when these hint at a tonic chord there is always an added diatonic dissonance to cloud the issue, as in the C♯ bass to the B major harmony which introduces these textures in bar 27.

Traditionally, composers used contrast in key and thematic material to structure their music. There are no such contrasts here – in fact, the opening two-bar motif is heard in one form or another throughout the movement. Instead, Reich structures his music through the careful control of texture.

The first section (bars 1–26) is characterised by a steady build-up of contrapuntal complexity with parts entering in pairs like this:

✦ Two parts in the first two bars,

✦ Four parts in bars 3–8,

✦ Two more parts are added at bar 9, but initially these double existing strands for four bars, so a real six-part texture doesn't emerge until bar 13,

✦ A seventh part is added from bar 21.

In the second section (bars 27–65), clarinets 1–6 continue with various permutations of this contrapuntal texture, but the live clarinettist breaks free to take on a more soloistic role. This section is also distinguished by the addition of six dissonant four-part chords, each played as repeated semiquavers. These fade in and out on clarinets 7 and 8 plus two bass clarinets. The first two last for six bars and the third for eight, after which the pattern repeats.

Listening guide

In exam answers you may need to clarify that your references to keys and chords in this work are to the printed score rather than to their actual sounds.

Ex. 12

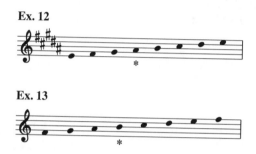

Ex. 13

A homorhythmic texture is a type of homophony in which all the parts move in the same rhythm (as often happens in simple hymn tunes).

Bar numbers given here are those in the score. In performance, many of the two-bar units are of course repeated.

The homorhythmic texture thus introduced makes a vivid contrast with the continuing counterpoint, but finally the chords disappear, leaving six more bars of fading counterpoint, followed by a cheeky three-note fragment of the opening motif in the final two clarinet parts.

The technique of **phasing** used in this work can be most clearly seen in the opening bars. For clarity Example 14 *below* shows only the upper of each pair of parts and omits the repeat signs. When the live clarinet enters in bar 3 it plays the same motif as clarinet 7, but half a beat later. When heard against the original motif (which continues in clarinet 7) it is a half-beat out of phase, and this is what creates the **canon**:

Ex. 14

Only four notes are imitated at this point – the greyed-out notes are replaced by rests. But look at bar 5 and you will see that the canon continues out of phase despite the missing notes. Reich fills in one more note (A♯) in bar 6 – and after this the live clarinet gets to play the entire canonic entry, still half a beat out of phase. Now look at the live clarinet entry in bar 13 of the score. Do you see that it has now moved one whole beat out of phase? The importance of the phasing process is that it causes expected rhythmic accents to be thrown 'out of sync', giving rise to complex new patterns as metrically different versions of the same idea are heard simultaneously.

The repetitions of the two-bar patterns create melodic **ostinato** patterns which centre on the hypnotic alternation of the chords of E major and F♯ major, but the phasing causes the chords to overlap and change at different times in different parts. The harmonic basis of the work can more easily be seen if we show the chords like this:

For clarity pairs of parts that are a 10th apart have here been printed a 3rd apart.

Ex. 15

The constant overlap of these two chords generates numerous diatonic dissonances as the texture thickens, but the repetition blends them into a gentle wash of harmonic colour, and the use of a hexatonic (six-note) scale for the contrapuntal parts avoids the particularly pungent clash of D♯.

However, with the arrival of the homorhythmic interjections comes the first appearance of D♯ and therefore much more gritty harmony. The three different chords heard in this section are B/C♯ in bars 27–

32, a chord based on 4ths (E, A♯, D♯, G♯) in bars 33–38, and F♯/G♯ in bars 39–46 (they are then repeated). These chords do not have a harmonic function – there is no progression towards a tonic. Their purpose is to provide contrast with the two chords of the counterpoint by adding to the dissonance level, as well as by offering a contrasting texture and different style of rhythm.

A notable aspect of the work is its use of a single instrumental colour (clarinet tone in the score, but Reich has also approved a saxophone arrangement of the work) and the use of technology (multi-track recording) to enable all 11 parts to be delivered by a single performer. The wide range of the clarinet (extended by the inclusion of bass clarinets), its distinctively different timbres in low, middle and upper registers, and Reich's control over textural change ensure plenty of variety.

Private study

1. Explain the difference between a contrapuntal texture and a homorhythmic texture, giving examples of each from *NAM 12*.

2. Define what is meant by phasing, giving an example from bar 21 onwards in *NAM 12*.

3. 20th-century music is often divided into tonal and atonal styles. Is *NAM 12* tonal?

4. To what extent do you feel that playing to a backing tape in *NAM 12* compromises the spontaneity of live performance?

In answering this question, you may want to consider the implications of Reich's title.

Sample questions

In the exam there will be three questions on the special focus works, from which you must choose to answer **two**.

1. Compare Shostakovich's approach to tonality in *NAM 9* with Reich's approach to tonality in *NAM 12*.

2. Show how Shostakovich achieves unity in his use of melodic material in *NAM 9*.

3. How does Reich create variety in *NAM 12*?

Continuity and change in rhythm, texture and timbre

For examination in summer 2006 and 2007

You do not need to study this topic unless *20th-century art music* is the Area of Study that you undertook for AS Music and which you are now extending for A2.

Before starting work on this topic you need a thorough understanding of the material on *20th-century art music* in the AS Guide (pages 40–52). Remember that for A2 the topic draws on works from across the **entire** Area of Study, not just those in one of the two lists, A or B.

It is important to remember that **texture** refers primarily to the number of simultaneous parts in a passage of music and the way in which they relate. At A level you should beware of describing texture in vague terms such as 'thick', 'thin' or 'open'. Generally you will need to be prepared to use precise technical terminology.

Introduction

For instance, you may need to describe a texture not only as contrapuntal but also as consisting of two-, three- or four-part counterpoint, and you may need to indicate whether the type of counterpoint is fugal, canonic or just freely imitative. Similarly, you may need to describe a texture as not just homophonic but as melody-dominated homophony ('melody and accompaniment') or homorhythmic (all parts moving in the same rhythm).

Timbre (pronounced *tam-bruh*) refers to tone colour. The clarinet has a different timbre to the trumpet, but the clarinet also has different timbres in various parts of its range. The timbre of an instrument can also be affected by the way it is played, for example by using a mute or plucking a string instead of using the bow.

One of the principal characteristics of 20th-century music is its diversity, so you should not be surprised to find more contrasts than similarities between the pieces in this area of study.

Stravinsky

NAM 7   CD1 Tracks 7–9
Academy of St. Martin-in-the-Fields
Conducted by Neville Marriner

Perhaps more than any other composer, Stravinsky is famed for establishing rhythm as one of the most potent elements in music, most notably in his ballet score *The Rite of Spring* (1913). But in *Pulcinella* Stravinsky's rhythms are mainly, but not exclusively, those of the 18th-century composers whose music he arranged. The three predominant rhythmic features of the **sinfonia** are:

+ **Quadruple metre** ($\frac{4}{4}$ time) with phrases that mostly begin with a quaver **anacrusis**, following the pattern set at the start, where the movement opens with an up beat quaver before bar 1

Ex. 16

+ The **dotted patterns** shown in Example 16, including both off-beat (b) and on-beat (c) versions of the dotted semiquaver pattern – the latter is a prominent feature of the oboe melody in bars 6^4–9 and in the related violin melody in bars 36^4–39

+ **Syncopation** – first appearing in the melody of bar 1, but later occurring in more extended form (as in bar 40, first violin).

All three rhythmic features are typical of many late-baroque allegro movements such as this, but Stravinsky makes numerous changes to enhance and extend their impact:

+ When the opening two-bar figure is repeated, the semiquavers of bar 1^2 are changed to a tripping dotted pattern in bar 3^2

Although often ascribed to Pergolesi, the source of the sinfonia is the first movement of a trio sonata by Gallo, probably written about 1750.

+ The syncopation in the second half of bar 1 (just a single G in Gallo's original) is emphasised by all the wind instruments, as well as by violas and by the double-stops in the second violins

+ Additional syncopation is used by Stravinsky in the parts that he adds or adapts, such as the second violin part in bars 5–6

+ Other added parts often have a distinctive rhythmic character, such as the bassoon and cello countermelodies in bars 7–10 or the energetic second violin and viola figure in bars 31–32

+ In bars 11–12 Stravinsky deliberately skews the quadruple metre by inserting an extra beat ($\frac{2}{4}$ + $\frac{3}{4}$ = five beats), allowing a crafty extra repetition of Gallo's little cadence figure. (The only other addition to the basic structure of the original movement is the interpolation of bar 18 with its 'marking time' effect.)

- Anacrusic starts are sometimes supressed, as in bar 33 where the first horn omits the first note of the theme (this is because Stravinsky has sneakily given the violins an extra twiddle, thus displacing the end of their phrase (Example 17)

- Instrumental doublings are used to bring subsidiary musical features to the foreground, such as in bar 14, where the repetition of the little scalic figure by the second bassoon is highlighted by the off-beat entry of solo cello and bass, both parts marked with some suitably fierce articulation – notice how all of these parts drop away and the dynamic collapses to *p* for the actual cadence in bar 15.

Ex. 17

In addition, Stravinsky adds copious ornamentation such as trills (*tr*) and grace notes (the notes in small print in the first violin parts of bars 5 and 6) of the type generally improvised by performers when playing the bare notes of baroque music. While he was not aiming to recreate a baroque performance, these add to the general rhythmic bustle of the movement and contribute to the amalgam of 18th- and 20th-century styles that is neoclassicim.

Gallo's original movement used a typical trio-sonata texture of two melodic parts in **free counterpoint**, played by two violins, above a functional bass part moving mainly in crotchets and quavers, and played by a cello. This texture would usually have been filled out with chords played on a harpsichord.

In free counterpoint there is no imitation between the melodic strands.

Stravinsky does not include a part for harpsichord, which was still regarded as an obsolete instrument in 1921, but he fills out the original parts by thickening the texture, often adding diatonic dissonances to the actual or implied harmonies of the original. The orchestral textures are not always as dense as they appear on the page, because often various parts **double** each other – for instance, the solo strings play the same notes as their orchestral counterparts at the start, while bassoons, cellos and basses all play slightly different versions of the same notes.

The combination of double-reed instruments and strings is found in much baroque music, and Stravinsky appropriates the baroque division of strings into *concertino* (solo) and *ripieno* (orchestral) sections. However, in the early 18th century the *concertino* most commonly consisted of two violins and a cello, not a string quintet. Horns were rarely used before 1750 and, lacking valves, would find the type of melodic solo seen in bars 33–34 virtually impossible.

Notice that Stravinsky avoids the use of clarinets – they didn't regularly appear in orchestras until the late-18th century.

Typical orchestral horn parts from the late 18th century can be seen in *NAM 2*, which dates from 1767.

Stravinsky employs numerous contrasts in the movement, although moments of simple three-part texture (such as in bar 15) are rare. For example, in bars 7–9 the semibreves of the original first-violin part are developed into a sustained backing for solo strings which accompanies not only the original second-violin part (now on oboe) but also Stravinsky's new countermelody for bassoon. The string timbre of bars 9–11 contrasts vividly with the double-reed timbres that follow it. In bars 24–34 Stravinsky uses **antiphonal exchanges** between strings, wind (with solo violin) and then three-part solo upper strings. Next, the full body of high strings (in a quite high **register** and without double basses) are used in bars 31–32, contrasting with the timbre of horns and bassoons in bars 33–34.

Although the source of this movement has been ascribed to both Pergolesi and Martini, it is now established that it comes from a keyboard suite by Carlo Monza, published in Italy about 1735. Monza followed his gavotte with six *doubles* (variations in shorter notes), of which Stravinsky used the first (*Double en gigue*) and fourth.

Scholars have been well exercised in trying to trace the true sources of the various pieces in *Pulcinella* that Stravinsky had assumed were all by Pergolesi. However, you may be relieved to know that you will not be asked questions about Stravinsky's sources in the exam.

The metronome mark at the start of this variation should read ♩.=100, not ♩=100. The dot is missing in earlier editions of the *New Anthology*.

Remember that when using the bass clef, the horn in F sounds a 4th higher than written, rather than the usual 5th lower.

Stravinsky also sometimes changes Monza's Alberti patterns into arpeggio figuration, as in bar 67.

The **gavotte** is a fairly lively baroque dance in **duple metre** (¢ means two minim beats per bar). In many gavottes the phrases begin with a two-note anacrusis (♩♩ |♩ ♩♩ |♩ etc) but that is not the case here. Rhythms are based mainly on the simple relationship between crotchets and quavers, with minims helping to mark the cadences. Shorter note values are written-out ornamentation, such as the turns in bars 1, 5 and 27 and the trill-like decoration in bar 31.

In the first part of the binary-form gavotte, Stravinsky gives the melody to oboe 1, while the bass of Monza's original two-part texture is assigned (with some changes) to bassoon 2, rounded off by horn 2 in bar 10. All other parts have been added by Stravinsky to thicken the texture.

At the start of the second part (beginning in bar 11) Stravinsky replaces Monza's walking bass of crotchets with minims for first bassoon, and adds a horn part of sighing appoggiaturas. At bar 15 the diagonal lines in the bassoon part indicate the use of **glissando** (unfortunately not played convincingly on the *NAM* recording). The **homophonic** texture and full wind scoring of bars 19–24 provide a climax and represent six bars in which Monza used a much fuller texture. However, Stravinsky doubles the melody in 6ths and omits the minim accompaniment in alternate bars. Instruments then drop away to provide contrast. A freely-inverted version of Monza's melody (and in a lower octave) is given to bassoon 1 at bar 25, and the gavotte ends with the delicate timbres of flute and bassoon in a two-part texture that is closer than anything else in *NAM 7* to the original source material.

Perhaps the most characteristic timbral feature of the gavotte, and its two variations, is the use of wind instruments throughout.

The first variation was styled *gigue* by Monza. The *gigue* (or jig in English) was a baroque dance in fast **compound time**, although Stravinsky here indicates a fairly leisurely tempo. Its rhythmic impetus comes from the mainly quaver movement in the melody (varied by ♩ ♪), which is assigned to the first oboe throughout. Monza's bass, which consisted entirely of broken chords in quavers, is considerably simplified and allocated to the second horn, low in its range, in the the first part of the variation and to second bassoon in the second part. In bars 43–50 the accompaniment is further simplified to mainly dotted minims, and its notes are altered to provide more diatonic dissonances, such as the D-major chord in the brass that sounds against G-major harmony in the woodwind on the first beat of bar 44. This chordal texture is replaced by free counterpoint in the woodwind for the remainder of the variation.

In the second variation, the melody is shared between flute and horn timbres while Monza's **Alberti bass**, typical of much keyboard music of the age, is transferred to bassoons. The happily gurgling result is totally *atypical* of baroque instrumentation, as are the rapid flute scales that decorate the melodic line and the entry of the oboe on an unprepared major 7th (F♯) in bar 79. Notice how Stravinsky exploits the very characteristic sound of the bassoon's high register (notated in the tenor clef) in bars 74–76. The melody and accompaniment mainly follows the two-part texture of Monza's original, occasionally bolstering this with one or two added parts.

Stravinsky's source for the *Vivo* is the last movement of a sonata for cello and continuo by Pergolesi – it actually was by him this time! It was written in a two-part texture throughout – a melody for cello in its high register and a purely supportive lower part that would have been played by another bass instrument and that also formed the basis for improvised harmonies played on a chordal instrument, such as a harpsichord or lute.

The most characteristic rhythmic feature of the movement derives from the **Scotch snap** shown in Example 18a. This is the reverse of the normal dotted-pattern, because the shorter note comes first. Pergolesi uses two short notes, rather than one, before the dotted note, producing an even snappier version of the rhythm, and his notation is shown in Example 18b. If you compare this with bar 2 of *NAM 7* you will see that Stravinsky curtails the third note to make the rhythm crisper still. Pergolesi uses the same pattern in **augmentation** (notes of twice the length, shown in Example 18c) throughout the rising and falling sequential melody of bars 6–13.

Ex. 18

Stravinsky assigns a much-altered version of Pergolesi's lower part to the orchestral double basses (relieved by the trombone in bars 31–37). The cello melody is allocated to the solo double bass until bar 52, after which it is shared with the trombone. Although the double bass sounds an octave lower than written, the music lies in a very high register, helping to produce a rather comical, strained tone. The trombone also **doubles** this melody at the start, adding short **glissandi** (which most players deliberately smear) to help set the slap-stick tone of the movement. This 'circus music' style is enhanced by an entire vocabulary of neoclassical humour:

The reason for all this hilarity is that in the original ballet score of *Pulcinella*, the *Vivo* accompanies a bizarre scene in which the supposed corpse of Pulcinella comes back to life and the girls of Naples discover that they have been flirting with their own boyfriends in disguise, in the belief that each was really the philanderous Pulcinella.

✦ Brazen brass entries (bar 6)

✦ Effects such as **du talon** in bar 12 – an instruction for string players to use the lowest part of the bow which, together with the accents, is intended to produce deliberately rasping tone

✦ Lightning changes in dynamics – *sub.* **ff** in bar 17 followed by *sub.* **p** for the last quaver of the pattern in bar 18

sub. is an abbreviation for *subito*, the Italian for 'suddenly'.

✦ Use of a total silence on the first quaver of bar 33 to create a cheeky 'boom-boom' perfect cadence in the rest of the bar – and destabilising both chords of that cadence by including the tonic (G) in the D^7 chord, and then leaving the second oboe stuck on F♯ while everyone else plays a chord of G major

Another example of a destablised cadence can be seen in the last two bars of the movement, where Stravinsky replaces Pergolesi's V–I bass with III–I (A–F).

✦ The use of a **heterophonic texture** in bars 38–45 to create a deliberate smudging of the loud melodic line (this is easier to see in the score than to hear on the *NAM* recording)

In a **heterophonic texture**, different versions of the same melody occur at the same time – compare the four melodic parts in bars 38–45.

✦ The addition of a tonic pedal in bars 46–51 (F in the cellos) to smudge Pergolesi's bass of F and E in alternate bars, enhancing the bleary-eyed effect of the solo bass reaching high in its range to an almost blues-like flat 3rd (this brief plunge into the tonic minor occurs in the original cello sonata)

✦ The rhythmic dislocation caused by omitting expected notes – for instance, at the start of bar 55 the tonic note at the end of the principal theme is replaced by silence, leaving an unresolved leading-note at the end of the previous bar.

Webern

pizz. (pizzicato) – pluck the strings
arco – bow the strings
mit Dämpfer – with a mute
Dämpfer auf – mute off

Both of these terms, and the mirror canons mentioned below, are explained in the AS Guide, page 45.

In early music a **cantus firmus** was a melody around which composers would construct a contrapuntal composition. Here we use the term to refer to the saxophone's presentation of the complete prime order of the note row in bars 6–10, followed immediately with its transposition by a tritone (to start on G) in bars 11–14.

Ex. 19

①	②	③
Saxophone	*Piano*	*Violin*
Bars 1–2	Bar 3	Bars 3–4

Unlike the movement by Shostakovich in *NAM 9*, written for the traditional medium of the string quartet with its blend of similar instruments, Webern's four instruments have **highly distinctive timbres**. The saxophone deserves special mention. It was invented in about 1840 but was rarely used in art music before 1920. Then it became more widely known through its adoption by jazz bands, and started to appear in works by composers such as Milhaud, Gershwin, Walton (*Façade*) and Ravel (*Bolero*). Although the saxophone can produce a very powerful sound, Webern clearly understood that it is also capable of the subtlety of tone and dynamic needed for good balance in small-scale chamber music such as *NAM 8* – notice how he requires quiet playing both in the lowest register (first note of bar 8) and near the top of the range (bar 27).

Webern also exploits extremes of range in the violin and clarinet parts. Notice that the pianist, while being faced with many wide leaps, rarely has to play more than one note at a time in each hand and that the violinist, as well as changing frequently between plucking and bowing, is also sometimes required to clip a mute to the bridge in order to produce a quieter, more veiled timbre.

The four instruments mainly play one at a time with little overlap, apart from bars 22–23 where the central climax is delineated by a thicker texture, wider range and louder dynamic level. They also play few notes in succession – mainly just two- and three-note cells – but almost every note is given its own indication of dynamic and articulation. As Webern's teacher Schoenberg noted, in music of this concentration and intensity the slightest nuance conveys an almost unbearable significance.

Webern's sparse use of resources in *NAM 8* is largely due to his **pointillist** texture and use of **Klangfarbenmelodie**. The fragmentary melodies and irregular entries require an acute sense of rhythmic pulse, and the sudden and frequent wide leaps across different registers need to be executed without losing a sense of line – a point that particularly concerned Webern at the first performance of his Symphony, Op. 21 (1928).

Despite the frequent lack of melodic overlap in the parts, the texture can be described as **contrapuntal** throughout, not least because of Webern's use of **mirror canons** that weave around the saxophone's **cantus firmus** in bars 6–14. The central part of the movement (bars 16–27) is a canonic development of motifs from the introduction. It is followed in bar 28 by a recapitulation in which the saxophone cantus firmus is redistributed between clarinet, violin and saxophone, while the mirror canons continue in the piano.

Webern writes most bars in $\frac{3}{8}$ time, although he occasionally groups nine quaver beats into units of $\frac{4}{8}$ and $\frac{5}{8}$ rather than three bars of $\frac{3}{8}$. However, at the slow speed indicated by the metronome mark and confirmed by the tempo direction *Sehr mässig* (very moderately), there is little obvious sense of regular metre in the fragmentary melodies. Without a clearly defined pulse, what might *appear* on paper to be complex syncopation certainly does not sound as such. Webern derives many of the rhythms in *NAM 8* from three rhythmic cells. The first appearance of each is shown in Example 19. See if you can trace their use elsewhere in the movement.

The most obvious timbral contrast between this quartet movement and the one you have just studied is Shostakovich's use of a string quartet. The blend and versatility of two violins, a viola and a cello had made this the most popular medium for chamber music since the middle of the 18th century, and Shostakovich was to write 15 works in this genre, mostly in his later years.

NAM 9 gets much of its dark quality from a low dynamic level, minor mode, long-held pedals and consistent use of a **low tessitura** in all four parts. The highest note is the first violin's F in bar 95 (only just into the middle range of the instrument), while at bar 28 the second violin, viola and cello each sit on their lowest note for more than 17 bars of double pedal. There are contrasts in texture (the **fugal** opening, the melody over the accompaniment of a double pedal at bar 28, the use of a **countermelody** at bar 55, and the **chordal homophony** in bars 79–81), but for much of the movement all four instruments play long legato lines with few rests. The exceptions are the fugal opening and the brief passages of **two-part counterpoint** in bars 19–23, 45–49 and 112–117 (supported by a pedal note from bar 116 onwards).

Shostakovich requires no effects such as using a mute, pizzicato or double-stopping (playing two notes simultaneously) from his string players. The slow tempo, unchanging metre and simple rhythms add to the sombre tone and allow the performers to concentrate on beauty of tone in creating the deeply reflective mood of the music.

In 1937 John Cage took a job as accompanist to a contemporary dance company. From this grew a particular interest in exploring the rhythm of music, particularly through percussion-based works. In 1940 the dancer Syvilla Fort asked Cage to provide music for a new dance with an African theme. But there was a problem – and Cage found a solution, as the composer himself explains:

> I couldn't use percussion instruments for Syvilla's dance, though, suggesting Africa, they would have been suitable; they would have left too little room for her to perform. I was obliged to write a piano piece. I spent a day or so conscientiously trying to find an African twelve-tone row. I had no luck. I decided that what was wrong was not me but the piano. I decided to change it. Besides studying with Weiss and Schoenberg, I had also studied with Henry Cowell. I had often heard him play a grand piano, changing its sound by plucking and muting the strings with fingers and hands.

Cage then describes how he experimented with different objects to modify the tone, and how these modified tones could be changed again by depressing the damper (soft) pedal while playing.

When Cage moved to New York in 1942 he was unable to take his percussion instruments with him, and turned again to the prepared piano for its potential as a one-man percussion ensemble. It figured prominently in his music over the next few years, starting with *Amores* (1943), his first concert work to include prepared piano. Cage used relatively few preparations at first, and sometimes (as in *Amores*) gave general indications about the aural effects he wanted, rather than the very detailed instructions and measurements seen on page 167 of the *New Anthology*. However, Cage later found that being so specific could also be misleading, because of the varying string-lengths and construction of different pianos.

Shostakovich

NAM 9	CD1 Track 11
Coull Quartet	

Cage

NAM 10	CD1 Tracks 12–14
Joanna MacGregor	

Cage originally wrote this account for the foreword to Richard Bunger's book *The Well-Prepared Piano* (1973). A revised version appears in the preface to *Cage's Prepared Piano Music Volume 1* (Peters Edition).

Amores I can be found in the 1986 edition of the *London Anthology of Music*, No. 109.

To appreciate the timbral changes brought about by preparation, it is essential to listen to the music rather than read about it. Study the table of preparations on page 167 of the *New Anthology* and then make your own notes on the timbres produced by 'mutes' (as Cage termed them) of different sizes, shapes and materials when used on strings of different pitch, and the ways in which these timbres change when either of the piano pedals are used.

```
×4   4 3 2 3 4   4 3 2 3 4   4 3 2 3 4   4 3 2 3 4
×3   4 3 2 3 4   4 3 2 3 4   4 3 2 3 4
×2   4 3 2 3 4   4 3 2 3 4
×3   4 3 2 3 4   4 3 2 3 4   4 3 2 3 4
×4   4 3 2 3 4   4 3 2 3 4   4 3 2 3 4   4 3 2 3 4
```

Cage's use of the **prepared piano** represents a fundamental break with the past of the sort not seen in the work of such conservative composers as Shostakovich. The example of the latter's piano music given in *NAM 25* was composed two or three years **after** *NAM 10*, although you may well feel that it sounds very much earlier in style. Even in comparison with Webern's atonal piano part in *NAM 8*, Cage's prepared piano seems to inhabit a totally new timbral world.

Rhythm is fundamental in the *Sonatas and Interludes*. Cage had been developing musical structures without recourse to pitch since his percussion works of the late 1930s. His solution was to adopt duration as the main structural element – an idea that possibly arose from his work with dancers. In his *First Construction (in Metal)* of 1939 we see a simple version of the principle that underpins *NAM 10*. The first 16 bars form a unit of five phrases with the bar-lengths $4+3+2+3+4$. The entire 256 bars consists of 16 repetitions of this unit, in the order $4+3+2+3+4$ (see *left*). Cage called this process of large structure replicating small structure 'micro-macrocosmic'. Today we would recognise it as the fractal structure seen in many features of the natural world.

The structures in the *Sonatas and Interludes* are more complex than the simple $16^2 = 256$ formula of *First Construction (in Metal)* because Cage uses irregular lengths for his basic units. In the AS Guide we showed how the first sonata is built on a seven-bar unit whose 28 crotchets are arranged in the pattern $4:1:3 + 4:1:3 + 4:2 + 4:2$. The whole sonata mimics this pattern by using seven-crotchet units in multiples of 4, 1, 3 (repeated) and 4, 2 (repeated).

The rhythmic structure of Sonata II is based on the asymmetric 31-crotchet unit of bars 1–9:

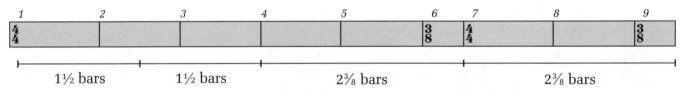

Again the whole sonata mimics this pattern by using 31-crotchet units in the multiples 1½ (repeated) and 2⅜ (repeated):

Bars 1–9	31 crotchets	$= 1 \times 31$
Bars 10–14	15½ crotchets	$= \frac{1}{2} \times 31$
Bars 15–23	31 crotchets	$= 1 \times 31$
Bars 24–32	31 crotchets	$= 1 \times 31$
Bars 33–37	11½ crotchets	$\approx \frac{3}{8} \times 31$

Notice how these sections are delineated by the double barlines in *NAM 10*, and how the final section involves a slight mathematical approximation to fit with the practicalities of clear notation.

Sonata III is based on a unit of 34 crotchets (bars 1–8):

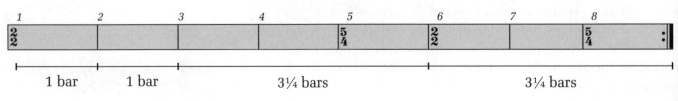

Like the other sonatas, the proportions of this pattern (1:1:3¼:3¼) also provide the proportions of the entire movement:

Bars 1–8	34 crotchets	= 1 × 34
Bars 1–8 repeated	34 crotchets	= 1 × 34
Bars 9–32	110½ crotchets	= 3¼ × 34
Bars 9–32 repeated	110½ crotchets	= 3¼ × 34

This careful attention to proportionality makes its impact in a subconscious way. Aurally more obvious is the fact that, because the two sections of the macrocosmic binary form are repeated, the microcosmic structures of the individual sections also create paired units (this is particularly evident at the start of Sonata I, where bars 3–4 form a varied repeat of bars 1–2).

Rhythm, or more precisely note lengths, used in this way has little precedent before Cage and so represents one of the many areas of great change seen during the course of 20th-century art music. However, there are other rhythmic features in NAM 10 that may seem more familiar. For instance, when the six-beat phrase at the start of Sonata II is answered by the left hand Cage substitutes a crotchet rest for the note in the middle of the pattern. This rest falls on a strong beat and so creates **syncopation**, an effect which is enhanced by the **metrical displacement** of the repeated four-quaver motif shown in Example 20. Such jazz-like rhythms permeate much of this sonata. For example, the metrical displacement of the repeated figure in bars 7–8 is essentially the early-jazz device of 'secondary rag', in which a three-beat figure is repeated across the fourfold beat of quadruple time. A cascade of rag-like syncopation follows in the rhythmic repetitions of bars 10–14.

Ex. 20

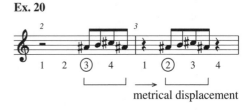

metrical displacement

Rhythmic manipulation plays an important role in the third sonata. For instance, the first section consists of three statements of the opening right-hand figure, in the second of which the final note is truncated to a crotchet. The initial three demi-semiquavers of this motif are **augmented** to eight times their value in bar 13. This new version then becomes the subject of other types of transformation – retrograde order in bar 14, extended into bar 15 by sequence.

Cage's textures are really quite simple. The first sonata is mainly **chordal**, with clear **homophony** in its final section. The second begins with a **monophonic** texture (one note at a time), becoming **two-part** from bar 10 onwards. The third sonata employs a largely two-part texture. However, be aware that these terms are normally used to refer to music in which clearly-defined pitch plays an important role. We are extending their normal use by employing them to describe the music of NAM 10 (and of NAM 11 below) in which many notes are of inderminate pitch.

If Cage's *Sonatas* seem to show little continuity with earlier music, Berio's *Sequenza III* might appear to be a total break with the past. But just as Cage wrote a table of preparations to prescribe specific timbres for each prepared note, so Berio gives full details to explain the **extended vocal techniques** required to produce the various timbral effects he wants and how he has notated them. Study these

Berio

NAM 11	CD1 Track 15
Cathy Berberian	

notes on pages 171–172 of the *New Anthology* carefully, and then compare what you have read to what you hear on the recording. Berio specifies the precise ways in which vocal timbre should be modified through means such as gradually changing vowel sounds and special techniques ('trilling the tongue against the upper lip', 'dental tremolo' and so forth).

Compare *Sequenza III* (1966) with the much earlier *Pierrot Lunaire* (1912, *NAM 40*). Schoenberg was one of the first composers to use the voice in new ways, but he is far less explicit in how his *Sprech-gesang* should be interpreted. However, just as performances of *Pierrot* differ radically from one reciter to another, and Cage's sonatas can sound very different on different pianos, despite careful following of the preparation instructions, so performances of Berio's *Sequenza* can vary widely when given by other performers capable of realising the virtuoso vocal techniques required.

As in *NAM 10*, an important aspect of the work is the selection of the raw materials from which it is formed. The text is short and simple, and Berio's setting is concerned not so much with the meaning of its words as their potential to be changed in order, exaggerated, distorted and blurred into other vocal events, such as coughing and laughing, which in turn are transformed into displays of coloratura virtuosity. There are many precedents in light opera and music-hall songs for musical representations of effects such as laughter, but *Sequenza III* inhabits a new, under-explored world on the very border between music and language, with its huge variety of rapidly changing vocal techniques and timbres.

Berio encourages a dramatic performance by means of cue words (tense, witty, etc) that are unrelated to the poem. He indicates that these may be used by the performer as triggers for bodily and facial gestures but also warns that literal expressions of these emotional states should be avoided – their purpose is to focus the colour and intonation of the voice. In other words *Sequenza III* is not a piece about a dramatic situation – it is itself the drama. It is music theatre.

Timbre, allied to drama, is an essential element in *Sequenza III*. The texture could be said to be **monophonic** throughout, since the soloist produces only one sound at a time – variety comes from the extraordinary range of vocal timbre. And while the composer gives occasional indications of rhythm by means of headless notes, there is no sense of regular pulse or metre, and so we can describe the entire piece as being **without clear metre** and in **free rhythm**.

NAM 12	CD1 Track 16
Roger Heaton	

Reich

As is so often the case with minimalist styles, there is a sense of coming full circle as we return to this work. Gone are the free rhythms of Berio, the complex proportions of Cage and the almost timeless quality of Webern. Instead we re-enter the familiar world of music with a recognisable pulse and regular metre.

However, the rhythms of *NAM 12* are clearly more complex than the (mainly) regular patterns and phrases in Stravinsky's dance music for *Pulcinella*. The most notable rhythmic feature in the second movement of *New York Counterpoint* is **syncopation**. This is present from the outset in the opening two-bar motif. But it doesn't *sound* like syncopation, because at the beginning of the movement there is nothing but this rhythm. Without other parts to lay down a well-defined pulse there is no clear sense of a regular beat for the syncopation to 'bite' against. As the canonic pairs enter, their phasing initially adds to the rhythmic complexity rather than helping to clarify it. The effect on the listener is that the pulse only gradually comes into focus and an awareness of the underlying **triple metre** comes some bars later. It's a typically Reichian aural illusion because the regular pulse and metre have actually been present since bar 1.

All of the melodic material is based on the opening two-bar motif, albeit often rhythmically displaced through phasing. The only other rhythmic feature occurs in the blocks of chords that are overlaid in the second half of the piece. Their constant repeated semiquavers are designed to offset the rhythmic complexity of the canons.

The texture of the movement was discussed on pages 55–56, and its use of timbre on page 57.

Private study

1. (i) What do you notice when you compare the horn writing in *NAM 7* with Haydn's horn parts in *NAM 2*?
    (ii) What is the main reason for such differences?

2. State what is meant by a heterophonic texture and give an example of such a texture in the *Vivo* of *NAM 7*.

3. What is a *Klangfarbenmelodie*?

4. Explain what is meant by rhythmic augmentation, giving an example using music notation.

5. To what extent does *NAM 10* support John Cage's description of the timbre of a prepared piano as 'a percussion orchestra under the control of a single player'?

6. Give the meaning of each of the following: *mit Dämpfer*, *du talon*, dental tremolo.

Sample questions

In the exam there will be two questions on this topic, from which you must choose to answer **one**.

(a) Compare the importance of rhythm in the works by Berio (*NAM 11*) and Reich (*NAM 12*).

(b) Compare and contrast the textures and timbres used in the quartets by Webern (*NAM 8*) and Shostakovich (*NAM 9*).

(c) How do the orchestral timbres used by Stravinsky in *NAM 7* reveal that *Pulcinella* is a 20th-century work?

Music for small ensemble

Special Focus Work for 2006 and 2007

NAM 18   CD2 Track 7
Guarneri Quartet with
Peter Serkin (piano)

Brahms: Scherzo and Trio from the Piano Quintet in F minor

Before starting on this section you should work through (or revise)
the information about the context and structure of this music given
on pages 62–64 of the AS Guide. Make sure that you understand
all of the terminology used on those pages.

The tumultuous, angry **Scherzo** has two fast dotted-crotchet beats
per bar. When it goes into $\frac{2}{4}$ the new crotchet beat is played at the
same tempo as the old dotted crotchet (and vice versa when $\frac{6}{8}$ time
returns). Apart from melodic and harmonic links between sections
you should notice that the whole movement is unified by a few
related rhythms in $\frac{2}{4}$ or $\frac{6}{8}$ time. The most important are:

✦ The four-note rhythm marked *y* in Example 1 *below*. It becomes
an important feature in bars 24–46 and a pounding **ostinato** in
bars 124–143.

✦ The ♩ 𝄾 ♩ pattern in bars 13–14 (effectively a dotted rhythm).
It too becomes a frenetic ostinato in bars 57–67 (lower strings).

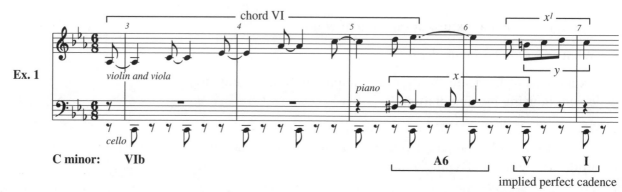

Ex. 1

This structure is complicated, so it may help
to refer to the table on page 72 to see how
it all fits together.

Theme A (bars 1–13¹): C minor

The structure of the Scherzo is **episodic** (meaning that it proceeds
in a succession of distinct sections) and is based on the three themes
identified as A, B, and C below.

The first theme has five elements:

1. An on-beat **tonic pedal** (cello) which continues until bar 12.

2. A **syncopated arpeggio** of A♭ major which turns out to be chord
VI of C minor when the implied perfect cadence (shown in
Example 1) has been heard.

3. A piano **motif** marked *x* in Example 1. This chromatic four-note
figure is in the shape of an inverted turn and, in various keys
and variously manipulated, it appears many times in both the
Scherzo and Trio. It is thus as much a unifying device as the
characteristic rhythms discussed earlier. Its first variant (x^{1})
appears in the violin and viola parts as a five-note diatonic
figure (containing motif *y*) in rhythmic diminution.

4. An **augmented 6th chord** resolving to chord V. This particular
augmented 6th is sometimes known as a German 6th and it is
this type that recurs throughout the Scherzo at significant

points. In minor keys it consists of chord VI plus an augmented 6th above the root, as shown in Example 2:

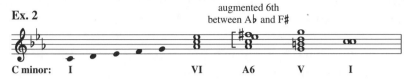

Ex. 2

augmented 6th
between A♭ and F♯

C minor: I   VI   A6   V   I

The notes of the augmented 6th all sound within the bracketed area marked **A6** in Example 1. However, you might find it easier to understand the same augmented 6th as it appears in the compressed version of this theme in bars 38–39 of *NAM 18*.

5. A **sequential** ascent of an octave starting in bar 9 (first violin and viola) followed by a descent to the cadence in bars 12–13. This is **imitated** in the piano part a fourth lower and one beat later.

Theme B (bars 13–21): C minor

The second theme starts with a five-bar melody that circles around the dominant. It contains two more manipulations of motif x. Both of them (x^2 and x^3 in Example 3a *below*) are free inversions of the motif marked x^1 in Example 1, *opposite*.

This is followed by the viola melody shown in Example 3b *below*, which turns out to be a ghostly foreshadowing of the theme of the next section (shown in Example 3c *below*). While the viola plays this melody the first violin plays a skeletal version of it, pizzicato and an octave higher. Two or more different but simultaneous versions of the same melody is known as a **heterophonic** texture. The sepulchral atmosphere is completed by the accompanying pizzicato chords that end with a **phrygian cadence** (IVb–V in bars 20–21) with no 3rd in the dominant chord.

Theme C (bars 22–37): C major

The previous minor-mode theme contrasts strongly with the major key and confident, swaggering march style of this section. It has just one repeated element – the seven-bar melody in Example 3c *below*. This contains several transformations of motif x, notably an **augmentation** of motif x^2 that is only slightly obscured by the rhythm of motif y in bar 24. This rhythm is heard three more times in bars 26–29 and, as we have already noted, it will become a unifying force element throughout the rest of the movement.

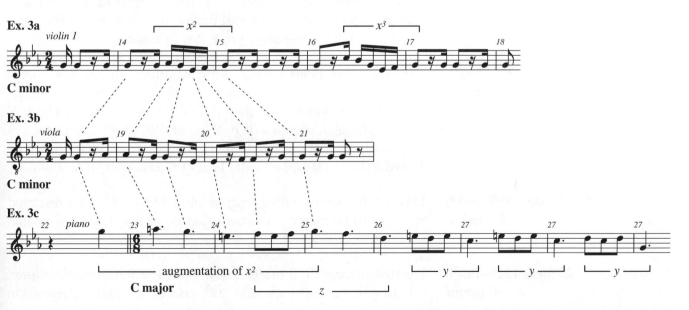

Ex. 3a
violin 1
C minor

Ex. 3b
viola
C minor

Ex. 3c
piano
augmentation of x^2
C major

The rest of the movement is based on themes A, B and C:

A¹ (bars 38–45):
C minor

Condensed versions of the arpeggio motif and the motif based on an augmented 6th chord, with rhythm *y* in the piano part.

A² (bars 46–57):
C minor modulating to G minor

A repeat of bars 2–8 followed by a reworking of the ascending sequence (compare bars 52–57 with bars 8–13). The section ends with another phrygian cadence (VI/IVb–V in G minor).

B¹ (bars 57–67):
G minor modulating to V of E♭ minor

The music in bars 57–61 is a transposed restatement of bars 13–17. This is transposed into B♭ minor in bars 61–65. The original phrase is extended by sequential repetitions of a new version of motif *x* (second violin, bars 65–66) which start in D♭ major and ends with a phrygian cadence in E♭ minor (bars 66–67). This leads to …

Fugato (bars 67–100):
E♭ minor until bar 88

A **fugato** is a fugal section within the context of a longer movement. Here it forms the central part of Brahms' episodic structure. The fugue subject (viola, bars 67–71) is the first four bars of theme B. As before it revolves around the dominant – in this case the dominant of E♭ minor. This is answered by the right-hand piano part (bar 71). There are further entries of the subject starting in bars 76 (violin) and 84 (viola). These are combined with no less than three **countersubjects**:

1. piano left hand, bar 67 (next heard in the viola part starting at bar 71)

2. piano left hand, bar 71 (next heard in the viola part starting at bar 76)

3. viola, bar 80 (next heard in modified form in the second violin part starting at bar 84).

In bars 88–100 all of these melodies are fragmented into tiny cells (illustrated in the AS Guide) in a complex **five-part contrapuntal texture** as the music modulates through F minor (bars 92–93), the dominant 7th of A♭ major (bars 94–95) and B♭ minor (bars 95–97) before ending on the dominant of E♭ minor (bar 100).

This extended contrapuntal passage in the remote mediant minor key (E♭ minor), along with the rapid modulation through so many other keys, intensifies the menacing atmosphere of the music before it ushers in a recapitulation and further development of the three principal themes, which are presented in this order:

B² (bars 100–109¹):
E♭ minor

The violin part, apart from a couple of tiny modifications, comes from bars 13–21 transposed from C minor to E♭ minor. The harmonic progression retains the original minor version of chord V and the phrygian cadence (IVb–V in bars 107–108), but instead of the ghostly bare 5th in bar 21 there is now a triumphant **tierce de Picardie** (bar 108) and an extra beat of repeated dominant notes.

C + A¹ (bars 109²–132)
E♭ major

This section begins with a recapitulation of bars 22–45 transposed up a 3rd to E♭ major – another example of the many 3rd-related keys in this movement.

A¹ (bars 132²–158¹):
C minor

The first ostinato rhythm slides down to G, the dominant of C minor, ushering in a repeat bars 125–132¹, now in the tonic. The section ends with a tumultuous reworking and sequential extension of the second part of theme A (bars 9–12) underpinned by a diatonic **circle of 5ths** (bars 149^2–152^1 repeated in the next four bars).

This huge development of theme B begins with a rising sequence based on bars 13–14 which reaches the dominant of A minor (bars 163–165) before another rising sequence (bars 166–169) passes through F minor and G minor before returning to A minor. This key is confirmed by an imperfect cadence (I–IV–V in bars 169–170). These rapid modulations start again in bar 172 but this time they lead to an imperfect cadence in the tonic key of the whole Quintet (I–Ib–V in F minor in bars 175–176).

B^3 (bars 158–176): C minor modulating to V of F minor

This whole section, in which the rhythms and motifs of the previous section are combined with the augmented 6th of section A^1, is really an extension of chord V of F minor with which the section begins. This interpretation is confirmed by nine imperfect cadences in this key in bars 184–190 and the almost obsessive repetition of the four-semiquaver group from motif x^2 now in F minor rather than C minor. The reason becomes clear when the Scherzo is repeated after the Trio, for this passage leads directly into the two unaccompanied F naturals at the start of the last movement of the Quintet. But it serves equally well as a bridge to the C major tonality of the Trio, which is in **ternary** form.

B^3 + A^1 (bars 176–193): F minor

The piano's 16-bar melody and the rescored repeat contain motif z (see Example 3c on page 69), in C major, G major and B major. Otherwise this section contrasts strongly with the cerebral gymnastics of the Scherzo.

D (bars 193–225): C major with subsidiary modulations to G and B major

The time signature changes and a new version of the first counter-subject reappears in the cello part of bars 226–233. In these bars it is freely imitated in the right-hand piano part and both parts are accompanied by a new countermelody in the string parts. All three parts are then contrapuntally inverted in the next eight bars (the countersubject from the fugato now in the right-hand piano part, its imitative partner in the violin part and the new countermelody in the left-hand piano part. Although the musis is chromatic, these three contrapuntal strands are anchored to the key of C major by the dominant pedal that runs through all 16 bars.

E (bars 225–241): V of C major

The diatonic melody of section D returns, but the mood is darkened by chromatic harmony (V^7d of IV resolving to IVb in bars 242–246) and a chromatic descent from B♭ to F in the bass part. Brahms composes a new ending which begins with a type of plagal cadence (ii^7b–I in bars 252–254) and which ends with diminished 7ths (VII^{b7}) twice resolving gently to chord I (bars 255–256 and 257–258). The last 13 bars contain a tonic pedal (cello then piano) that balances the effect of the dominant pedal which ran all the way through section E. The syncopations in the last four bars warn of the imminent return of the Scherzo.

D^1 (bars 241^2–261): C major

While the structure of the brief Trio is fairly simple, the Scherzo is a complex construction in which Brahms modulates to distant keys – even the important keys which dominate large sections are 3rdrelated, such as C minor in the first section and E♭ minor in the fugato. To help you retain an overall view of the whole movement, we have summarised our analysis in the following table:

Form		Bars	Tonality
Scherzo	A	1–13	C minor coloured by an augmented 6th chord in bars 5–6
	B	13–21	C minor ending on chord V without a 3rd
	C	22–37	C major (march-like theme in compound time)
	A^1	38–45	C minor with an augmented 6th twice resolving to V
	A^2	46–57	C minor modulating to V of G minor
	B^1	57–67	G minor modulating through B♭ minor and D♭ major to V of E♭ minor
	Fugato	67–100	E♭ minor with transitory modulations in bars 88–98
	B^2	100–109	E♭ minor
	$C + A^1$	109–132	E♭ major
	A^1	132–158	C minor (including a repeat of bars 125–132^1, now in the tonic)
	B^3	158–176	C minor modulating to V of F minor
	$B^3 + A^1$	176–193	F minor
Trio	D	193–225	C major with sequential modulations through G major and B major
	E	225–241	V of C major (note the dominant pedal in the piano then cello parts)
	D^1	241–261	C major coloured by the subdominant key (bars 242–246), and chromatic chords borrowed from the tonic minor (bars 252–257)

Private Study

1. (a) Name the pitch of the viola's first note in bar 2.

   (b) After this first note, how does the viola part relate to the first violin part in the rest of bars 3–17?

2. Give an example of double-stopping in the first violin part.

3. Explain what is meant by a phrygian cadence, and state where one occurs on page 235 of the *New Anthology*.

4. Define the term fugato.

5. What is a tierce de Picardie?

6. Name the chord used in bars 126–127.

7. In which bars **of the Trio** does Brahms use a diatonic circle of 5ths progression?

Sample questions

In the exam there will be three questions on this work, from which you must choose to answer **two**.

(a) Explain how bars 38–67 derive from the first 21 bars of the movement.

(b) Write a detailed account of the fugato in bars 67–100.

(c) Show how the Trio is related to the Scherzo and yet contrasts with it.

Continuity and change in structure and tonality

You do not need to study this topic unless *Music for small ensemble* is the Area of Study that you undertook for AS Music and which you are now extending for A2.

Before starting work on this topic you need a thorough understanding of the material on *Music for small ensemble* in the AS Guide (pages 53–66). Remember that for A2 the topic draws on works from across the **entire** Area of Study, not just those in one of the two lists, A or B. When studying this topic it is important to be aware that tonality refers to the relationship of keys in music (and for exam purposes that also includes modes) – it is nothing to do with the tone of musical sounds.

Although the title *Sonata pian' e forte* (a piece with soft and loud bits) must have seemed modern in 1597, this is one of Gabrieli's most old-fashioned compositions, certainly as regards its tonality and structure. The work is in the **dorian mode on G** (Example 4) but, as was customary in the late 16th-century, accidentals are introduced for two principal purposes:

✦ To form cadences on most degrees of the modal scale. For centuries it had been accepted that the seventh degree of the scale should rise a semitone to the tonic in perfect cadences and should fall a semitone in imperfect cadences. In most modes there is a semitone between the seventh and eighth degrees, but in the dorian mode on G an accidental (F♯) needs to be used to form a perfect cadence on the tonic. You can hear this effect in the perfect cadence in bars in bars 8–9.

✦ To form major chords at the end of phrases. For centuries it was customary to end phrases on an octave, a bare 5th chord, or a major triad (never a minor chord). In the dorian mode on G a natural sign is needed to turn the tonic chord of G minor into a G major triad, hence the natural sign in the second trombone part in bar 9, beat 1. This raised 3rd is, of course, a **tierce de Picardie.** Listen carefully and you ought to be able to spot dozens of them in this piece.

So, although the score looks quite chromatic, the aural effect is modal because nearly all of the accidentals are needed for the two purposes we have explained.

There are about 40 cadences in this sonata – that's about one every other bar! This is an important point because it means the music hardly ever gets an opportunity to remain in one key for an appreciable length of time, so harmonic progressions in the modern sense hardly exist.

The one exception is the **circle of 5ths**. The easiest to understand is the one in bars 36–41 where you can trace its pattern of alternate rising 4ths and falling 5ths in the bass part. But listen to the chords above this bass pattern. What you are hearing is a series of perfect cadences which, in a more tonal context, could belong to the keys D, G, C, F and B♭. It is important to notice that these are all degrees of the dorian mode on G (I, III, IV, V and VII). Cadences are also formed on the second degree of the mode, but these are a special

Gabrieli

NAM 14 CD2 Track 3
His Majesty's Sagbutts and Cornetts
Directed by Timothy Roberts

Ex. 4

Giovanni Gabrieli was organist at St. Mark's, the principal church of the island state of Venice in northern Italy. Its exterior, which has hardly changed since Gabrieli's day, is shown on the front cover of this book.

Ex. 5   **Phrygian cadences**

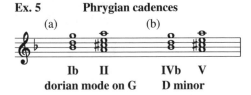

        Ib   II   IVb   V
        dorian mode on G   D minor

This is the same type of cadence that we encountered on page 69, but in a minor key these two chords are described as IVb and V, as shown in (b) *above*.

type of imperfect cadence originally associated with the phrygian mode and so known as the **phrygian cadence** (Example 5). These cadences occur in bars 16–17, 58–59 and 69–70. If we think in terms of D minor, each of them consists of the progression IVb–V.

This tonal restlessness made it difficult for composers to write extended compositions in which tonality could be used to help define structure. In this piece some sense of tonal architecture arises from the fact that more than half of the cadences come to rest on the dominant or tonic. This impression of a newly-emerging tonal style replacing ancient modality is wonderfully confirmed by the final plagal cadence (the only one in the sonata). Here the E♭s strongly suggest the key of G minor rather than the dorian mode on G.

Another way of giving a composition a sense of shape is melodic repetition. There's plenty of it, including:

✦ Direct repetition (e.g. the **antiphonal exchanges** in bars 45–49)

✦ **Close imitation** and **canon** (e.g. cornet and viola in bars 75–79)

✦ **Sequences** (e.g. cornett in bars 39–41[1])

✦ Modified repetition in an **antecedent–consequent** pair (that is, a 'question and answer'), such as viola in bars 14–21.

But all of these are local events – there is none of the *recapitulation* of melodic material that we shall later find in simple structures such as the ternary form of *NAM 19*, bars 1–8 and 58–65.

Holborne

NAM 13   CD2 Tracks 1–2
Rose Consort of Viols

Given that they were published within two years of each other it is difficult to account for the difference in tonal style between Gabrieli's sonata and Holborne's dances. Difficult – but it is not impossible when we remember that the sonata was written for the church while the pavan and galliard were written for the home – perhaps for the sole pleasure of the performers, perhaps for dancing, but probably for both.

Secular music had, since medieval times, been much more tonal than church music. Perhaps the most important reason for this was that much secular music was meant for dancing, and what dancers listen out for is a clear indication of pulse, metre and cadence. With ensemble music this means that chords need to change in time with the rhythm and metre of each type of dance, and that cadences, particularly at the end of a section, should be blindingly obvious (and therefore probably tonal).

In Elizabethan England the **galliard** was a lively dance in fast triple time, often with a syncopated 'hop, skip and jump'. It usually fell into three self-contained phrases, each of them ending on a chord lasting for a whole bar. The first section of Holborne's *Ecce quam bonum* galliard illustrates these features to perfection and shows how the harmonic rhythms of the largely tonal progressions aid and abet the rhythms of the diatonic melody.

The key of D minor is obvious throughout the first eight-bar section, despite the lack of key signature (B is flattened by an accidental where required, following the convention of the time). It divides

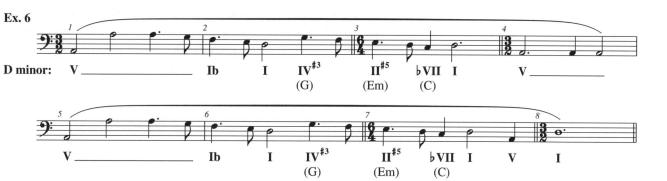

Ex. 6

into the two four-bar phrases shown in Example 6. The first phrase ends with an imperfect cadence (I–V). The second is identical except that the imperfect cadence is replaced with a perfect cadence (V–I). The dancers have got their blindingly obvious tonal cadences at the end of two balanced phrases (an antecedent and consequent pair again) that could have been in the satchel of an 18th-century dancing master.

Now look at the harmonic progressions that lead to these cadences and notice that:

✦ Chord V changes to chord Ib at the bar line

✦ The changes of chord in bar 2 coincide with the minim beat

✦ The changes of chord in bar 3 emphasise the syncopated 'hop skip and jump' (we have added time signatures in Example 6 to make Holborne's change of metre clearer)

✦ 11 of the 17 chords are tonics or dominants of the key of D minor and only six are modal (the chords of G, E minor and C derive from the dorian mode).

Turning back now to the stately D major **pavan**, you can hear a tonal structure of remarkable clarity and simplicity in its final section (bars 34–59). There are four phrases defined by cadences in the keys of D major and its dominant, A major:

Phrase 1 (bars 34–42): D major
After a descent from the dominant to the tonic the arch-shaped melody rises from the tonic to the upper tonic, then falls back to the lower tonic. This is harmonised with a **tonic pedal** followed by what was to become a very common tonal progression: II–Ib–V–I.

Phrase 2 (bars 43–49): D major modulating to A major
This begins with a segment of a **circle of 5ths** that is entirely diatonic apart from the C♮ in bar 46 (a tiny sign of lingering modality). The phrase ends with a modulation to A major and a perfect cadence in this new key.

Compare the diatonic simplicity of this progression (VI–II–V–I–IV in D major) with the tonal restlessness of Gabrieli's circle of 5ths in bars 36–41 of his sonata.

Phrase 3 (bars 50–54): D major modulating to A major
The return to D major happens without a modulation (another sign of modal thinking), but the phrase ends with another perfect cadence in A major (VIIb–I in bars 53–54).

Phrase 4 (bars 54–58): D major
A dominant pedal reflects the tonic pedal at the start of this section, and a perfect cadence in the tonic brings this entirely tonal phrase to an end.

Thus we can see that while Gabrieli was still working in a modal idiom in *NAM 14*, Holborne was adopting a more tonal style which, in this section of the pavan, defines a ternary *tonal* structure (D major – A major – D major) expressed through four phrases whose tonal cadences also reflect these keys.

Corelli

NAM 15   CD2 Track 4
Fitzwilliam Ensemble

We carefully selected the phrases from Holborne's paired dances to illustrate the difference between his tonal structures and those of Gabrieli. With this movement by Corelli, written some 90 years later, there is no need to do so because there is no longer a trace of modality. *NAM 15* has the style of a gigue, a lively dance in compound time. As in Holborne's dances, changes of chord underline the metrical flow of the music. But what really concerns us is the way Corelli uses tonality to define a clearly articulated **binary form**. From a tonal point of view the first section (bars 1–19) can be divided into three sections:

✦ Bars 1–8 are in the tonic key of D major

✦ Bars 8–11 modulate from the tonic to the dominant

✦ Bars 11–19 are in the dominant key of A major, confirmed by the inverted tonic pedal in the second violin part and the perfect cadence in the last two bars.

The second section (bars 20–43) reveals long-term tonal planning. From a tonal point of view it can be divided into four sections:

✦ In bars 20–23 the music modulates back to the tonic (D major)

✦ In bars 23–32 Corelli embarks on a more adventuous tonal journey that takes him from D major to **related minor keys** (B minor in bars 26–28 and E minor in bars 28–32)

✦ In bar 32 a **modulating circle of 5ths** begins with the tonic chord of E minor and then passes through *related major keys* (A major, D major and G major in bars 33–35) that balance the minor keys of the previous section

✦ In bars 36–43 the homeward journey is begun with a modulation back to the tonic (the harpsichordist will play a C♯ in the second half of bar 36 to complete V^7 of D major), and the music remains entirely diatonic in this key until the final perfect cadence.

Unlike the sonata and dances we have already studied, this movement is unified by the two motifs heard in the first bar, a technique that is used more rigorously by Haydn in our next piece.

Haydn

NAM 16   CD2 Track 5
The Lindsays

Although we have moved on in time by nearly another 90 years, there are direct connections between Haydn's finale and both the dances by Holborne and the trio-sonata movement by Corelli. Corelli's gigue and bars 1–36 of this movement are both examples of binary form, but they differ in that:

✦ The first section of *NAM 15* modulated to the dominant but the first section of Haydn's movement (bars 1–8) consists of two balanced four-bar phrases, the first of which modulates from the tonic key (E♭ major) to the dominant (B♭ major, bars 3–4), while the second returns to the tonic.

Compare this antecedent–consequent pair with those we discovered in the sonata by Gabrieli and the dances by Holborne.

♦ The second section of Corelli's gigue starts in the tonic and modulates through several related keys before returning to the tonic. This contrasts sharply with the music in bars 8–36 of Haydn's finale. It remains firmly in the tonic throughout, but Haydn uses a dominant pedal to arouse expectation in much the same way as Holborne does in the last section of his pavan. This expectation is satisfied when the whole of the first section is repeated in bars 28–36, thus completing a section in **rounded binary form** which is, surprisingly, simpler than that of Corelli.

Haydn now uses the whole binary structure as flanking sections of a **ternary structure**, the central section of which (bars 36–70) contains passages in the subdominant (A♭ major) and *its* relative minor (F minor). The movement ends with a long section (bars 107–172) in which dominant pedals (shades of Holborne again) are used to generate terrific anticipation. This is satisfied, not by a grand reprise of the first theme, but by tiny damp squibs derived from it.

Bars	Form	Key
‖: 0–36	ABA	E♭ major :‖
36–70	C	A♭, Fm, E♭
71–107	ABA	E♭ major
107–140	C^1	E♭ major
140–148	A	E♭ major
148–152	Adagio	E♭ major
152–172	A^1	E♭ major

This analysis of the structure is summarised in the box (*right*) – but the frequent returns of the A section in the tonic key may make you feel that the movement is more like a rondo form, as shown in the diagram on page 59 in the AS Guide.

There are no connections between Haydn's comic use of tonality and any of the music we have so far studied, but we will discover equally silly tonal japes when we later study Poulenc's trio.

By the end of the 18th century composers were able to give shape to extended movements such as *NAM 17*. Furthermore they confidently handled a wide vocabulary of chromatic chords that could be used simply to provide colour or to effect more wide-ranging modulations.

In the Septet, **chromatic harmony** appears as early as bar 5 where there appears to be a modulation from the tonic key of E♭ major to the subdominant key of A♭ (bars 6–7). This interpretation is proved wrong when a **German augmented 6th** (C♭–E♭–G♭–A♮ in bar 7) resolves to chord V of the home key (E♭ major) in the next bar.

This simple dominant triad appears on the first beat of every subsequent bar until bar 15. Sometimes it is approached with diatonic harmony (bars 8^2–10^1), sometimes with a tonic chord borrowed from the parallel minor (bars 11^2–12^1) and sometimes with a secondary dominant (V^7 of V on the third beat of bars 12–14).

Finally, a timid chromatic progression in bar 16 leads to an explosive version of V^7 (bars 17–18). By approaching the dominant from so many different tonal angles, Beethoven whips up expectation for a return of the tonic in much the same way as Haydn does in the coda of his finale. But here the effect is magisterial rather than silly, and in the Septet the resolution of V^7 is worth waiting for because it's the beginning of a wonderfully effervescent sonata-form allegro that sparkles all the more for its proximity to the solemnities of the introduction.

Similar tactics allow Beethoven to hold our interest throughout the long *Allegro con brio*. It has the three principal sections of a **sonata form** movement plus a vastly extended **coda** lasting 54 bars:

Beethoven

NAM 17   CD2 Track 6
Berlin Philharmonic Octet

When studying *NAM 17* remember that the clarinet in B♭ sounds a tone lower than printed, and that when in the treble clef a horn in E♭ sounds a major 6th lower than printed (when in the bass clef it sounds a major 3rd higher).

Form	Bars	Section	Keys
Exposition	18–39 40–52 53–98 98–111	First subject Transition Second subject Codetta	E♭ major E♭ major modulating to B♭ major B♭ major B♭ major
Development	111–153	B♭ major (bars 111–113) modulating (114–115) to C minor (116–120). Then modulating (121–123) to A♭ major (124–128) and next modulating (129–131) to F minor (bar 136). Finally Beethoven modulates back to E♭ major (bars 138–140). The development ends with extended dominant preparation (bars 140–153).	
Recapitulation	154–181 182–187 188–233	First subject Transition Second subject	E♭ major and A♭ major V of E♭ major E♭ major
Coda	233–288		E♭ major, A♭ major and E♭ major

Although the structure is much more complex than Haydn's finale there is never any doubt about the succession of keys, thanks to Beethoven's strongly functional (that is, key-defining) harmony. Several important features should be noted:

The **exposition** is characterised by two principal thematic groups (known as subjects), the first in the tonic key and the second in the dominant, while the **development** is a dramatic central section in which Beethoven reviews some of the melodies of the exposition while taking us on a tour of related keys. This contrast between two clearly defined keys in the exposition and tonal instability in the development is typical of classical sonata-form structures.

In bar 140 a dominant pedal (shades of Holborne and Haydn) begins in the viola and transfers to the horn in bar 148. Meanwhile the bass stalks up and down chord V^7. Both events create tension which is finally released by the tonic chord in bar 154, marking the start of the **recapitulation**. This a reprise of the exposition with some modifications. There are two that are particularly relevant from our point of view.

The first is the dramatic plunge into A♭ major that starts in bars 166–169 where the chords (E♭^{7}/D♭ and A♭/C) are *almost* the same as those in bars 5–6 (E♭^{7}/B♭ and A♭/C). The big difference between these two passages is that in the introduction Beethoven returns to the tonic key of E♭ major immediately after the German augmented 6th in bars 7–8, whereas here he remains in A♭ major for 12 bars. Only then does the same German 6th (C♭–E♭–G♭–A♮ in bar 181) resolve to chord V of E♭ major (bar 182).

The second is that all of the music in bars 47–110 is repeated, but transposed to the tonic key, in bars 182–245.

So Beethoven has expanded a chromatic progression in the introduction from four bars to 17 bars and has done this to prepare the listener for a transposed repeat of 63 bars from the first section. Most listeners will not perceive what is going on, but it is by such strategic, long-term tonal planning that classical composers were able to engineer their vastly extended structures. All are, however likely to recognise the **ternary structure** of these three sections.

Finally, the **coda** deserves special comment. The function of a classical coda is to emphasise the home key by such devices as tonic pedals and, as we saw in *NAM 16*, repeated perfect cadences in the tonic. Beethoven's coda does not follow these aims. Instead he writes an extended section which has many characteristics of a development. Certainly it begins with a traditional **tonic pedal** (cello and bass, then horn, in bars 233–241) and continues with perfect cadences in E♭ major (bars 242–245), but suddenly Beethoven introduces chromatic harmony (bars 248 and 272–274) and a modulation to the subdominant in bars 288–265. These tonal features need a bucketful of perfect cadences in E♭ major to restore the home key. Beethoven provides ten of them in the last 13 bars.

Brahms

NAM 18   CD2 Track 7
Guarneri Quartet with
Peter Serkin (piano)

We dealt with the structure and tonal scheme of *NAM 18* at the start of this chapter, and so we will confine discussion here to a few additional points about continuity and change.

In many of his works Brahms revealed a deep respect for musical traditions of the past. In *NAM 18* this is evident in his use of:

✦ The piano quintet (a small genre within chamber music, but one that dates back to the late 18th century)

✦ A Scherzo and Trio format (the Scherzo and Trio replaced the Minuet and Trio as the preference for the third movement of multi-movement works back in the time of Beethoven)

✦ Simple ternary form for the Trio

✦ Fugal textures and contrapuntal techniques

✦ The phrygian cadence, used by Gabrieli and that occurs several times in *NAM 14*, more than 250 years later.

Brahms himself would have recognised continuity in this last point – he knew most that there was then to be known about ancient music, he edited early music for scholarly editions, and he made use of themes by Bach and Handel in his own compositions.

But the popular description of Brhams as a 'conservative' composer is not entirely justified. The syncopated first theme of *NAM 18*, his use of remote 3rd-related keys, rapid modulation and chromatic harmony all reflect changes in musical style that were becoming widespread during the romantic period.

This duality of continuity and change in Brahms' music can be illustrated by looking at his use of the German augmented 6th chord. The version in bars 126–127 of *NAM 18* uses exactly the same notes (C♭–E♭–G♭–A♮) that Beethoven used in bar 7 of the Septet. But while for Beethoven this was a one-off dramatic effect, for Brahms it is a thematic element that he employed throughout the Scherzo.

Poulenc

NAM 19   CD2 Track 8
Nash Ensemble

Although called a sonata there is no element of continuity between the sonatas of Gabrieli and Corelli on the one hand and this witty ragbag of neoclassical tricks on the other. The focus is on the melodies, which are even more **diatonic** than Haydn's and as much given to **triadic figures** and **antecedent–consequent pairs** as any classical composer. A comparison of the eight-bar trumpet melody at the beginning of *NAM 19* with the eight-bar melody at the start of *NAM 16* will reveal how much fun Poulenc had. This is not to suggest that he had 'The Joke' in mind when he wrote the sonata, but who knows? Let's make a comparison of those first eight bars:

Haydn	Poulenc
eight-bar theme forming an antecedent–consequent pair	eight-bar theme forming an antecedent–consequent pair
antecdent ends in dominant consequent ends in tonic	antecedent ends in tonic consequent ends in dominant
a couple of chromatic notes	no chromatic notes
one triadic figure lots of scalic figures	six triadic figures a few scalic figures

But there are also contrasts:

+ Haydn's anacrusic melody ends at its pre-ordained place (on the strong beat of bar 7) while Poulenc's wicked parody ends lamely on a weak beat (bar 8, beat 4).

+ The first three of Poulenc's triadic figures are all the same and the last three are very simple variants. When they are developed in bars 21–25 there's disagreement about whether the music is in the major or the tonic minor (a parody of similar portentous tonal devices in passages like bars 8^2–12^1 of Beethovens Septet).

+ Poulenc uses the rather obvious device of semiquaver scales to move his music forwards – they must be played *très précis* (very precisely), to the doubtless consternation of the hornist! Haydn gets by perfectly well without any sort of link between his opening two-bar phrases.

The whole movement is in **ternary form** with a short **coda** in the last four bars. The fast flanking sections (bars 0–25 and 57^4–85) are in G major and the slower central section (bars 26–57^3) in E♭ major and B♭ major.

One of Poulenc's witticisms are the passages in which a return of the opening motif (the descending triad) suddenly attempts to announce a false reprise – which just as quickly then peters out (bars 21^4–25 and 39^4–41^1). Also unusual is the reuse in the final A section of material from the B section of the ternary form – bars 66–71 are a rescoring and transposition to G major of bars 48–53.

Poulenc tends to alternate between sections of **functional harmony** such as bars 1–8, in which primary triads clearly define keys (despite occasional **diatonic dissonances** of the sort illustrated on page 65 of the AS Guide), and sections in which chromaticism is deliberately used to destabilise the tonality. For instance, in bars 9–15 the mainly root-position triadic harmony in G major outlined by the trumpet and trombone is assaulted by F♮s and E♭s from the horn. Similarly, far from defining tonality, the cadence in bar 29 leaves the ear wondering quite what key has actually been reached!

While *NAM 19* is in ternary form, it is far removed from the large-scale exposition-development-recapitulation plan of *NAM 17*, and its use of 3rd-related keys has little in common with *NAM 18*.

Don't forget that the horn in F sounds a perfect 5th lower than printed.

?

1. (i) How does the dorian mode differ from the minor scale?

(ii) Which work in this Area of Study uses the dorian mode?

2. On page 74 we used the expression 'antiphonal exchange'. What does this mean?

3. Explain what is meant by an 'antecedent–consequent pair'.

4. In the second section of *NAM 15* Corelli modulates through the keys listed in the table *below*. Complete the table by showing how each of these keys relates to D major:

Bars	Key	Relationship to D major
26–28	B minor	
28–32	E minor	
32–33	A major	
33–34	D major	tonic
34–35	G major	
35–43	D major	tonic

5. What is meant by 'rounded binary form'? (Carefully reread the first paragraph of page 77 if you are unsure.)

6. (i) What makes the development section of Beethoven's Septet less tonally stable than the exposition?

(ii) In what way(s) does the coda of Beethoven's Septet differ from codas in earlier works such as *NAM 16*?

7. On page 80 we used the expression 'functional harmony'. What does this mean?

Sample questions

In the exam there will be two questions on this topic, from which you must choose to answer **one**.

(a) Show how *NAM 13* and *NAM 14* differ in their respective composer's approach to tonality.

(b) Explain the importance of tonality to the structure of music in the classical period, using examples from both *NAM 16* and *NAM 17*.

(c) Compare and contrast the structure and tonality of *NAM 15* and *NAM 19*.

Keyboard music

There are *two* Special Focus works, *NAM 20* and *NAM 23*, both o
which must be studied if you are taking the exam in 2006 or 2007

Sweelinck, Pavana Lachrimae

Special Focus Work 1 for 2006 and 2007

NAM 20   CD2 Track 9
Peter Seymour (harpsichord)

Before starting on this section you should work through (or revise
the information about the context and structure of this music giver
on pages 68–69 of the AS Guide. Make sure that you understand
all of the terminology used on those pages.

The title

The pavan was a stately dance of the 16th century in slow o
moderate **simple duple time**. Listen to the recording. In the firs
few bars you will probably feel four crotchet beats to the bar (a:
indicated by the **C** time signature). But if you listen to the first 1€
bars you should be able to detect a much slower underlying pulse
of two minims to the bar – the simple duple metre that is so typica
of this courtly dance (although the performer's use of *rubato* is, to
say the least, unhelpful).

The pavan (which is an English spelling) originated in Italy, hence
Sweelinck's Italian spelling, *pavana*. *Lachrimae* means tearful anc
is a reference to the words in the first bar of Dowland's lute song
(*NAM 33*) on which the pavan is based. You need to be aware o
this connection for it explains not only the title but also why the
motif of a falling 4th (both perfect and diminished, and often fillec
in with passing notes) is such a prominent feature of the pavan.

The melodic structure

Bars			
1–16	A	Dowland bars 1–8
17–32	A^1	Variation on A
33–48	B	Dowland bars 9–16
49–64	B^1	Variation on B
65–81	C	Dowland bars 17–24
82–98	C^1	Variation on C

The structure of NAM 20 can be represented as $AA^1BB^1CC^1$, in
which A, B and C are free transcriptions of the three strains o
Dowland's lute song, each followed by a variation (A^1, B^1 and C^1)

Theme A (bars 1–16)

The first 16 bars constitute a varied transcription of bars 1–8 o
Flow my tears. On paper they look different because Sweelinck has
doubled Dowland's note values. He also made some changes to the
melody that show how one great composer responded creatively to
material he borrowed from another musical genius.

Example 1 shows all of the changes Sweelinck made to Dowland's
vocal melody in this first section (we have doubled Dowland's note

Ex. 1

values to make it easier to understand them). Some variants have to do with the change of medium. So, because a note played on a harpsichord dies away almost immediately, Sweelinck repeats the first C instead of tying it. Other changes derive from the keyboard style of the period. Thus the minim G♯ in bar 14 of the song becomes a written-out trill and turn in the pavan.

Other melodic variants are more creative. In bar 11 Sweelinck replaces Dowland's expressive falling phrase with a semibreve A, falling to G♯ at the start of bar 12. Why? Firstly, melodic simplicity helps focus attention on the **phrygian cadence** at this point, which helps to clarify the regular four-bar phrase structure (particularly important in the absence of Dowland's rhyming text). Secondly, it throws into relief Sweelinck's **melodic inversion** of the falling 4th figure in bar 12, thus preparing the way for Dowland's own inversion that appears faithfully transcribed in bars 65–66 of the pavan.

The phrygian cadence consists of the progression IVb–V in a minor key. It is a type of imperfect cadence that is characteristic of renaissance and baroque styles.

Variation A (bars 17–32)

Example 2 shows that the melody of bars 17–20 of the pavan are an elaborate variant of the first four bars of the pavan.

Ex. 2

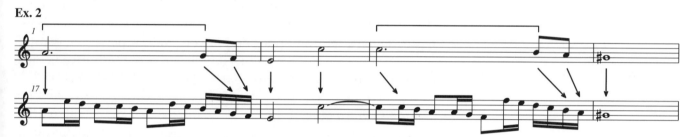

Every pitch of the original melody is preserved, but Sweelinck separates the bracketed notes with stepwise decoration, the falling outlines of which mirror the 'falling tears' of the song and the falling motifs that are so prominent in both song and pavan. Such lavish ornamentation is evident again in bar 23 where the F and D minims from bar 7 are reduced to semiquavers at the start of each four-note group. Similarly, Example 1 *opposite* shows that bar 10 of the pavan is a variant of two minims in Dowland's song, but, although all six pitches of bar 10 of the pavan are present in bar 26, they are inundated with semiquaver figuration. In the next bar only the first and last notes correspond with the pitch of the single semibreve that fills bar 11 of the pavan. We have already noticed the cadential flourish that replaces Dowland's minim G♯ (Example 1, bar 14). Now compare this with the more elaborate variant in bar 30 and the stepwise figuration that follows it.

> **Important note**
> During the course of these pages we have often referred to Dowland's *Flow my tears* because comparisons with this song, which is readily available in the *New Anthology*, greatly help in understanding Sweelinck's work and in clarifying his expressive intentions. However, be aware that you are not *required* to know Dowland's lute song.

Sweelinck's variation technique is not confined to just the tune. In bar 18, for instance, the bass is allowed a share of the melody by repeating the treble of the previous bar (with one slight change). The same technique is used in bar 24 where the middle voice is allowed a moment of glory. In the following bar the bass is allowed its say as it rises to join the start of a long passage of semiquaver figuration in the treble part (and similarly in bars 28–29).

Theme B (bars 33–48)

Theme B is a slightly varied transcription of bars 9–16 of *Flow my teares*. The chief differences are the addition of a passing note between each of Dowland's expressive rising 3rd figures (imitated by the two lowest parts in bars 39–41) and the addition of cadential ornamentation in bars 35 and 45–47.

Variation B (bars 49–64)

To see precisely how Sweelinck varies the melody of theme B try writing out both melodies, one above the other, using Example 1 on page 82 as a model. You may wonder why, in bar 51, instead of adding ornamentation to the melody of bar 35, Sweelinck removes the last four quavers and returns to Dowland's original melody. The answer lies in the lower parts. In bar 50 the alto part imitates the treble part of the previous bar and this more contrapuntal texture continues when the bass enters imitatively in bar 51. Had Sweelinck preserved the cadence figure of bar 35 it would have distracted attention from the bass imitation – so, as in bar 50, he writes a very simple treble part.

This reversal of roles is maintained right through to bar 55 – the original treble melody is preserved while the performer is required to demonstrate good left-hand technique in the rapid passagework. We have already noticed how Sweelinck adds a passing note to Dowland's rising-3rd figure; in bars 55–57 he adds a quaver before this so Dowland's 'teares, and sighes, and grones' becomes a lively dialogue between the upper and lower pairs of parts. You should now be able to describe how Sweelinck varies the **imitative texture** of the next three bars (compare bars 42–44 with bars 58–60).

Theme C (bars 65–81)

This is a varied transcription of bars 17–24 of Dowland's song. By now you should be able to recognise Sweelinck's cadential ornamentation and his in-filling of the characteristic diminished 4th, but you should recognise the fact that the melodic lines of the lower parts are often just as important as the treble melody. Notice, for instance, the **strict imitation** of the first five treble notes in the tenor part (bars 66–68) and the way the alto imitation of the first three notes a 3rd lower continues to form a lovely modal arch in the same bars. Notice too the way the commonplace cadential figure (tenor, bar 79) leads to a restatement of the falling 4th figure that so dominates both the song and the pavan.

A tierce de Picardie is a major 3rd in the final tonic chord of a minor-key passage. It was common in the last bar of any sort of minor-key music in this period, but placing the sharpened 3rd in the treble was unusual, and it makes Sweelinck's ending seem more optimistic than Dowland's.

It is in the last five bars that Sweelinck strays furthest from his vocal model. In bar 77 his ascending passing notes between G♯ and C continue on upwards to reach E, the highest pitch of Dowland's song and the note that its composer reserved for the word 'Happie'. Sweelinck then follows Dowland's melody a 3rd higher to reach a joyful **tierce de Picardie**.

Notice too the three-beat lute interlude at bar 20 in the song, where the singer's rests help to highlight the climactic entry on 'Happie' – this is reflected in the six-beat harpsichord interlude in *NAM 20* (bars 72–73) where the change of texture similarly highlights the high treble entry. Bar 19 of Dowland's song exceptionally contains six beats and this carries over to the pavan, in which Theme C and its variation are 17 (not 16) bars long. This irregularity can be heard in the assymetric phrase structure – for instance, the first phrase begins at the start of bar 65 and ends on the minim A in bar 69 – 4½ bars. The second begins at bar 69[3] and ends in bar 72 – 2½ bars.

Variation C (bars 82–98)

In the first four bars of the variation the complex counterpoint of Theme C disappears in favour of semiquaver figuration and a new and simpler point of imitation (bar 83, treble and bar 84, tenor). In bars 90–92 Sweelinck's variant of the falling 4ths from bars 73–75 echoes the tied rhythm in the tenor part of bars 89–90 in a rare example of a melodic sequence.

As you read this section bear in mind that Sweelinck preserved a good deal of Dowland's melodies in this work. Melodic movement is mostly **conjunct** (stepwise). When there is a leap the melody usually returns within the leap or moves on by step – the more triadic movement in bars 36–37 is a rare exception.

The slow descent from tonic to dominant in bars 1–2 had long been associated with anguish in vocal music, but when this falling perfect 4th is transposed in bars 3–4 its effect is intensified by transformation into a **falling diminished 4th** (C–G♯) – an interval that was hardly ever used in 16th-century polyphony, but employed throughout the 17th century to signify extreme anguish. Notice that the transposition brings about an upward leap of a minor 6th in bar 2, another interval often associated with grief.

In the discussion *below*, we use x to represent the falling 4th motif, and y to represent the interval of a 3rd, which is another important unifying element in the music. However, before studying this account, be sure to read the margin note, *right*. In Theme A:

+ Motif x (bars 1–2) falls a perfect 4th from tonic to dominant

+ Motif x^1 (bars 3–4) is a transposition of motif x which falls a diminished 4th

+ Motif x is repeated with a simple rhythmic alteration in bar 5

+ Motif y (bar 6) consists of two notes forming an ascending 3rd

+ Motif y^1 (bar 7) is an inversion of motif y

+ A transposition of motif y^1 occurs in bar 9

+ In motif y^2 (bar 10) the falling 3rd (B–G♯) is disguised by ornamentation

+ Motif x^2 (bar 12) is an inversion of motif x^1 with slight rhythmic alterations.

You should be able to spot many later manipulations of these two motifs in Themes B and C. In the variations, most of Dowland's tightly-knit motivic work is lost in the elaborate figuration but Sweelinck still retains some of the original motifs and introduces new manipulations of his own. For example, in section A^1 the descending sequence of three-note motifs in bars 17 and 19 derive from motif y^1 (bar 7) and foreshadow the inverted form of this motif in the rising sequence of bars 39–41. Similarly the three-note figure in bar 21 comes from the first and last notes of motif x and foreshadows the simpler statement of this idea in bar 36. Finally, look at the soprano melody starting in bar 49 (imitated a bar later by alto and then bass parts). Example 3 shows how it, too, is formed from versions of x (solid brackets) and y (dashed bracket).

Melodic style

It is unlikely that Sweelinck himself would have thought of manipulating motifs in the way we have described here. Most of the connections arise logically from the type of pattern-based style he used.

Ex. 3

Textures

It would make life easy if composers were to limit themselves to totally chordal textures on the one hand and totally contrapuntal textures on the other. Alas, real composers are rarely so obliging. In the pavan there are five basic types of texture:

1. A single, relatively fast melody or figuration contrasting with a slow **homophonic accompaniment**. This first appears in bars 11–16 where the melodic interest passes from the alto to the soprano, then tenor, then soprano again, and finally back to the tenor. An even clearer example occurs in bars 94–98.

2. A texture in which a theme passes from one part to another while other parts provide a subservient accompaniment, as in bars 17–19 where almost identical melodies are heard first in the soprano, then the bass, and then the soprano again.

3. An **imitative texture** in which a melodic idea presented in one part is copied approximately or exactly in another part while the melodic line of the first part continues to unfold. Imitation first appears in bars 42–45 where the four-note figure in the soprano part is repeated two octaves lower in the bass (with the first note augmented from a crotchet to a minim). Then, in quick succession the motif is heard in the tenor (overlapping the end of the first bass statement), the soprano (overlapping the end of the tenor) and the bass again (overlapping the last note of the tenor part and the last three notes of the soprano part).

Note the difference between the imitative texture of bars 42–45, in which the contrapuntal parts overlap, and the 'type 2' texture of bars 39–41, in which they do not.

4. The most rigorous type of imitation is **canon**, in which an extended melody (rather than a short motif) is repeated note for note (possibly transposed) by another part a short distance later, while the first melody continues to unfold. The only canon in the pavan is in bars 91–93 where the soprano part (starting on the D on the third beat of bar 91) is copied note for note a compound 4th lower by the bass part (starting on the high A on the second beat of bar 92 and shortening the first note to a tied crotchet). The canon ends on the first bass note of bar 94.

5. **Free counterpoint**, in which a number of independent and more or less melodic strands are woven together, as in the first eight bars of the pavan. Here the supremacy of the soprano melody is challenged by the tenor in the first two bars, then by the alto in bars 2–4 (the first three notes imitating the tenor, the last four imitating the soprano). Only the bass part lacks any melodic interest (its long sustained notes simply provide a firm foundation for the harmonies formed by the contrapuntal upper parts). After another point of imitation (bars 5–6) the music becomes more homophonic until it comes to rest on chord V, with its much decorated 3rd (G♯) in bar 8. This freely contrapuntal texture with brief points of imitation is, in fact, very common in instrumental music of the 16th and early 17th centuries.

Tonality and harmony

Sweelinck's variations were written at a time when renaissance **modality** was giving way to the **tonal system** of major and minor keys. Example 4 on the next page shows the underlying harmonic progressions of Theme A. It illustrates many features of this transitional harmonic style and clarifies the tonal structure. We have used a $\frac{2}{2}$ time signature because the pavan was a dance in slow duple time and, with only a very few exceptions, the **harmonic rhythm** conforms to this metre – in other words, the fastest rate of chord change is normally the minim beat.

Ex. 4

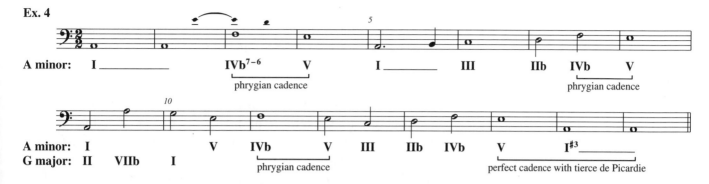

There are cadences at the end of each four-bar phrase, all in the key of A minor, and every chord derives from the harmonic or melodic minor scales of this key. Chords I, IVb and V dominate the harmony. These primary triads (plus chords II and VI) are said to be functional because they define the tonality. Yet despite this **functional harmony** and clear **tonal cadences** the music still has a decidedly modal feel. Why? There are several answers:

✦ The first three phrases each end with a **phrygian cadence** (see page 83) giving a somewhat archaic, modal tinge.

✦ Chord III in bar 6 has a modal feel because in this C major chord the sharpened leading note (G♯) is replaced with G♮ (from the descending melodic minor scale but also the aeolian mode).

✦ The only sort of modulation is a brief visit to G major in bars 9–10. This again sounds much more like a modal relationship than the modulations to the dominant or relative major that are commonplace in later tonal styles.

✦ In the G major chord at the start of bar 10, the G♮s in the bass and alto parts are immediately contradicted in the second half of the bar by the G♯s in the melody – such **false relations** are one of the most characteristic sounds of modal polyphony.

The most pungent example of this device is the **simultaneous false relation** in bar 96 where the treble G♮ (the highest note in the pavan) sounds against the sustained G♯ on the bass stave.

The majority of chords in *NAM 20* are root-position triads and most of the rest are triads in first inversion. The harmony is **diatonic** (meaning that there is no significant use of chromatic notes).

The only dissonanances that occur on minim beats are **suspensions**, such as the 7–6 suspension sketched in with the small notes in Example 4 *above* (compare this with bar 3 of *NAM 20* to see how this suspension, like many others in the piece, is decorated with an ornamental resolution). Equally common is the 4–3 suspension in which a 4th above the bass (regarded as a dissonance in this period) resolves to a 3rd, as with the upper part's A in bar 37 that resolves by falling to G♯ above the bass E.

Read the glossary entry on suspensions in the AS Guide if you are unsure about the meaning of this term.

Passing notes abound in *NAM 20*. When they occur *off the beat* they hardly sound dissonant. This is true in bar 1 where the tenor B links the harmony notes A and C, and is also true of the quavers which similarly link the harmony notes A and E in the treble part of the same bar. But when passing notes occur *on the beat* as **accented passing notes** they sound decidedly dissonant, as is the case with the alto B in bar 7, which clashes with the minim A in the tenor.

Another type of melodic decoration that occurs throughout Swee-linck's variations is the **auxiliary note**, which moves by step from a harmony note and then returns. For instance, in the melody at the start of bar 23 the harmony note F is decorated with **lower auxiliaries** on E. Similarly, in the second half of bar 26 the harmony note G♯ is decorated with both a lower auxiliary (F♯) and an **upper auxiliary** (A). The **appoggiatura** is, in effect, a suspension without its preparation. It is rare in music of this period, but a fairly prominent example occurs on the second minim beat of bar 68, where the soprano leaps to A (forming an unprepared dissonant 7th with the tenor) before falling to the harmony note G♯. In fact, the piquant harmony throughout bars 65–69 deserves particular attention since it includes:

✦ Four bars of **dominant pedal** (on E) starting in bar 65

✦ Passing notes on A in both the tenor and soprano of bar 65

✦ A long **upper auxiliary** on C in the soprano of bar 66 that turns chord V into a sexy augmented chord (C–E–G♯)

✦ The use of the **aeolian mode** (G♮ in the alto part) in a passage of otherwise tonal harmony – and this G♮ also forms a **false relation** with the tenor G♯ in the previous bar

✦ A **consonant 4th** formed by the soprano A sounding against the bass E in bar 67 (in the approach to a cadence the otherwise 'forbidden' unprepared 4th from the bass was allowed within certain strict parameters and was commonly used at the time, although this is the only example in Sweelinck's pavan)

✦ the **parallel 7ths** at the start of bar 68. They are caused by the simultaneous resolution of the **suspension** in the treble part and the **lower auxiliary** in the tenor part. Such offbeat dissonance is fairly common in this period and, as we shall see, very common in late baroque music

✦ the **bare-5th chord** in bar 69, which was uncommon in this period and very rare in later baroque styles.

Keyboard style

In the 16th century instrumental music grew out of vocal styles. In *NAM 20* this is apparent in Sweelinck's transcriptions (the main A, B and C sections). These could, with only the slightest adaptation, be performed by a quartet of competent singers because:

✦ Four-part texture is maintained almost throughout

✦ All four individual parts have ranges that correspond with the ranges of SATB voices

✦ Parts move largely by step, with any disjunct intervals being carefully embedded, and there are few repeated notes (unlike most instrumental music of any period).

None of this would be out of place in 16th-century vocal polyphony. Even the cadential ornaments in sections A and B are of a type that would have been added to the music by skilful soloists.

If possible, try to play bars 65–69 on the sustained sounds of an organ (genuine or synthesised) – or, better still, sing it with friends: the apparently mild dissonances will then become positively succulent (especially if you sing the alto part).

But when we hear the variations it is immediately obvious that the festoons of ornaments that twine about Dowland's chaste melodies are virtually impossible to sing. The most extreme example starts in the bass in bar 28 and passes to the uppermost part in bar 30. This type of figuration is designed for a keyboard instrument – we can describe it as an **idiomatic** keyboard style. Notice, however, that as with most music of this period there are no dynamic or phrasing marks (compare this with the proliferation of markings that Debussy provides to guide the interpretation of *NAM 24*).

NAM 20 is written for the harpsichord or a similar contemporary plucked-string keyboard instrument such as the virginal (or virginals). In the early 17th century such instruments had a range of about four octaves, of which Sweelinck modestly uses just under three.

Private Study

1. Explain what is meant by a phrygian cadence and identify an example of one on page 247 of the *New Anthology*.

2. Describe the texture used in bars 49–52.

3. What term describes the relationship between G in the bass of bar 53 and G♯ in the melody of the same bar?

4. Identify one example of each of the following three types of melodic decoration in bar 87: an appoggiatura, a passing note, an upper auxiliary note.

5. In bar 90 the B in the tenor part clashes with C in the bass. What is this type of dissonance called?

6. Explain what is meant by idiomatic keyboard writing and give an example from *NAM 20*.

Schumann, Three pieces from Kinderscenen

Special Focus Work 2 for 2006 and 2007

NAM 23   CD2 Tracks 13–15
Alfred Brendel (piano)

Before starting on this section you should work through (or revise) the information about the context and structure of this music given on pages 72–73 of the AS Guide. Make sure that you understand all of the terminology used on those pages.

The first piece is in **rounded binary form** – ‖: A :‖: BA :‖ – in the key of G major. Note that this is *not* the same as ternary form. Its other main structural features are:

Von fremden Ländern und Menschen

✦ Balanced **periodic phrasing** (2+2+4 bars in the first section, shown by Schumann's phrase marks) – typical of music from the preceding classical period (such as the two-bar phrasing at the start of *NAM 22*)

✦ An A section that does not modulate and that is repeated almost exactly when it returns in bars 15–22

✦ A central B section (bars 9–14) that is melodically distinct from section A and that makes only fleeting reference to a different key (E minor)

✦ A rhythmic ostinato formed by the triplets in the inner part that continue throughout the piece.

The melody is simple, repetitive and entirely diatonic – features reflecting the style of the innocent German folk songs that so pleased the growing middle classes of the early romantic period.

However, Schumann's harmonisation is sophisticated:

✦ A **diminished 7th** appears in the very first bar

✦ **Unrelated** triads of B and G major are juxtaposed in bar 12

✦ A **circle of 5ths** appears in bars 9–12 (modified by a first inversion triad in the second half of bar 10 and the chromatic progression we discussed above in bar 12).

This combination of a simple diatonic melody with subtle and sometimes ambiguous harmonic touches, in a texture of **melody-dominated homophony**, is typical of Schumann in his dreamy romantic mode. The effect is enhanced by the frequent rhythmic blurring caused when the dotted patterns coincide with triplets, often tempting the performer to use **rubato** (encouraged by the ritardando followed by a pause in bars 12–14).

By 1838 the piano could be found in middle-class homes throughout western Europe, and Schumann's **idiomatic** writing exploits some of its most characteristic features. The articulation of the uppermost part as a song-like melody depends on the performer's ability to play it louder than the lower parts (despite the fact that the highest notes of the accompaniment must be played with the right-hand thumb). Although it is possible to give a *cantabile* rendition of the melody without the sustaining pedal, Schumann's romantic style demands the sustained resonance that can only be achieved through its careful use. The artful two-part counterpoint between the outer parts in bars 9–14, with continued harmonic filling, is typical of romantic textures that are enhanced by the sustaining power that pianos had by this time achieved.

Hasche-Mann

This is another rounded binary-form movement with tell-tale signs of romanticism, such as the sudden intrusion of an unrelated key (C major in bars 13–15) and the abrupt shift (there is no modulation) from the C major chord to V^7 of the home key (B minor) in bar 15. Once again a constant rhythm, this time semiquavers, is heard in one part or another right through to the final bar.

The game of blind-man's bluff is evoked by scurrying semiquavers. The prominent flattened leading note (A♮) in bar 2 comes from the use of the descending melodic minor scale, but A♯ appears at the end of both four-bar phrases. This tonal ambiguity is mirrored by the use of chord V with a minor 3rd (bars 2 and 6) and then a straightforward tonal cadence (V^7–I in B minor) in bars 4 and 8.

In the **tonal sequence** of bars 9–12 Schumann avoids clearly defined tonal centres by the use of **interrupted cadences** in G major (bars 10–11) and E minor (bars 12–13). Like a disorientated, blindfolded child, the music seems to get stuck on a chord of C (bars 13–15). Indeed, we seem to be in the *key* of C major judging by the alternating C and G^7 chords above the **double pedal** on C and G. But in bars 15–17 the tonic key is regained by the appearance of chords V^7 and I of B minor. In retrospect it turns out that the C major triad is a **neapolitan chord** in root position (a major triad on the flat supertonic). The texture is again melody-dominated homophony, with a difficult leaping accompaniment for the left hand to suggest the jerky, lurching movements of the blindfolded child.

Note that the F♯ in bar 11, beat 2 (left hand) should have a down-stem to show that it is part of the bass countermelody and is to be sustained as a crotchet.

Rubato literally means 'robbed' and refers to shortening some beats and lengthening others in order to give an expressive, free feel to the pulse. The use of *rubato* is often associated with romantic piano music.

The ABACABA **rondo form** of this piece is classically symmetrical. The periodic phrasing is also similar to many classical phrase structures, but the rondo theme is less integrated with the episodes (section B in bars 9–12, repeated in bars 37–40, and section C in bars 21–28) than the much longer and more complex sonata-rondo structures of classical music.

The romantic style is evident in the luscious melodic and harmonic **chromaticism** of the rondo refrain (the A sections) which alternate with the more **diatonic** style of the intervening episodes. By now you should be able to analyse the harmony in the sequence of bars 9–12, where the keys are E minor and C major, and the passage where Schumann subtly avoids exact sequences (bars 25–28).

Schumann's idiomatic piano writing includes the use of a bass melody accompanied by right-hand staccato chords (bars 9–12 and 37–40) and syncopated *sforzandi* in the 'frightening' central episode, which is also differentiated from the other sections by its new rhythm pattern and loud dynamic. The memory of a childhood scare lasts for only four bars and then the remainder of the episode wends it way back to the soothing mood of the rondo refrain.

Private study

1. Describe the texture **and** form of 'Von fremden Ländern und Menschen' using appropriate technical terms.

2. (a) What is a neapolitan chord?

   (b) Name the triad that would form a neapolitan chord in the key of A minor.

3. If a rondo form is described as ABACA, what name is given to (i) the recurring A sections and (ii) the intervening sections?

4. What does diatonic mean?

Sample questions

In the exam there will be three questions on the special focus works, from which you must choose to answer **two**.

(a) Describe Sweelinck's use of variation technique in *NAM 20* by comparing bars 17–32 with the first 16 bars of the work.

(b) Contrast Sweelinck's approach to tonality in *NAM 20* with Schumann's approach to tonality in *NAM 23*.

(c) Describe what is meant by idiomatic keyboard writing, illustrating your answer by reference to specific passages in both the special focus works you have studied.

Continuity and change in harmony and melody

For examination in summer 2006 and 2007

You do not need to study this topic unless *Keyboard music* is the Area of Study that you undertook for AS Music and which you are now extending for A2.

Before starting work on this topic you need a thorough understanding of the material on *Keyboard music* in the AS Guide (pages 67–77).

Remember that for A2 the topic draws on works from across the **entire** Area of Study, not just those in one of the two lists, A or B.

We dealt thoroughly with Sweelinck's melodic and harmonic style at the start of this chapter, so we won't revisit the pavan now. You must, however, make sure you understand all the points about melody and harmony in that section, including the meaning of the terms printed in bold, before you read on.

Bach

NAM 21   CD2 Tracks 10–11
András Schiff (piano)

$$\| : \quad \begin{matrix} D \\ I \end{matrix} - \begin{matrix} A \\ V \end{matrix} \quad : \| : \quad \begin{matrix} Bm \\ vi \end{matrix} - \begin{matrix} Em \\ ii \end{matrix} - \begin{matrix} D \\ I \end{matrix} \quad : \|$$

Fortspinnung is a German word meaning 'spinning out'.

The clear tonal scheme of Bach's binary-form Sarabande is shown *below left*. This assured handling of tonality as a structural device distinguishes Bach's dance from Sweelinck's variations, written more than a century earlier and which remain in a modal A minor almost throughout. The two composers also handle melody differently. Although Sweelinck manipulated motifs in various ways to help unify what might otherwise have been a rather episodic structure, there are also passages of semiquavers that are purely ornamental and non-thematic. Bach took motivic manipulation (**inversion**, **intervallic augmentation** and so on) to extremes and combined it with **simple repetition** and **sequential repetition** to produce a type of continuous melodic development called *Fortspinnung*. For instance, see if you can trace his use of the three-note figure from bar 1 of the Sarabande through the rest of the movement (its distinctive demisemiquaver rhythm makes it easy to recognise). This process of *Fortspinnung* is even more evident in the Gigue, in which Bach combines rounded binary form (like that in the Sarabande) with fugal textures.

Where Sweelinck's melodic lines are mainly conjunct Bach's leap as often as they step, sometimes quite unexpectedly (as in bars 2 and 14 of the sarabande). Such disjunct motion often serves a harmonic purpose. For instance, it is immediately obvious that the melody in bar 1 of the gigue is an arpeggio of D major, followed by the dominant 7th of G major in the next bar. These are the tonal anchors on which the other bars depend – we expect the C♮ in bar 2 to resolve down to B, and in bar 3 it does. **Triadic melodies** (a term used even when many of the implied chords are dominant 7ths) like this indicate a radical change from the conjunct, modal melodies of the renaissance to the dominance of major and minor keys in the baroque period.

Bach's harmony is **functional**. This means that nearly all of the chords define keys which in turn help define the form of each movement. Cadences are particularly vital in this process. Thus the two-part binary form of the Sarabande is defined by its tonal structure like this:

✦ In the first section, the tonic key of D major is confirmed by two perfect cadences (bars 3–4 and 4–5). After passing through the keys of A major and E major the goal of the first section (the dominant, A major) is established by perfect cadences in bars 8–9 and 11–12 (the F♮ in bar 12 is a **chromatic auxiliary note** which does not affect the key).

✦ The second section starts in the dominant and the harmony then briefly establishes a number of **closely related keys** (B minor, E minor and A major again). A long passage in the tonic key is required to balance this tonal upheaval. This is provided in bars 29–38, in which material from section A returns in D major. Only the two **secondary dominants** (bar 30 and the last quaver of bar 32) disturb the diatonic harmony of this final section.

You may recall that we found a rare example of a melodic sequence in Sweelinck's pavan. Bach, in contrast, makes frequent use of sequences of all kind. That heard in bars 5–6 of the Sarabande is a **real sequence** in which every note of both parts is transposed up a perfect 5th (or down a perfect 4th). Real sequences always cause a change of key and are far less common than **tonal sequences** (like that in bars 9–10 of the Gigue, in which the sequential repetition is adjusted to avoid accidentals and so remain in the key of D major). Bach also sometimes treats only the melody sequentially (as with the groups of four demisemiquavers in bar 19 of the Sarabande) and sometimes only the harmony is sequential (as in bars 25–27 of the same movement, above which the melody varies in each bar).

Suspensions play an important role in Bach's harmonic vocabulary. They can sometimes be identified by the presence of a tie between the preparation and the dissonance, as in bars 5 and 6 of the Sarabande. But don't assume that any tie indicates a suspension – the tied As in bar 7 are both consonant with the underlying A-major harmony, so there is no suspension here.

Like the Sarabande most of *NAM 22* has a two-part texture, but the right-hand melody totally dominates a left-hand accompaniment that often consists of simple broken chords, making it easier for us to understand Mozart's use of harmony. Even when the left hand is given melodic snippets (as in bars 35–36) it soon reverts to providing a **functional bass** (bar 37), **block chords** (bars 45–49), or the clichéd figuration of the **Alberti bass** (bars 57–58 and 71–80).

Whereas Bach concentrated on the monothematic elaboration of a few pervasive motifs, Mozart uses two self-contained and clearly differentiated main themes (called the **first subject** and the **second subject**) in his sonata-form movement, the structure of which is outlined in the table, *right*.

The movement begins with the first subject in B♭ major. It features an accented dissonance on the first beat of each of bars 1–4. If you are in a pedantic frame of mind you could identify which is an **appoggiatura**, which a **suspension** and which are **accented passing notes**. However, we will refer to the dissonance and its resolution as simply the 'appoggiatura motif'.

The appoggiatura motif appears no less than ten times in the first subject (bars 0^4–10) and is scattered throughout the rest of the movement (often in varied forms) thus unifying its contrasting sections. Notice how sometimes there is an **anticipation** between the dissonance and its resolution (bar 1), sometimes it is **inverted** (bar 14), sometimes it is **rhythmically diminished** (bar 7) or **augmented** (bar 63) and sometimes it is **chromatic** (bar 27).

Such motivic-based writing links Mozart with Bach and Sweelinck, and remained a characteristic feature of numerous styles of music throughout the next two centuries.

A secondary dominant is a chromatic chord that resolves to one of the triads of a major or minor key (other than I) *without* bringing about a modulation.

Mozart

NAM 22	CD2 Track 12
Alfred Brendel (piano)	

Bars	
1–63	An **exposition** of the main themes, grouped into two opposing tonal centres (tonic and dominant: B♭ and F)
63–93	A **development** of these themes passing through several keys (notably F minor, C minor and G minor in bars 63–86)
93–165	A **recapitulation** of the principal themes in the tonic

Like Bach, Mozart writes melodies that define tonality and suggest specific chords – a clear example can be seen in bar 22, where the melody ends with a flourish of pure C major to announce the arrival of the F major second subject in the next bar. But bar 22 also shows the much wider range of Mozart's melodic writing, in the dramatic plunge from the highest register to the lowest.

The F major melody at the start of the second subject (bars 23–30) consists of two four-bar phrases. Such **balanced** or **periodic phrasing** is typical of the classical style. If we now compare these two phrases with the two four-bar phrases that follow we will see that the first of each pair (bars 23–26 and 31–34) are almost identical, but that the second of each pair (bars 27–30 and 35–38) are quite different. The music in bars 23–30 sounds like a question because it ends in 'mid air' on the dominant. It is known as an **antecedent**. The music in bars 31–38 sounds like an answer because it ends with the finality of tonic harmony. It is called the **consequent**.

The phrases in the first subject each begin with an anacrusis (up-beat) of either four or six semiquavers, so they don't literally fill two full bars, but each one spans approximately eight beats of $\frac{4}{4}$ time and so by convention are called two-bar phrases.

Together the antecedent and its consequent make a complete 16-bar melody. While such perfectly symmetrical phrasing is common in the classical period, composers knew when to avoid the obvious. For instance, the ten-bar melody that forms the first subject consists of *five* two-bar phrases.

1		2	3	4	
Bb	Gm/Bb	Cm	F⁷	Bb	
I	vib	ii	V⁷	I	

Mozart's harmony in this work is also typical of the period, being mainly simple and entirely functional, as in the first four bars shown *left*. In the first subject, chords I and V^7 predominate, ensuring tonal stability, and these remain the most frequently-used chords throughout the exposition (which ends at bar 63).

Ex. 5

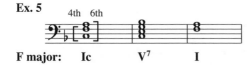

F major: Ic   V⁷   I

The chord that is most characteristic of the classical style is the **cadential** $^6_4$. Its name indicates that it is formed from notes that are a 6th and a 4th above the bass (chord Ic, as shown in Example 5) and that it is used in cadences – either as the first chord of an imperfect cadence (Ic–V) or as an approach chord to a perfect cadence (Ic–$V^{(7)}$–I).

Clear examples of the cadential $^6_4$ in F major can be seen in the second subject, occupying one beat at bar 37^3, two beats in the first half of bar 53 and four beats in bar 57 (the last of which is shown in compressed form at the start of Example 5). Every time it appears before a cadence, Ic resolves to $V^{(7)}$, and this in turn resolves to a tonic chord to complete a perfect cadence. The cadence in bars 57–59 (with an Alberti bass, triadic figuration and a long trill) is one of the most typical sounds of classical music – and one that distinguishes this style from baroque and romantic styles.

Mozart also uses chromatic chords, the most common of which is the secondary dominant, especially V^7b of V as occurs on the first beat of bar 121. The first chord is C^7 (in first inversion) and it resolves to F (chord V of Bb major). The entire passage is in the key of Bb major, confirmed by the cadence in bar 122. So, because it does not cause a modulation, C^7 is a secondary dominant. Two other secondary dominants can be seen in the **harmonic sequence** of bars 143–146 – V^7b of II in bar 143 and V^7b of VI in bar 146. Compare these two progressions with bars 67–70, where Mozart uses **diminished 7th chords** (bars 67 and 69) in a similar way.

In the cadence at the end of this passage, the expected F major chord in bar 70 is replaced by an abrupt switch to F minor. This is not a modulation, it's simply a dramatic change to the **tonic minor.** This is rare in baroque music, but is quite common in the classical period and almost a cliché in 19th-century romantic styles. More remarkable is the chromatic chord in bar 76 – a triad of E♭ minor, unrelated to the chords before and after. It sounds logical because the ear accepts the G♭ as a chromatic passing note between G in the bass of bar 75 and F in the bass of bar 76, and because of the E♭ pedal heard throughout bars 75^2–78^2. Try playing this passage omitting bar 76 and you will hear a simple diatonic modulation from C minor to B♭ major which lacks the pathos of Mozart's chromatic interpolation.

The last chromatic chord Mozart uses in this stormy development section is the **augmented 6th**. This occurs on the last beat of bar 80, where it consists of E♭–G–B♭–C♯ (the interval of an augmented 6th between E♭ and C♯ gives the chord its name). The key in bars 80–86 is G minor and this augmented 6th and the other two (bars 82^4 and 84^4) all resolve in the normal way to chord V. Mozart then leaves G minor to begin a passage of **dominant preparation** (bars 87–93) in which chord V^7 of B♭ major is coloured by chromatic G♭s in the left hand and chromatic ornaments in the right. This is all designed to raise expectation for the return of the tonic key and first subject, which happens at the start of the recapitulation on the last beat of bar 93.

We discussed the three short character pieces from *Kinderscenen* earlier in the chapter. Take the opportunity to revise this section, noticing particularly Schumann's use of periodic phrasing in the melodies of the first and third movements. By now such balanced phrasing was becoming old-fashioned, but it suits the somewhat nostalgic recollection of past times in these 'Scenes of Childhood'. In contrast, Schumann's harmonic vocabulary is often more forward-looking, especially in its frequent use of chromatic harmony and its sometimes surprising juxtapositions of chords.

Schumann

NAM 23	CD2 Tracks 13–15
Alfred Brendel (piano)	

In *NAM 24* Debussy carries to extremes the tendency towards modality that we noticed in Schumann's *Hasche-Mann*. In many ways it is more modal than even Sweelinck's pavan, for Debussy wrote his Sarabande to reflect an ancient and elegant world, albeit in modern terms. That modernity is seen principally in his chord vocabulary, but first let's look at Debussy's melodic style in this work.

Debussy

NAM 24	CD2 Track 16
Zoltán Kocsis (piano)	

The melody of the first section (bars 1–22) conforms to the pitches of the **aeolian mode** on C♯, shown in Example 6. But each of the first six phrases ends on the dominant (bars 2, 4, 16 and 18) or the second degree of the mode (bars 8 and 14). Only at the end of the last phrase (bars 19–22) does the melody end on the tonic, with the fall from F♯ to C♯ implying a plagal cadence. Such phrase endings are common enough in medieval plainsong, but in this context the long wait for the tonic sows the seeds of the deliberate tonal ambiguity that distinguishes this piece from the earlier keyboard pieces we have studied.

Ex. 6   aeolian mode on C♯

At the start of the second section (bars 23–72) modality evaporates in a welter of chromatic discords, and when the first theme returns (bar 42) the first bar is harmonised with a D major chord that is foreign to the aeolian modality of the melody. However, the movement ends with a modal cadence (B to C♯), and chromatic pitches in the melody occur in only 14 of the Sarabande's 72 bars. Other melodic features worth noticing are:

+ The large **range**, which extends from the bass melody in bars 20–21 to the high E in bars 38 and 39

+ **Conjunct movement** interspersed with 3rds and, less frequently, perfect 4ths, 5ths and octaves

+ An almost complete **absence of triadic melody** (it would be at odds with Debussy's quasi-modal style)

+ The regular two-, four- and six-bar phrasing (defined by the second-beat minims and the final dotted minim in bars 1–22) broken only by **cross-phrasing** in bars 38–41 and the **hemiola rhythm** (effectively six bars in duple time instead of four bars in triple time) in bars 67–70

+ The frequent use of **repetition** and the infrequent **sequences** (which are, in any case, usually inexact).

When you read these notes on Debussy's harmony, it is important to remember that Debussy does not generally use chords such as the dominant 7th in a functional way – in other words, he doesn't employ them to establish clearly-defined keys, he uses them for colour. The one exception is in bar 55, where the D♯ major harmony sounds like a dominant chord, terminating the phrase in bars 50–55 with an imperfect cadence, and then resolving to chord I (G♯ minor) at the start of the next phrase in bar 56.

In our study of earlier keyboard music we have seen that the chief agents for establishing tonality are perfect and imperfect cadences. Both are almost completely absent in the Sarabande. Debussy's cadences are breathing points in the musical flow, established by longer chords and a temporary cessation of dissonance, and they more often end indecisively with a major or minor triad on degrees of the modal scale other than the tonic. In the first section there are four cadences that end with *minor* triads on the dominant (thus including the modal flat 7th B, rather than the leading-note, B♯), one that ends with a major triad on ♭VII (B major in bar 8) and another that ends with a triad of D♯ major in bar 14.

Even when the melody ends on the tonic at the close of the first section (bar 22), the lack of any chords (modal or tonal) leaves us with no absolutely clear sense of tonality. Only at the very end is there a cadence that confirms the C♯ minor tonality suggested by the key signature – and it is, of course, a modal cadence. It remains for us to catalogue the most important types of **non-functional chords** that Debussy uses.

+ *NAM 24* begins with a **half-diminished 7th** consisting of a diminished triad (D♯–F♯–A) plus a minor 7th (C♯) above the root

+ The next chord is a **minor 7th** consisting of a minor triad (F♯–A–C♯) plus a minor 7th (E) above the root

+ The third chord is a **dominant 7th** in third inversion (the first two chords are then repeated in reverse order, so every chord in bar 1 is some kind of 7th chord)

+ The parallel perfect 5ths and octaves throughout the first four bars in the right hand are an important element in Debussy's harmonic style. Such **parallelism** is common throughout the work, especially in bars 50–65.

- The last chord in bar 6 is a **major 7th** (E–G♯–B–D♯)

- **Unrelated triads** of A major and F♯ major occur in bars 9–10

- The chain of **parallel dominant 7ths** in bars 11–12 is built on a bass part that moves through notes of the **whole-tone scale**

- Bars 23–28 use **quartal harmony** – chords based on 4ths rather than the 3rds of traditional harmony (most of the chords in this passage contains three perfect 4ths)

- A major 13th chord occurs on beat 2 of bar 31 – it consists of the root (E), the 3rd (G♯), the 7th (D, written **enharmonically** as C𝄪), the 9th (F♯) and the 13th (C♯) – it doesn't resolve functionally to A major but is instead followed by a chord of G♯ minor

- In bars 63–65 Debussy seems to be reaching back to the dark ages with parallel **bare 5th** chords.

Remember that Debussy's ambiguous tonal style can often be seen most simply in his **modal cadences**. The one in bar 2 consists of a triad of E major followed by G♯ minor, the latter's anticipation on the second quaver further clouding the effect. The same rhythmic effect occurs in the modal cadence at bar 14, where the falling perfect 5th in the bass suggests a perfect cadence, but the lack of a leading note of D♯ major (C𝄪) denies it.

The Prelude has a simple ternary structure that is largely defined by the contrast between tonal and chromatic harmony:

A	bars 1–12	mostly diatonic A major tonality
B	bars 13–22	tonally ambiguous chromatic harmony
A¹	bars 23–28	mostly diatonic A major tonality

Like Bach's dances, the Prelude is based on a limited number of motifs that are heard in a variety of guises throughout most of the movement. In this case there are just two, both heard in the first bar (the semiquaver figure and a three-note leaping quaver figure). These form the basis of a **diatonic** theme which, with the underlying tonic pedal, could hardly state the key of A major more strongly. The melody forms an arch that rises from the tonic and falls back to the dominant in bar 3 and then, through stepwise semiquavers, regains the tonic once more. But its most obvious feature is its frequent wide leaps of a 7th, octave, 9th or 10th.

The pedal points on I, VI and V (A, F♯ and E respecitvely) anchor the music to the tonic key of A major, even when chromatic triads are introduced in bar 10.

Bar 13 begins with an ascent through the first five notes of a scale of C♯ major scale followed by a descent through an incomplete chromatic scale decorated with sleazy diatonic and chromatic **upper auxiliaries**. The chromatic descent is arranged in **melodic sequences** of six quavers each (with some subtle 'wrong notes'). This central section of the Prelude is characterised by such foreign chords as F major in bar 18 and A♭ major in bar 19, and by chromatic melodies, both almost negating a sense of tonality. Almost, but not quite, because:

Enharmonic notation gives this passage a daunting appearance, but if it helps you could think of the complex-looking chord on the last beat of bar 30, for example, as simply a triad of B♭ minor in disguise.

Can you spot the misprint that makes a dissonant nonsense of one of the chords in these bars?

Shostakovich

NAM 25   CD2 Track 17
Tatiana Nikolayeva (piano)

- The implied triad of C♯ major in the first two beats of bar 13 is related to chord I of A major by the common note C♯ (which is maintained as another tonal anchor for three bars)

- The chord of F major is a triad on the flattened 6th of the scale of A major (a chromatic chord not uncommon in Bach's music)

- The chord of A♭ major contains the leading note of A (A♭=G♯)

- The chord of D♭ major (bars 21–22) contains the 3rd of the tonic chord of A major (D♭=C♯).

It is the enharmonic equivalence of D♭ and C♯ which facilitates Shostakovich's jump straight from this last chord back to chord I of A major, implied by the left-hand melody in the first three beats of bar 23. From here to the end an **inverted dominant pedal** is heard above three **plagal cadences** formed by the chords IIb and I, the last of which is over a tonic pedal. The use of pedals to create tonal anchors is the most important feature of the harmony – well over half of the Prelude's 28 bars contain a pedal on one or other of the pitches of the tonic chord, helping to create its serene mood.

The left-hand part in bars 23–25 presents the original theme in its simplest form. Shostakovich detaches the last six notes of this melody and, after a beat's rest, repeats them as an independent motif in bars 25–26. He then detaches the first four notes of this motif to form the final motif in bars 26–27, after another beat's rest. This melodic technique is called **fragmentation** and it provides a magical conclusion to the Prelude.

The Fugue is one of the most remarkable pieces to have come from the 20th century, not so much for what Shostakovich has put in it, but for what he has deliberately left out. The work contains **no discords** – not even passing notes. This absence of dissonance, along with the entirely **triadic** nature of the fugal subject (bars 1–4), accounts for the movement's feeling of serenity.

In the exposition (bars 1–14) the four-bar subject uses entirely tonic harmony. The same melody, but in the dominant (the answer) is stated by the left hand in bars 5–8, while the right hand continues with a **countermelody** (known in fugal terms as a countersubject). After two intervening bars, the tonic chord is heard again throughout bars 11–14, where the subject is stated in the bass part.

The **rate of change** of chords is slow (every four bars) whenever the subject or its answer are stated. Shostakovich reserves faster harmonic rhythm for the intervening episodes, such as that in bars 15–20, where chords mostly change every two beats. This is an important factor contributing to variety throughout the fugue. The lack of dissonance in the movement means that the only method of generating tension is side-stepping to unrelated keys or triads.

In the episodes, motifs from the exposition are manipulated in a similar manner to the way Mozart manipulates motifs in the development section of the sonata-form movement we studied earlier. Bars 15–16, based on chords Vb and IVb, are repeated in sequence in bars 17–18, based on chords IIIb and IIb. This first episode ends with chord Ib in bar 20 followed by more rapid alternations of tonic and dominant harmony in bar 21.

Although plagal cadences usually consist of a IV–I progression, IIb–I is an alternative. Chord IIb has a similar function to IV, with which it has two notes in common (including the same bass note).

This version of the theme is so close to the melody in the first bar of Bach's Prelude in D major from his second book of 48 Preludes and Fugues that there can be little doubt that Shostakovich intended this Prelude to be an affectionate caricature of several of Bach's musical mannerisms.

Don't be misled by the apparent discord on the first beat of bar 58 – the C♭ is a misprint and should be C♮.

The subject (inner part) and answer (inner part then treble) return in bars 21–28, now based on chords VI and III – minor triads that give the passage a modal feel. This pattern of fugal entries alternating with episodes continues, but the first move away from A major doesn't come until the middle of the third episode (bars 41–46). This is brought about not by modulation but by changing the tonic chord to A minor (C♮ in bar 43), which is the same as chord III in the new key of F major. However, the **perfect cadence** that confirms this key does not arrive until the end of the episode (bars 46–47). This the first of only four definitive perfect cadences, the others being in A major (bars 69–70 and 91–92) and F♯ major (bars 85–86).

The chords of A minor and F major share the common note A. Similar **tertiary** relations are apparent in the chromatic chords that colour the otherwise diatonic harmony in the final section of the Fugue (bars 62–99):

The term 'tertiary' refers to keys or chords that are a 3rd apart.

- In bars 82–84 triads of A major and C major are linked by the common note E

- In bars 84–87 triads of A major, C♯ major, F♯ major and F♯ minor are linked by the common note C♯

- In bars 87–88 triads of D major and F♯ major are linked by the common note F♯.

On the final page of the Fugue long bass notes reassert the tonic key, those in bars 62–69 forming a **dominant pedal** in preparation for the condensed entries of the subject (known as a **stretto**) that begin in the tonic at bar 70. The long bass notes in the last 18 bars refer back to the same pitches that were pedal notes in the Prelude (A, F♯, E and C♯) – all asserting the A major tonality.

Private Study

1. Which of the tied notes in bars 23–24 of *NAM 21* indicate the use of a suspension?

2. Why can the Gigue in *NAM 21* be described as monothematic?

3. Identify the chords used in bars 159 and 160 of *NAM 22* and the types of melodic decoration used in bars 164 and 165.

4. Give an example of periodic phrase structure in *NAM 23*.

5. What term describes the harmony in bars 67–70 of *NAM 24*?

6. What is meant by a tertiary relationship?

Sample questions

In the exam there will be two questions on this topic, from which you must choose to answer **one**.

a) Compare and contrast Schumann's use of melody in *NAM 23* with Mozart's use of melody in *NAM 22*.

b) How does Shostakovich's use of harmony in *NAM 25* contrast with Debussy's use of harmony in *NAM 24*?

c) In what ways does Bach's approach to melody and harmony in *NAM 21* differ from Sweelinck's approach in *NAM 20*?

Sacred vocal music

Gabrieli, In ecclesiis

Special Focus Work for 2006 and 2007

NAM 27   CD3 Track 2
Gabrieli Consort and Players
Directed by Paul McCreesh

Before starting on this section you should work through (or revise) the information about the context and structure of this music given on pages 86–88 of the AS Guide. Make sure that you understand all of the terminology used on those pages.

The **structure** of *In ecclesiis* is largely determined by the Latin text. Gabrieli relishes the opportunities to deploy his lavish choral and instrumental resources in such a way that each successive sentence clearly contrasts with the next by virtue of huge changes of texture and instrumentation.

Bars		
1–5	A	First vocal solo
6–12	B¹	*Alleluja* refrain
13–24	C	Second vocal solo
25–31	B²	*Alleluja* refrain
31–39		Instrumental *Sinfonia*
39–61	D	First vocal duet
62–68	B³	*Alleluja* refrain
68–94	E	Second vocal duet
95–101	B⁴	*Alleluja* refrain
102–118	F	*Tutti* (everyone)
119–129	B⁵	*Alleluja* refrain

The acclamation *Alleluja* appears five times in the text. Gabrieli sets it like a **refrain** in which the same principal melody and chord progression is used every time it appears. These choral sections alternate with settings of the rest of the text for solo voices, each with different melodies and chord progressions. The result is similar to a **rondo,** but the alternation of solo and chorus sections also makes it similar to a concerto movement. In the middle there is an instrumental interlude which Gabrieli calls a *sinfonia*. The entire structure is summarised in the table *left*.

In the early 17th century the **tonal system** of major and minor keys was starting to appear, but the influence of modality was such that cadences (primarily perfect) could occur on almost any degree of the scale, and this leads us to hear what appear to be constantly changing keys. For instance, we might be tempted to think that there are cadences in the keys of C, G, D and A major in bars 62–66. But Gabrieli would probably have thought of these as cadences on the third, seventh, fourth and first degrees of the **aeolian mode** (if he even thought of them as cadences!). Nevertheless, A minor is the tonic key because all of the most important sections end with a perfect cadence in this key, and at the end a plagal cadence in A minor follows the massive perfect cadence in bars 115–118.

The aeolian mode can be found by playing the 'white notes' on a keyboard from A up to A an octave higher.

Gabrieli follows a widely accepted tradition in earlier music that important sections must end on a unison, an octave, a bare 5th or a *major* triad. To avoid ending on a minor triad, many cadences conclude with a **tierce de Picardie** (a major 3rd in the tonic chord at the end of a section in a minor key).

In the account that follows we have used translations that are more literal than those given on page 538 of the *New Anthology*.

A (bars 1–5)

In ecclesiis benedicite Domino (Bless the Lord in the churches)

Gabrieli wrote only the lower of the two staves at the bottom of each system in this work (the *Basso per l'organo*). The chords implied by this bass would be played on chordal instruments (here, the organ) with some degree of improvisation. The second stave up is a modern editor's suggestion of how to realise this *basso continuo* part.

This first solo section is scored for a countertenor with a **continuo** accompaniment that runs all the way through the work. The term used to describe such a texture in early 17th century music is **monodic**. Although starting on a chord of A major, the **ostinato** figure in the bass of bars 3–5 is clearly in A minor (the C♯s are all Picardy 3rds). The repetition of *benedicite Domino* ensures the text will be heard in large reverberant churches such as St. Mark's in Venice.

There are many examples of such repetition in this work and in most sacred music of the time. Some think the repeated phrases should be sung more quietly, like an **echo**.

B¹ (bars 6–12)

The first choral refrain begins with an F major triad in which the C♮ forms a **false relation** with the C♯ of the Picardie 3rd in the continuo realisation at the end of bar 5. Root-position chords a major 3rd apart with false relations are such a common feature in this motet that we will only mention them again in passages where Gabrieli is clearly using them as an expressive resource. The refrain is strongly contrasted with the previous section in:

✦ Vocal scoring, which consists of four-part **choral homophony** alternating and combining with a countertenor solo

✦ Texture, which is basically homophonic but with **imitation** between alto 1 and tenor parts in bars 10–11

✦ Metre – triple time changing to quadruple time without a break

✦ Harmony and tonality – the passage ends with primary triads in root position that define the tonic key (IV–I–V–I#3 in A minor)

✦ **Syncopated rhythm** – the first alto part in bar 11 is not only syncopated but also uses a cadential device called a **consonant 4th** (an unprepared 4th above the bass, in this case the alto A, which is treated as though it wasn't technically dissonant).

C (bars 13–24)

In omni loco dominationis benedic anima mea Dominum
(In every kingdom bless the Lord O my soul)

This has the same monodic texture as section A, but a baritone replaces the countertenor. Notice:

✦ The **harmonic and melodic sequences**, which entail repetition of the text to ensure that no words will be missed

✦ The syncopated setting of *dominationis* to express the joy of the faithful in every kingdom

✦ Perfect cadences on C, A and E (the notes of an A-minor chord)

✦ An *ascending* **circle of 5ths** in bars 17–20 (C–G–Dm–Am–Em–B).

B² (bars 25–31)

The second choral refrain is the same as the first, except that the soloist is now a baritone singing the same melody as the countertenor in section B¹, but an octave lower. The end of this section overlaps with the start of the next.

Sinfonia (bars 31–38)

For Gabrieli and his contemporaries, *sinfonia* ('sounding together') meant a purely instrumental composition with no solos or, as here, an instrumental interlude in a vocal composition. The most striking features are:

✦ **Idiomatic instrumental writing** associated with new rhythmic patterns such as rapidly-repeated notes in dotted rhythm (much easier for instruments than voices) and long notes followed by rapid four-semiquaver groups

✦ **Imitation** on three different subjects (bars 32–33, 35–36 and 36–38)

- A striking **augmented triad** (F–A–C♯) on the third minim beat of bar 31

- An equally striking **false relation** between the viola's C♯ at the start of bar 34 and the second cornett's C♮ on the next beat.

D (bars 39–61)

In Deo salutari meo et gloria mea, (God is my salvation and glory,) *Deus auxilium meum et spes mea in Deo est* (God is my help and my hope is in him)

Nearly all of the features we have so far discussed are present in this third solo section. It is a **duet** for alto and tenor who, in the last four bars, compete with the cornetts in a display of **vocal virtuosity**. Try to distinguish between **canonic imitation** (*Deus auxilium meum et spes mea* in bars 50–54) and simple melodic exchanges (*in Deo est* in bars 57–60) in which there is no contrapuntal overlap. This section includes a root-position triad that is *not* on one of the degrees of the aeolian mode (the B♭ triad in bar 57). It adds the sort of **chromatic colour** that Gabrieli explores more fully in the *tutti* at the end of the motet. Nevertheless, there is still no doubt that A minor remains the tonic.

B³ (bars 62–68)

The third choral refrain is the same as the first except that:

- the tenor is assigned the principal solo melody

- a new solo **countermelody** is sung by the alto

- the soloists are accompanied by the instrumental ensemble rather than just the continuo instruments.

E (bars 68–94)

Deus noster, te invocamus, te laudamus, te adoramus
(Our God, we call upon you, we praise you, we worship you)

A **melisma** is a group of notes sung to one syllable.

This duet for countertenor and baritone begins with a **melisma** that draws attention to the word 'God'. Limited **word painting** of this sort is typical of sacred music of the 16th and 17th centuries.

Libera nos, salva nos, vivifica nos (Set us free, save us, enliven us)

The ideas of freedom and liveliness are represented by sudden changes of metre and syncopation (a more obvious example of word painting). This whole section begins and ends in the tonic key of A minor.

B⁴ (bars 95–101)

The fourth choral refrain is the same as the first apart from the new countermelody for solo baritone. Gabrieli reduces the accompaniment to just continuo instruments in order to allow the next section to make its full, glorious impact.

F (bars 102–118)

Deus adjutor noster in aeternum (God is our helper for evermore)

This section differs from all others because, for the first time, Gabrieli deploys his full resources in homophonic and contrapuntal textures, mostly in a large number of independent melodic strands. It starts with harmonic progressions designed to thrill the wealthy nobility of Venice into believing they could be hearing the music of heaven itself within the opulent surroundings of St. Mark's (the exterior of which is shown on the front cover of this book).

Gabrieli creates his moment of typically early-baroque drama by setting the key word *Deus* ('God') to massive chords a 3rd apart. In bar 102 these are F major and D major, linked by the common note A but supercharged by the **false relation** between the outer parts (F in the bass on the first beat and F♯ in cornetto 1 on the second). Both chords are repeated a step higher in the next bar.

In the second and third minim beats of bar 104 an **unprepared 7th** (D) is followed by **échappées** (labelled in Example 1a *below*). These change the dominant 7th into a first-inversion **augmented triad** (E–G♯–C). We previously noticed this chord in the *sinfonia* – here, although it still only lasts for a crotchet, its effect is hugely magnified by the clash between C (chorus, alto 1 part) and B (chorus, tenor part). When the setting of *adjutor noster* is repeated, scored for all performers (bars 105–107), the effect of these very advanced harmonies is even more magnificent.

Gabrieli then repeats these six bars a 4th higher, starting at bar 108. But instead of a literal transposition, which would have assigned chords of C major and A major to bar 109, he ratchets up the drama still further by changing these chords to G major and E major so that the entire progression in bars 108–109 now descends in 3rds: B♭–G, G–E, as shown in Example 1b:

These progressions of descending 3rds in semibreves may remind you of the setting of the same word (*Deus*) in bars 50–51.

An échappée is a melodic dissonance that leaves a harmony note by step and returns to the next harmony note by a leap in the opposite direction.

Ex. 1a

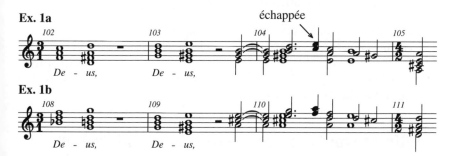

Ex. 1b

Gabrieli increases the impact of this change by reserving the entry of the brass for the second evocation of *Deus* in bar 109, where these new chords appear. After this the rest of this six-bar passage is also rescored, then just the setting of *adjutor noster* is repeated in sequence in bars 113–114.

The **tonal scheme** underlying these passages is clear, despite the striking juxtaposition of unrelated chords at their starts:

✦ V$^{(7)}$–I in the keys of A minor and D minor (bars 103^6–107)

✦ V$^{(7)}$–I in the keys of D minor, G minor and C major (bars 109^6–114^4), leading without a break to:

✦ A *long* dominant pedal (the text means 'evermore'!) ending with the most decisive perfect cadence in A minor in the whole piece (bars 115–118).

Although the tonic chords of the keys Gabrieli visits are based on degrees of the aeolian mode, such long-term tonal planning is more typical of the late baroque than of early 17th-century music. To add to the tremendous sense of anticipation engendered by alternating tonic and dominant chords over a dominant pedal, two **canons** are combined in bars 114–117. The first is in the choral alto and tenor parts, starting with the minim E in bars 114 and 115 respectively.

The second is for all four soloists, starting with the tied E in the countertenor part of bars 114–115 and imitated at an interval of two beats in the bass, tenor and alto parts.

B⁵ (bars 119–129) This extended refrain has three perfect cadences and a plagal cadence, and now involves all voices and instruments. Notice the dramatic silences which allow the mighty *Alleluja* to echo around the large spaces of St. Mark's, Venice.

 Private study

1. What type of instruments are the cornetts used in this work?

2. Explain each of the following terms and give an example of its use in *NAM 27*: basso continuo, monodic texture, aeolian mode, tierce de Picardie, false relation, melisma, canon.

3. How does Gabrieli allow for, and make the most of, the resonant acoustics of St. Mark's in this work?

Sample questions

In the exam there will be three questions on this work, from which you must choose to answer **two**.

(a) Show how the newly-emerging tonal system of major and minor keys is used by Gabrieli in *NAM 27*.

(b) Discuss Gabrieli's use of textures and instruments in bars 31–61 of *In ecclesiis*.

(c) Comment on the form of *In ecclesiis*, showing how Gabrieli acheives both unity and variety in the work.

For examination in summer 2006 and 2007

Continuity and change in structures and tonality

You do not need to study this topic unless *Sacred vocal music* is the Area of Study that you undertook for AS Music and which you are now extending for A2.

Before starting work on this topic you need a thorough understanding of the material on *Sacred vocal music* in the AS Guide (pages 78–90). Remember that for A2 the topic draws on works from across the **entire** Area of Study, not just those in one of the two lists, A or B. It is important to be aware that tonality refers to the relationship of keys in music (and for exam purposes that also includes modes) – it is nothing to do with the tone of musical sounds.

Taverner *O Wilheme, pastor bone* has **two main sections** of similar length (bars 1–32 and 33–67). Both begin with a two-part texture followed by a three-part texture and both end in a full five-part texture. This division (which is not binary form) reflects the two stanzas of the text. There is also tonal contrast between F major and G minor:

NAM 26   CD3 Track 1
Christ Church Cathedral Choir
Oxford
Conducted by Stephen Darlington

Bars 1–22³ are in F major, with five cadences ending on the tonic.

Bars 22⁴–52³ are in G minor, beginning with a tonic triad and continuing with an imperfect cadence in G minor (I–V in bars 23–24), answered by a perfect cadence in this key in bars 26–27. There are six more cadences in G minor, some ending with a **tierce de Picardie** (which does not change the tonality).

Bars 52⁴–67 return to F major. These bars begin with a **false relation** between the Picardie 3rd in the treble part and the minor 3rd in the mean part (where a new sentence of the text begins). F major is not fully established until the perfect cadence in bars 55–56. The motet ends with a decorated plagal cadence.

The structure is largely governed by the rhyming text and it is defined by changes of texture and structural cadences. The first of the two main sections consists of:

✦ *O Wilhelme, pastor bone.* (bars 1–7). A duet for boys' voices is answered by the same text set for three-part lower voices. The treble melody is repeated in the countertenor part and this second phrase ends with a modal cadence (II–I).

✦ *Cleri pater et patrone,* (bars 7–13). Another duet for boys' voices is this time answered by all five parts. The mean part in bars 7–10 is repeated (apart from just one note) an octave lower in the bass part of bars 10–13, linking these two phrases, the second of which ends in a modal cadence (IV–III with a suspension).

✦ *Mundi nobis in agone* (bars 13–16). A five-part **homophonic** texture. The phrase ends with a decorated modal cadence on the tonic and **contrapuntal overlapping** links it to …

✦ *Confer opem, et depone Vitae sordes,* (bars 16–28): The **antiphonal exchanges** between boys and men of bars 1–10 resume here, followed by a more **contrapuntal** style as G minor supplants F major from bar 22. The passage ends with an imperfect cadence in G minor in bar 28.

✦ *Et coronae Coelestis da gloriam.* (bars 29–32). The setting of the first verse of the text ends with a modal cadence in which the final chord includes Picardie 3rds in treble and countertenor.

The structure of the second section (bars 33–67) is similarly governed by the words:

✦ Antiphonal exchanges in bars 33–47, concluded by a perfect cadence in G minor.

✦ Five-part homophony with some independent movement (bars 48–56¹), ending with a perfect cadence in F major.

✦ Five-part counterpoint with free imitation (bars 56²–67), ending with a decorated plagal cadence in F major.

Like *O Wilheme, pastor bone* the structure of *In ecclesiis* is largely determined by its Latin text but, as we saw earlier, Gabrieli makes no attempt to conceal the joins between the end of one sentence and the start of the next. Instead, he uses these divisions as a cue to make the sections of his work as contrasting as possible.

The **tonal scheme** of *In ecclesiis* is clear, despite the modality of some of its melodies and chord progressions. By 1612 composers were moving away from the sort of modal cadences we noticed in Taverner towards cadences that could be said to be in a key. We saw only a few reminders of modality in *NAM 27* – although one survivor, the *tierce de Picardie*, appears at least as frequently in Gabrieli's sacred concerto as it does in Taverner's motet.

Gabrieli

| *NAM 27* | CD3 Track 2 |
| Gabrieli Consort and Players |
| Directed by Paul McCreesh |

For more detail on tonality and structure in *In ecclesiis*, be sure to revise the first part of this chapter.

Bach

NAM 28 CD3 Tracks 3–6
Yorkshire Bach Choir, Fitzwilliam
Ensemble, Clare Mathias (alto)
Conducted by Peter Seymour

The distinct sections of *In ecclesiis* foreshadow the multiple movements of Bach's cantatas. This work has seven movements in all, but the four printed in the *New Anthology* are representative of some of the most common types used by Bach:

I.   An extended movement for chorus and instrumental ensemble

II. A *recitativo accompagnato* (a term for recitative accompanied by an ensemble of instruments, as opposed to the faster-moving *recitativo secco* in which the voice is accompanied by continuo instruments only)

III. An ancient **chorale melody**, harmonised by Bach in four-part homophony (the very chromatic style and **melismatic** ending in this are not typical of his many simpler harmonisations)

IV. An **obbligato aria** (the term refers to an obligatory instrumental solo, played here on the oboe, that is almost as important as the vocal part) with an acccompaniment for continuo instruments.

The structure of the first movement has much in common with *In ecclesiis* in that it based around a repeating refrain. This is known as a **ritornello** (literally a 'little return') because it comes back in abbreviated form during the course of the movement.

The key is G minor and the full ritornello is heard at the start, ending at the perfect cadence in the tonic in bars 11–12. Chunks of the ritornello return between the **choral episodes.** These choral episodes have another link with *NAM 27* – they all contain canonic parts for the chorus, including a **four-part canon** starting in bar 88. In addition, the wind parts play a simultaneous **two-part** canon, the melody of which is based on that of the cantata's final chorale (not included in *NAM 28*). It is little wonder that Bach is regarded as the greatest master of counterpoint!

However, the ritornello form of this movement differs from the rondo-like structure of *In ecclesiis* in that here are no obvious breaks between sections. Despite Bach's **chromatic harmony**, the tonal scheme is remarkable for modulating only to related minor keys (in keeping with the sombre text).

There is no continuity between earlier works we have studied and the extreme chromaticism and wide-ranging modulations to unrelated keys of the **recitative** that forms the second movement.

Similarly, there is no connection between these earlier works and the simple, diatonic phrases of the **chorale melody** in the third movement – nor is continuity evident between earlier music and Bach's expressive and highly chromatic harmonisation of it.

The fourth movement is another ritornello structure which is so easy to understand that we can represent its form diagrammatically in the table on the next page. Compare it with the table on page 100, which summarises Gabrieli's more complex structure.

The most significant distinction between the **tonality** of this fourth movement and the tonality of *In ecclesiis* is that Bach visits only the keys most closely related to E♭ major, whereas Gabrieli's cadences fall on the degrees of the aeolian mode. Tonality has totally displaced modality.

A^1	Bars 0–16^2	Complete instrumental ritornello in the tonic key of E♭ major
B	Bars 16^3–38^2	First vocal solo, modulating from E♭ major through F minor to B♭ major
A^2	Bars 39^3–48^2	A partial repeat of two sections of the ritornello, transposed to B♭ major
C	Bars 48^3–56^2	Second vocal solo, beginning in C minor and modulating to A♭ major
A^3	Bars 56^3–60^2	A repeat of the first four bars of the complete ritornello, transposed up a 4th
D	Bars 60^3–79^2	Third vocal solo, modulating from F minor through related keys before returning to the tonic key of E♭ major in bars 78–79
A^1	*da capo* (Bars 0–16^2)	A reprise of the complete first ritornello, as directed by the instruction *D.C. (da capo) al fine* (play again from the beginning until the word *fine*)

This movement falls into three parts, the first **homophonic** (bars 1–22) the second **fugal** (bars 22–61) and the last (bars 62–82) a **contrapuntal** section for four soloists and (in the last six bars) the chorus. These **contrasting textures** remind us of the alternations between *soli* and *tutti* in Gabrieli's *In ecclesiis*, but here there are no breaks between sections – the whole movement is carried irresistibly forward by the **symphonic** orchestral writing.

These sections subdivide into smaller units distinguishable by changes of texture, as follows:

First section (bars 1–22)
D major tonality and diatonic harmony (apart from a few striking secondary dominant chords, such as those in bars 7 and 15).

✦ A^1 (bars 1–9^1) contains **antiphonal exchanges** between soloist and chorus (choir sopranos repeat the soloist's melodies).

✦ A^2 (bars 9–15^1) is a homophonic and abbreviated repeat of A^1.

✦ A^3 (bars 15–22^1) is a homophonic setting over a tonic pedal.

Second section (bars 22–61)
Much more chromaticism and modulations to related keys. Haydn's restricted modulations reflect Bach's similar tonal scheme in the fourth movement of Cantata 48.

✦ B^1 (bars 22–57^3) The setting of *in gloria Dei Patris* is a **fugue** subject and the setting of the word *Amen* is its countersubject. Throughout the fugal exposition (bars 22–30^1) the key is D major with passing modulations to the dominant (as is usual in fugal answers). The rest of the fugue moves through **related keys** such as B minor (bars 32–36) and A major (bars 37–39) before ending on the **dominant pedal** of D major (bars 54–57).

✦ B^2 (bars 57^4–61) form a **coda** that ends with a decisive perfect cadence in D major.

Third section (bars 62–82)
Diatonic harmony and D major tonality throughout.

C^1 (bars 62–71) The contrapuntal solo parts are accompanied by orchestral parts that form six perfect cadences over a tonic pedal.

C^2 (bars 71–82) is a repeat of C^1, with the chorus taking the last phrase and final perfect cadences.

Haydn

NAM 29   CD3 Track 7
Barbara Bonney (soprano)
London Symphony Chorus
City of London Sinfonia
Conducted by Richard Hickox

Because the same piece of music can often be viewed in more than one way, you should always give a reason for your opinion in an exam – for example, 'This is a three-part structure because …'.

Bruckner

NAM 30	CD3 Track 8
Christ Church Cathedral Choir Oxford,	
Conducted by Stephen Darlington	

Haydn's three-part tonal structure is a little like that of Taverner's motet (F major, G minor, F major). But you could regard *NAM 29* as a two-part structure (bars 1–22 and bars 22–82), just as Taverner's motet can be seen as a two-part structure determined by its text.

There is continuity between the tripartite structures of *O Wilhelme*, Haydn's mass movement and this motet. But in Bruckner's case we speak of simple **ternary form** because it includes a return to the thematic material of the first section as well as a return to the tonic key.

Section A (bars 1–12^1) is in C major with a brief visit to G major in bars 5–6. It sounds as though bars 5–8 are a sequential repetition of the first four bars, but Bruckner cunningly modifies the second phrase so that it returns to the tonic key of C major. The section comes to an end on the dominant chord of G major.

Section B (bars 12^2–29) begins with a G *minor* chord, the 3rd of which (B♭) forms a **false relation** with the B♮ in the G major chord at the end of the first section. This modal effect occurs in *O Wilhelme* – for instance, in bar 52, where G major and G minor chords are similarly juxtaposed. It is also used by Gabrieli – for example, in bar 34 of *In ecclesiis*, where A major and A minor chords are juxtaposed so that a false relation is formed between C♯ in the viola and C♮ in the second cornett. It may seem strange to find this element of continuity between works separated by three centuries, but Bruckner was involved in a movement which sought to replace symphonic church music (like Haydn's masses) with **modal** plainsong and renaissance-inspired polyphony.

This attraction to older music is confirmed by **phrygian cadences** (IVb–V) in D minor (bars 15–16) and E minor (bars 19–20). While there happen to be no phrygian cadences in the earlier music we have studied, they are a distinguishing feature of much renaissance and baroque music.

The feeling of mystery in the tenor entry at bar 21 is caused by the drop to a very quiet dynamic and by the appearance of just the tonic *note*. There is no tonal connection between this C and the B major chord in the previous bar. The tenor then begins a slow chromatic descent upon which chords of B major, G minor, A major and F minor are juxtaposed. It is only when the tenor arrives on G in bar 26, supporting a chord of G^7, that Bruckner prepares for the return of C major with four bars of diatonic harmony. There is no precedent for the chromatic mystery of bars 21–25 in any of the earlier works we have studied.

Section A^1 begins in bar 30 with a recapitulation of bars 1–10, but the final perfect cadence is delayed by modulation to E minor (with more chromaticism) in bars 40–42. The dramatic silence after *Deo* might remind us of the silences separating Gabrieli's colossal evocations of *Deus*, but the mood here is one of hushed contemplation.

Despite extremely chromatic harmonic progressions, Bruckner's motet only modulates to the related keys of G major, D minor and E minor. In this respect there is continuity with much of the sacred music we have already studied.

Most sections of this movement are constructed from one or more tiny motifs that are repeated hypnotically, often over **ostinato** bass patterns. Each of these sections corresponds with a musical setting of a phrase or sentence of Psalm 150, but sometimes an orchestral interlude appears between choral passages, and these too are based on similar melodic or rhythmic patterns.

In the aria from Cantata 48, Bach manipulated motifs taken from the oboe melody in the first ritornello to construct an entirely monothematic movement. Stravinsky unifies his work by the use of motifs derived from the **interlocked 3rds** first heard in the harp and trumpet parts of bars 29–31. The first is minor (G–Bb), the second major (Ab–C). If the order of 3rds is reversed and the motif starts on Bb the result will be Bb–D (major 3rd) and C–Eb (minor 3rd). These are the pitches (Bb, C, D and Eb) from which Stravinsky fashions the tenor melody of bars 4–8. Stravinsky himself pointed out the importance of the harp and trumpet motif, the first melodic idea he had when he began to compose the Symphony of Psalms.

There are many more motifs that derive from it, such as the piano motif in bar 38, but we have done enough to be able to see the difference between the techniques and aims of Bach and Stravinsky with regard to motivic manipulation. What matters most, of course, is the end result. In Bach's aria we can *hear* the growth of new melodies from the motifs in the first 16 bars, but in the Symphony of Psalms it is actual *melodies* that are heard, not the motifs concealed within them. No one hearing *NAM 31* for the first time could possibly know that the tenor melody in bars 4–8 derives from a motif of interlocking 3rds because it has not yet been played!

There are numerous other structural and tonal continuities and changes that we might observe. Let's identify some of them.

✦ The acclamation *Allelujah* appears five times in Gabrieli's *In ecclesiis*, each time with the same melody and harmony. The same word appears three times in the last movement of the Symphony of Psalms, each set to the same music. But Gabrieli's repeated *Allelujas* form a frequently recurring refrain, while Stravinsky's one-bar *Alleluia* marks the start and end of sections in a long and complex movement.

✦ In bars 4–6 the **bitonal** combination of a C major triad (outlined in the harp and piano parts) with the second tetrachord of the scale of Eb major (Bb–C–D–Eb) finds no parallel in any of the other works we have studied.

✦ In *O Wilhelme* and *In ecclesiis* juxtaposed major and minor triads brought about false relations between one phrase and the next. The same tonal effect is heard in bars 10–11 of this movement (E♮ and Eb in the alto and soprano parts of bar 10) but these happen mid-phrase.

✦ We saw that modality, in particular the aeolian mode, still played a role in *In ecclesiis*. All of the pitches in bars 14–22 of *NAM 31* derive from the aeolian mode on C (literally, because the ostinato bass is a double pedal formed from the tonic and dominant of the mode), but a sharpened leading note never appears in this passage, let alone a perfect cadence.

Stravinsky

NAM 32   CD3 Track 10
Westminster Abbey Choir
Directed by Martin Neary

The aeolian mode on C consists of the notes C–D–Eb–F–G–Ab–Bb–C.

◆ The first section ends with a **tierce de Picardie** in bars 21–22, but the cellos add a modern-sounding flat 7th (B♭).

Unrelated triads were juxtaposed in the last section of *In ecclesiis* and unrelated triads are heard one after the other in the horn parts of bars 35–40 in *NAM 31*. But Gabrieli's triads are a 3rd apart with one common pitch, while Stravinsky's chords are a tone apart (C major, D major and E major) with no common pitches between adjacent chords.

Tavener

NAM 31   CD3 Track 9
Choir of Westminster Cathedral
City of London Sinfonia
Conducted by James O'Donnell

Just as the apparent simplicity of Blake's 'Song of Innocence' hides a profound Christian doctrine, so Tavener's apparently simple musical setting of Blake's words hides a subtle approach to tonality.

In the first bar we hear a melody that, because it only contains four pitches, could be in either G major or E minor. This tonal uncertainty will not be resolved until the end of the first verse. Why the uncertainty? Could it be because Blake asks a fundamental question about existence? There is certainly no precedent for such profound simplicity in any of the other works we have studied.

In the second bar the trebles repeat the first melody while the altos sing an **exact inversion** of it. Using exact inversion results in a **bitonal** combination of tunes in G major (or E minor) and E♭ major (or C minor), rather like the combination of a melody in E♭ major with a chord of C in bars 4–6 of *NAM 31*.

Ex. 2

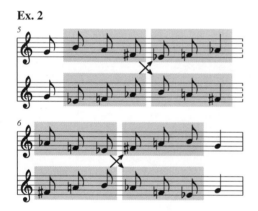

In bar 3 the melody starts with four pitches from the soprano part of the previous bar, and ends with three pitches from the alto part of that bar. Bar 3 is then repeated in retrograde order to form bar 4. This means that bars 3–4 start in G, change (there is no modulation) to E♭ then return (without modulation) to G. Bars 5–6 are formed from pitches in the two previous bars by exchanging cells of three notes in normal and inverted form, with the result that the alto part becomes a simultaneous inversion of the soprano part, as shown in Example 2. There are no precedents for this kind of approach to melody and tonality in any other work we have studied.

In bars 7–10, the opening one-bar melody is presented four times in succession, rhythmically augmented on its final appearance in bar 10, in a four-voice homophonic texture. The music in these bars is based entirely on the **aeolian mode** on E (E–F♯–G–A–B–C–D). The aeolian modality is confirmed by the perfect cadences (B minor –E minor) in which the 3rd remains unsharpened in the dominant chord. Diatonic and chromatic uncertainty has been resolved. By now you should be able to identify aeolian modality in *NAM 27* and *NAM 31*, as well as in this work.

All of the material in bars 1–10 derives from the opening bar. The second verse of the anthem follows exactly the same pattern as these ten bars, the only significant differences being the text (and changes in performing directions suggested by these new words) and octave doublings in bars 11–16. Using the same music for two or more verses of text is known as a **strophic** setting. There is no precedent for this type of structure in any other work we have studied but, as we have seen, the simple form and tranquil mood of *The Lamb* hides a wealth of melodic ingenuity.

Private study

1. (a) Explain what is meant by the following statement:
         Bars 1–10 of *NAM 26* consist of antiphonal exchanges.

    (b) What type of voice is meant by a 'mean' in *NAM 26*?

2. (a) Write a short paragraph comparing Bach's canonic writing
         in the first movement of *NAM 28* with Gabrieli's canonic
         writing, seen on pages 284–285 of the *New Anthology*.

    (b) What is (i) a recitative, and (ii) ritornello form?

3. In bar 9 of *NAM 29* the choir begins a varied repeat of bars 1–8.
    How does Haydn achieve a smooth transition to this section
    from the first eight bars of the movement?

4. Make a list of the the ways in which *Locus iste* (*NAM 30*) differs
    from renaissance motets such as *NAM 26*.

5. Explain the term bitonality, and give an example from either
    NAM 31 or *NAM 32*.

Sample questions

In the exam there will be two questions on this topic, from which
you must choose to answer **one**.

(a) Compare and contrast John Taverner's renaissance approach
     to tonality in *NAM 26* with the 20th-century approach of John
     Tavener in *NAM 32*.

(b) Contrast the structures of the **last** movement of NAM 28 with
     the structure of NAM 27.

(c) Compare and contrast the structure and tonality of *Locus iste*
     (*NAM 30*) with that of *The Lamb* (*NAM 32*).

Secular vocal music

There are *three* Special Focus works, *NAM 33*, *NAM 37* and *NAM 39*, all of which must be studied if you are taking the exam in 2006 or 2007.

Special Focus Work 1 for 2006 and 2007

NAM 33   CD3 Track 11
James Bowman (countertenor) with
David Miller (lute) and bass viol.

Dowland, Flow my tears

Before starting on this section you should work through (or revise) the information about the context and structure of this music given on pages 95–96 of the AS Guide. Make sure that you understand all of the terminology used on those pages.

In **strophic form**, the same music is set to successive verses of text.

This **ayre** is one of the finest **lute songs** ever written. It enjoyed fame throughout Europe during Dowland's life and for long after his death. The song is in **modified strophic form.** The first two verses are set to the same eight-bar melody (A), verses three and four to a second eight-bar melody (B), and verse five is set to a third eight-bar melody (C) which is repeated. We can therefore describe the form as AABBCC, but note that the repeat of verse five is not observed on the *New Anthology* recording.

Dowland adapted this song from a pavan for solo lute that he had composed earlier in the 1590s. He would therefore have written the words of *Flow my tears* to fit the pre-existing melody of his pavan.

The melodies divide into **asymmetrical phrases** that match the asymmetry of the verbal rhythms. For instance, the first two phrases begin on the beat in bars 1 and 3 respectively, but the third begins with a quaver **anacrusis** on 'Where' at the end of bar 4 and the last phrase begins at the end of bar 6 with a crotchet anacrusis. The result is that of the four phrases in Section A, only the first is exactly two bars long – the other three are each slightly less or slightly more than eight beats in length.

Syncopation is used to emphasise important words, such as 'fall' at the end of bar 1 and 'infamy' in bar 6. In section B silence is used to suggest sighs in the expressive **sequences** of bars 12–14, the gaps being filled by the **imitative** lute accompaniment.

Dowland uses the **melodic minor scale** in phrases that fall a 4th from tonic to dominant (such as 'Flow my teares') or from the mediant to the leading note (such as 'fall from your springs'). A similar fall from tonic to dominant, but in C major, occurs in bars 9–10, at the start of section B.

In various guises these falling figures occur ten times, becoming characteristic **motifs** that unify the song. The first to occur is an example of **word painting** (tears flow *down* the cheeks in the first verse and the lamps are turned *down* in the second verse). But after the first three beats the motif is manipulated to become an ever more potent expression of melancholy, for instance:

✦ In the setting of 'fall from your springs' the motif is **rhythmically augmented** and falls through the highly expressive interval of a diminished 4th.

✦ In bar 17 the diminished 4th version of the motif is **inverted**.

✦ In bars 20–21 the original motif is reduced to two notes falling a perfect 4th on the word 'Happie'. The first of these (E) is the highest note in the song. After this climactic point the perfect

4th is repeated at a lower pitch to form a **melodic sequence**, As the melody continues to fall in pitch from the climax in bar 20, the fall from mediant to leading note returns to provide a sharp contrast for the words 'they that in hell'.

✦ The interval of a diminished 4th between G♯ and C in bar 22 was normally avoided in music at this period, but here it links the setting of 'they that in hell' to the setting of 'Feele not the world's despite' to express the final mood of total despair.

The **harmonic progressions** are dominated by simple major and minor triads, as you can see in this skeleton of the first 10 bars:

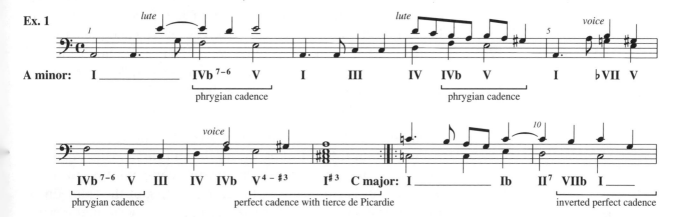

Ex. 1

✦ 34 of the 40 beats are occupied by **primary triads** in root position or first inversion, forming progressions in the key of A minor or C major. However, ...

✦ Chords III and ♭VII (a major triad on the flat 7th degree of the scale) derive from the descending form of the melodic minor scale – they add a touch of **aeolian modality** to the harmony each time they appear.

✦ Many of these chords are decorated with **suspensions** (melodic decoration has been omitted to clarify the 7–6 suspension in bars 1–2 and the 4–3 suspension in bar 7) or **accented passing notes** (the first B in bar 4 and the A in bar 9).

✦ These dissonant notes always herald a cadence. In Example 1 there are three **phrygian cadences** (a type of imperfect cadence consisting of chords IVb and V in minor keys), one **perfect cadence** and one **inverted perfect cadence** (inverted cadences have one or both of the cadential chords inverted).

✦ Expressive **false relations** occur between G♮ and G♯ in bar 5. In perfect cadences in a minor key it was customary to sharpen the 3rd of chord I. In bars 8–9 this **tierce de Picardie** (C♯) forms another false relation with the C♮ in the next chord.

Three-part counterpoint is evident in most bars of *NAM 33*. It consists of the vocal melody, a lute countermelody and a more functional bass part (played on a bass viol on the anthology CD). Notice the **canon** between voice and bass in bars 12–14, and the way the bass takes the leading role in the freely imitative exchange starting at bar 20, after which it descends to a low E on the word 'hell' (another example of word painting). Only in the first and last bars of each section is the texture more homophonic.

Special Focus Work 2 for 2006 and 2007

NAM 37   CD3 Track 15
Elly Ameling (soprano)
Jörg Demus (piano)

Haydn, My mother bids me bind my hair

Before starting on this section you should work through (or revise) the information about the context and structure of this music given on page 99 of the AS Guide. Make sure that you understand all of the terminology used on that page.

My mother bids me bind my hair was one of a series of settings of English verses that Haydn wrote to commission on a visit to England in the 1790s. The elegant but rather superficial style reflects the sentimental text of this *canzonetta* (little song).

The **strophic** structure of *NAM 37* is a form we encountered in the first two sections of Dowland's ayre. The difference is that Dowland's melody fits text perfectly, even when repeated (he wrote the words himself, to fit the melody) while the rests in the second half of Haydn's setting, which work fine for verse 1, sound absurd in verse 2, because they split words and syllables in a meaningless way ('And while ... I spin ... my fla - ... xen thread').

Each verse of the text consists of five lines of identical rhythm (ti-tum ti-tum ti-tum ti-*tum*, ti-tum ti-tum ti-*tum*). This unvarying metrical scheme is reflected in Haydn's **compound duple metre** and his four-bar phrasing. Only in his setting of the third line of the verses does he try to break free from the poem's rigid metrical pattern: in bars 17–21 he repeats 'and lace' (which becomes 'and sigh' in the second verse) to produce a five-bar phrase.

Every phrase of Haydn's vocal melody starts with an anacrusis and ends on the first beat of the bar. The song is clearly designed for amateur vocalists, and this is confirmed by the **doubling** of the singer's first three phrases in the piano part. Once the singer is launched he risks a little **heterophony** in bars 22–26 (where the pianist ornaments the vocal line) and he finally gives the piano accompaniment some limited independence in the last 12 bars.

Haydn's four-bar phrases are paired to form the **antecedent and consequent** (or 'question and answer') pattern that is so typical of late 18th-century music. This **periodic phrasing** is evident in the melody of the piano introduction, where the antecedent ends with an imperfect cadence and the answering consequent completes the musical sense by ending with a perfect cadence. The first eight bars of the vocal melody also form an antecedent–consequent pair, in which the answering phrase (bars 12^6–16) begins with a repetition of bars 8^6–10^5 but ends with a perfect cadence in the dominant instead of an imperfect cadence in the tonic.

The piano melody includes several **triadic figures,** but the singer is only allowed one (bars 8^6–9^5, repeated four bars later). For the rest the melodies are mainly **conjunct** and diatonic, but as soon as weeping is mentioned, Haydn responds with a **chromatic** descent through a perfect 4th (22^6–24^1). This touch of conventional word-painting is rather undermined when Haydn's diatonic version of this 'weeping motif' (still with customised sighs) ends with a pause on the highest note of the phrase for the ludicrous word 'creep'.

Other melodic features that are characteristic of the period as well as of the composer include the **free sequence** in bars 5–6, the **grace**

notes in bars 12 and 15, and the **fragmentation** and **manipulation** of poor young Lubin's phrase in the last four bars of the song,

The functional harmony uses mainly **primary triads**, along with the dominant 7th, in all inversions plus an occasional **chromatic chord**, such as the **diminished 7th** that adds a touch of chromatic colour in bar 6. Chord Ic appears as a **passing $^6_4$** and a **cadential $^6_4$**. Both of these progressions are hallmarks of classical style. **Tonic and dominant pedals** appear several times in this song. Those in bars 0–4 are typical of classical style because of the simple chords that appear above them and because they are lavishly decorated with **passing notes** in 3rds (bar 1^5), **an anticipation** (bar 1^6), **double appoggiaturas** (bar 2^1), **a suspension** (bar 2^4) and **diatonic and chromatic passing notes** (bar 3).

The **harmonic rhythm** (the rate of change of chords) in bars 0–16 is slow at the beginning of each phrase but speeds up towards the cadences (another feature of classical style). This first section is entirely in the tonic key of A major until the modulation to the dominant (E major) in bars 15–16. As the unfortunate lady becomes more twitchy, the rate of change speeds up until, in bars 17–21 there are four chords per bar. These bars remain in E major, after which a dominant pedal (initally supporting chromatic writing) prepares for the return of the tonic key, culminating in nearly two bars of dominant harmony (E major in bars 26–27).

The final section returns to the tonic of A major (with a brief visit to D major in bar 29). It starts with two four-bar phrases that form another antecedent–consequent pair, both ending with a perfect cadence in the tonic and both developing the halting rhythmic idea of bars 22^6–25. The final four-bar phrase forms a short coda that confirms the tonic key with three perfect cadences in A major.

Chord Ic is called a $^6_4$ because it is formed from notes that are a 6th and a 4th above the bass. A passing $^6_4$ occurs in the second half of bar 5, where its bass (E) acts as a passing note between F♯ and D♯ (bars 5–6). A cadential $^6_4$ is used in cadences – either as the first chord of an imperfect cadence (Ic–V) or as an approach chord to a perfect cadence (Ic–V⁷–I in bars 7^4–8).

Private study

1. (a) What is a phrygian cadence? Give an example of one on page 348 of the *New Anthology*.

   (b) In bar 22 on that page, G♮ in the bass is followed by G♯ in the melody (on the word 'hell') and then G♮ in the lute part. What name describes this sort of tonal conflict?

   (c) Give the bar number of a tierce de Picardie on page 348.

2. Explain each of the following terms:
   (i) ayre, (ii) canzonetta, (iii) strophic form.

3. Look at the chords in bars 30–39 of *NAM 37*. Why is this described as functional harmony?

4. Explain what is meant by periodic phrasing.

5. How do the textures used by Dowland and Haydn differ?

Fauré, Après un rêve

Before starting on this section you should work through (or revise) the information about the context and structure of this music given on pages 99 of the AS Guide. Make sure that you understand all of the terminology used on that page.

Special Focus Work 3 for 2006 and 2007

NAM 39   CD3 Track 17
Janet Baker (mezzo-soprano)
Geoffrey Parsons (piano)

Ex. 2a aeolian mode on C

Ex. 2b aeolian mode on F

Faure spent much of his youth and early manhood learning about **modes** and teaching modal theory – and it shows! If you sing or play the vocal part of bars 2–4, followed without a break by bars 6–8, you may feel some doubt about the tonality, but you will probably agree that you had ended on the dominant of C minor. Your doubts arose because all of the pitches of these six bars belong to the aeolian mode on C (Example 2a). Now sing or play the first seven bars of the melody including the bar we missed out earlier. You will probably feel happier to say the melody is in C minor. This is because bar 5 contains the leading note of C minor rising a semitone to the tonic (we accept the D♭ as local chromatic colouring that does not affect the tonality).

But this interpretation does not hold for the melody of bars 9–15, starting with *Tes yeux étaint plus doux* (your eyes were more tender). It seems to start in E♭ major (more tender than the aeolian mode?) but immediately gives way to F minor in bars 10–12[2] then E♭ minor in bars 13–15. After a repeat of the first ten bars of the vocal part the aeolian mode returns, this time on F (Example 2b) – notice the D♭ and E♭ *rising* to the tonic in bar 27. But throughout bars 26–31 this modality alternates with F minor – notice the raised leading note (E♮) rising to the tonic (F) in bars 25 and 28–29. Look on from here and you should now be able to identify a passage in B♭ minor, a passage in the aeolian mode on F and a longer passage in C minor.

What is Fauré up to? He seems to be changing from one key or mode to another and concealing the real tonal centre (C minor) until the end of the song. Why? The answer lies in the text, in which the poet recalls an image of his beloved but then awakes and implores the mysterious night to return him to the radiance of his dream. We all know that dreams often consist of changing and unfocused images that melt into one another and disappear when we awake to the cold light of day. This was the poet's experience, and Fauré responds with the elusive tonality of the first 30 bars and the emergence of C minor as the clear tonal centre at the end.

However, this is not the whole story, for the piano accompaniment simultaneously weakens the tonality/modality of the vocal part and strengthens it. This paradox can be illustrated by examining the harmonic progression of the first nine bars. It begins with a simple triad of C minor, but as sleep (*sommeil*) descends, so a series of sumptuous discords dissolve away the key of C minor.

Alternatively you could think of the chords in bars 3 and 4 as dominant 7ths, each with a suspension. In either case, note that the C in the piano part of bar 4 should fall to B♭ on the third beat of that bar.

Fauré's harmonisation of bar 3 comes as a wonderful surprise. It is chord V^9 of B♭ major (changing to V^7 on the last beat of the bar). But instead of resolving to chord I of B♭ the progression continues with V^9 (and V^7) of E♭ major.

The pattern changes slightly in bar 5, where Fauré uses V^{11}–$V^{♭9}$ of A♭ major. In bar 6 he steps off what has by now become a **harmonic sequence** of dominant discords to an **augmented triad.** The only connection between $V^{♭9}$ and this new chord is a common pitch (E♮/F♭). The E♮ rises to F, which becomes the 7th of V^7 in C minor, leading to the first perfect cadence in the tonic key in bars 7–9.

E♮ and F♭ are said to have an **enharmonic relationship** because the two pitches sound the same, despite their different notation.

Thus the C minor tonality/modality of the vocal part has been *weakened* by a harmonic progression that strongly hints at the keys of B♭, E♭, A♭ and F minor. But C minor tonality is *strengthened* by the roots of the chords in bars 1–9, which form a complete diatonic **circle of 5ths** that begins and ends on the tonic note of C minor. When the vocal part is added some delectable dissonances appear, the most pungent being the sounding together of the aeolian A♭ and B♭ against the G and B♮ of chord V^7 in bar 7. This type of conflict is resolved at the end of the song by the free inversion of the triplet figure so that both performers can at last agree that the song is indeed in the key of C minor.

It is Fauré's miraculous fusion of modality, major/minor tonality and extreme chromaticism that accounts for his distinctive style, but there are some other important points to notice:

✦ Fauré's **text-setting** is sensitive to the verbal rhythms of French, in which stresses often fall on the last syllable of a word, and final vowels that are normally suppressed in spoken French are restored when sung (hence the three notes used for *i-ma-ge*). The setting is mainly **syllabic**, apart from the short but exquisite melismas in, for example, bars 7 and 22.

✦ The vocal phrases are much longer than the mainly two-bar phrasing of *Flow my teares*. The triplets within Fauré's vocal melody create **cross-rhythms** against the even quavers that run throughout the piano accompaniment, blurring their regularity and adding to the dream-like atmosphere.

✦ The texture of the song is entirely homophonic, although notice that the bass of the piano accompaniment moves mainly in contrary motion to the vocal melody. This provides a contrapuntal backbone in passages such as the opening circle of 5ths and (particularly) in bars 36–47, where the interplay between voice and bass forms two-part counterpoint that guides the song back to the tonic with absolute inevitability.

✦ The first two stanzas of the poem are clearly separated by the singer's rest in bar 16 , but Fauré plunges straight into the third stanza on 'Hélas!' at the end of bar 30. Here is the structure:

	Bar 1	Piano introduction: repeated C minor triads announce the tonic key
A	Bars 2–16	Two seven-bar vocal phrases: the first in C minor, the second modulating to the relative major (E♭), followed by a one-bar piano interlude leading to …
A^1	Bars 17–30	A repeat of bars 2–11 followed by a modulation to V of F minor (bar 30)
B	Bars 30^3–38	Two four-bar phrases, the first in B♭ minor (containing the climax of the song in this distant key), the second returning to V of C minor
B^1	Bars 38^3–47	Two four-bar phrases derived from B, the first starting in C minor, the second ending with a perfect cadence in this tonic key
	Bar 48	Piano postlude: one tonic chord of C minor

The vocal melodies in each of the four main sections are unified by triplet figures that occur before all but one of the 12 cadences in the song, and by the interval of a rising perfect 4th that signals the beginning of each section. The latter may remind us of the recurrent motif of a 4th in *Flow my tears*.

Private study

1. Describe the texture of *Après un rêve*.

2. Complete this sentence: The clash between B♭ and B♮ in bar 7 of this song is an example of a simultaneous ...

3. How does Fauré achieve continuity between the phrase that ends in bar 8 and the new phrase that starts in bar 9?

4. Give an example of an enharmonic relationship in the piano part of bars 16–25.

5. Explain the terms syllabic and cross-rhythm, giving examples of each from page 364 of the *New Anthology*.

Sample questions

In the exam there will be three questions on the three songs you have studied, from which you must choose to answer **two**.

(a) (i) State what is meant by word painting in music and explain the use of this technique by Dowland in *NAM 33*.

(ii) Comment on Dowland's use of tonality in *NAM 33*.

(b) Compare and contrast the structures of the songs by Dowland and Fauré.

(c) Comment on Fauré's use of tonality and harmony in *NAM 39*.

Continuity and change in text-setting and handling of voice

For examination in summer 2006 and 2007

You do not need to study this topic unless *Secular vocal music* is the Area of Study that you undertook for AS Music and which you are now extending for A2.

Before starting work on this topic you need a thorough understanding of the material on *Secular vocal music* in the AS Guide (pages 91–105). Remember that for A2 the topic draws on works from across the **entire** Area of Study, not just those in one of the two lists, A or B.

Weelkes

NAM 34   CD3 Track 12
Purcell Consort of Voices
Directed by Grayston Burgess

Sing we at pleasure is typical of many short, simple and tuneful madrigals of the late 16th and early 17th centuries that in England were called **balletts**. They were characterised by lively triple-time dance rhythms and *fa-la-la* refrains, and were often written for five voices, as was *NAM 34*. Such five-part texture often included contrasted vocal groupings (such as SAA and ATB), although Weelkes does not make use of such a possibility in this short piece.

The Latin terms *cantus* (song) and *quintus* (fifth) refer back to a time when contrapuntal parts were added to the principal part given to the tenor, so *quintus* simply meant the fifth voice to be added to the polyphony. Here these historic names have no bearing on the importance of these two parts.

The **range of the voice parts** is typical of the period: two soprano parts, both with a range of a 9th (as indicated by the black noteheads after the clefs), an alto part with a range of a 7th and wide-ranging tenor and bass parts. All five voices are equally important in the varied homophonic and contrapuntal textures of *NAM 34*.

The English madrigalists were famous for their sensitive **text-setting** and *Sing we at pleasure* is no exception. The text consists of three rhyming couplets:

1. Sing we at pleasure, Content is our treasure. Fa la la …
2. Sweet Love shall keep the ground, Whilst we his praises sound.
3. All shepherds in a ring Shall dancing ever sing: Fa la la …

In his largely **syllabic** setting Weelkes frequently repeats phrases of this text and makes sure that the stressed syllables (underlined *above*) fall on the first beats of bars. The exception comes in his setting of 'Whilst we his praises sound' where every one of his five voices has its own distinctive part to play in a joyfully chaotic **imitative** texture. In this, most entries begin with a rising interval that ensures a musical accent on the stressed second syllable ('Whilst we'), but the **close imitation** means that this syllable falls higgledy-piggledy on all three beats.

This metrical confusion is set to rights in the **homophonic** setting of 'his praises sound' (bars 29–31), but he adds spice with **syncopation** on the second syllable of 'praises' (compare the soprano and tenor parts with the normal setting in the alto and bass parts).

In the *Fa, la, la* refrains Weelkes is not inhibited by verbal stresses and so can reflect the joy of the dancers in more complex syncopation. At the end of the first refrain, for instance, the alto has a field day with rhythms that disrupt the normal triple-time metre of the other parts. In Example 3 the alto part of bars 16^3–22^2 has been re-barred to show how the syncopation virtually imposes three different metrical patterns, including the **hemiola** that is such a feature of late renaissance and baroque music.

A hemiola is a rhythmic device in which two groups of three beats are articulated as three groups of two beats.

Ex. 3

The meaning of the text is reflected in cheerful **major keys**, with no hint of modality, and in the character of the melodic parts. At the start the **conjunct** ascent of the first soprano part to the highest pitch highlights one of the most important words ('pleasure') and contrasts with the falling contour of the melody in the next phrase (reflecting contentment). The almost stationary upper parts in bars 31–34 suggests the dancers calmly forming a ring and this contrasts with the melodic lines in bars 35–41, a conjunct ascent of nearly an octave to the highest soprano note on the key word 'sing'.

Leaps occur mostly in the bass part, as an inevitable consequence of it often having to supply the roots of primary triads, as in bars 31–34. But in bars 43–53 the bass is given such a hard time that the singer cannot fail to sound like a buffoon. Either Weelkes disliked basses or, more probably, he intended this comic melody to contribute to the general rustic rejoicing. That feeling is emphasised by cheerful **sequences** (as in the first-soprano part of bars 10–15 and 25–29) which simply spin out the melody.

Although the points in the two paragraphs *above* don't amount to word painting, Weelkes enjoys a musical play-on-words when he reaches the word 'ring' in bar 34. A ring is round, and a round is a type of **canon** – and this is precisely what follows in the canon between sopranos in bars 34^4–43^2. This is immediately followed by a more extended canon for the two sopranos (bars 43^3–52^1) that begins with an **inversion** of the first canonic subject (bars 34^3–43^2).

Of course an audience is unlikely to notice such sophisticated musical jokes, but remember that madrigals were written for *singers* to enjoy, not for passive *listeners* to hear.

The structure of the whole ballett follows the structure of its text: couplet 1 plus refrain (repeated), followed by couplets 2 and 3 plus refrain (repeated). But there is a difference that only the sopranos are likely to notice and relish. Whereas the first repetition is exact and indicated by repeat marks, Weelkes writes out the second repeated section (starting at bar 54^3) in order to swap the soprano parts round (a technique known as contrapuntal inversion).

Dowland

Although *Flow my teares* was published two years after *Sing we at pleasure*, we are returning to it now in order to see how the two works differ. Most obviously, Dowland's ayre is for solo voice with accompaniment, while Weelkes' ballett is for five solo voices and is usually performed without accompaniment.

The style of the two works is also completely different. The ayre is predominantly in a minor key, and its quadruple metre requires a slow tempo to reflect the doleful poem. Weelkes uses entirely major keys and a dancing triple metre that needs a fast tempo to reflect the general rejoicing of its text.

Dowland uses syncopation to highlight important words, whereas Weelkes uses it to capture the dance-like mood of his text. Dowland uses the interval of a falling 4th (and particularly the expressive diminished 4th) to unify his setting and underline the sadness of his poetry. Weelkes uses the pervasive dotted rhythm heard in the first bar of *NAM 34* to unify his setting and convey its happy rhyming couplets. This jollity also sees expression through simple triadic harmony and frequent perfect cadences, whereas Dowland's bitter mourning is reflected in his expressive suspensions, dissonant false relations and lamenting phyrgian cadences.

Compared with such differences, the similarities between the two pieces seem less significant. The vocal range of a 9th in *Flow my teares* is the same as that used by Weelkes in the soprano parts of *Sing we at pleasure* and the text in both works is set in a syllabic style. The musical structures of both pieces are based on the poetic structures of their texts and both are associated with dances types – the ballett began life as dance music, and *Flow my teares* has the tempo, metre and three-part structure of the pavan (as mentioned earlier, Dowland adapted the ayre from his own *Lachrimae pavan* for solo lute).

Monteverdi

The madrigal came to England from renaissance Italy, but if you compare Weelkes' ballett with the declamatory style of *Ohimè, se tanto amate* (published only three years later, in 1603) you will see little continuity between them, other than syllabic text-setting and Monteverdi's occasional use of imitation (although the tierce de Picardie in bar 39 will be familiar from our study of Dowland).

The principal reason for this was the creation in Italy of a new style of vocal composition called the ***seconda prattica*** (second practice). It was a revolution that sought to overthrow the conventions of renaissance polyphony (the *primo prattica* or 'first practice').

NAM 33   CD3 Track 11
James Bowman (countertenor) with David Miller (lute) and bass viol.

For more on Dowland's text setting and his handling of the voice, don't forget to revise the first part of this chapter.

NAM 35   CD3 Track 13
The Consort of Musicke
Directed by Anthony Rooley

Monteverdi put forward the argument that words must govern vocal music. Once this was accepted then conventions could be adapted or ignored in order that the music might most vividly express the mood and meaning of the text. So far as vocal writing and text setting are concerned, this **stile nuovo** (new style) is represented in *NAM 35* by:

✦ **Wide ranges** for all voices that allow Monteverdi to explore the varied timbres of different **vocal registers.** The tenor part covers a range of a 10th and all other voice parts cover an 11th.

✦ A declamatory style that allows the text to be delivered almost as fast as it could be said. Declamatory passages, such as the soprano and bass parts in bars 1–2, derive from the **recitative style** of recently-invented opera. Rhythms change with each new phrase of the poem (notice the almost chant-like passage starting at bar 47^2) and throughout the madrigal Monteverdi's melodies mirror the speech rhythms of spoken Italian.

We shall look at recitative in more detail in our study of the next secular vocal work.

✦ Expressive melodic lines that reflect the meaning of the words. At the start, for instance, the falling 3rds of *Ohimè* ('Ah me') suggest the way the voice falls on these syllables when spoken.

✦ **Disjunct** melodic lines, most notably in the alto part of bar 56. The madrigal was written for professional singers to perform to cultured audiences in the palaces of aristocratic patrons of the arts. The vocal parts often relate directly to the text as a form of **word painting.** The descending leap of a 7th in the bass part of bar 16 colours the text ('if I say alas') and the descent of the tenor from high to very low register in bars 20–21 vividly expresses the words 'if I die now'. In bars 49–52 the falling 3rd of *ohimè* is repeated over and over in **sequence** to express the thousand sweet 'Ahs' of the lovers, and the chromatic writing in these bars produces tortured **false relations** between the parts.

The fact that *Sing we at pleasure* was most probably intended for groups of friends to sing at home, while *Ohimè, se tanto amate* was written for professionals vocalists to perform to groups of admiring listeners, is one of the main reasons why voices are handled very differently in these two madrigals.

✦ **Tritones** and other melodic intervals that were forbidden in renaissance polyphony are used freely as an expressive resource. The melodic tritone in the *quinto* part between F♯ (bar 2) and C (bar 4) adds to the tortured dissonances and pregnant silences that Monteverdi uses to express 'Alas, alas, alas, alas'.

✦ Extremely **dissonant** harmonic intervals that reflect the mock agony of the poet, such as the unprepared 9ths between bass and *quinto* in bars 2 and 4 and the dissonances in bars 16–17.

✦ Contrasts in **texture** that are used to illustrate the words. In the first four bars, for instance, pairs of voices engage in a dialogue that suggests the alternating sighs of the two lovers.

✦ A **syllabic** setting that allows the audience to hear the words. The only **melismas** (bar 42) introduce semiquavers for the first and last time. Their lively rhythms express the delight the poet takes in the possibility that his lady might yet relent.

We have not found much continuity between the three pieces we have so far studied, even though they were published within five years of each other. But there *are* connections between Dowland's ayre, Monteverdi's madrigal and this recitative and air by Purcell.

Purcell

NAM 36   CD3 Track 14
Carolyn Watkinson (soprano)
with the English Baroque Soloists
Directed by John Eliot Gardiner

By the time Purcell came to write his opera Dido and Aeneas (1689), Monteverdi's recitative style (of which we saw some glimmerings in *NAM 35*) had become accepted throughout Europe as the best means of delivering operatic dialogue.

As in Monteverdi, so also in Purcell, the text of the short recitative in *NAM 36* is of paramount importance, so the accompaniment part (labelled *continuo*) consists merely of a functional bass line from which harmonic progressions could be improvised. This allows Dido to deliver the words with considerable rhythmic freedom, and that is the essence of **recitative**. Dido is contemplating suicide and as she does so, she becomes disorientated. And so does our sense of tonality as she sings a melodic phrase that begins in C minor, passes through F minor and ends in F major, all in the space of three bars. The wandering **chromatic melisma** with which Purcell sets the word 'darkness' perfectly expresses Dido's state of mind.

By now Dido is short of breath, so the text is fragmented by rests. They signify gasps or sighs (reminding us of Monteverdi's four exclamations of *Ohimè* at the start of *NAM 35*). As her spirits sink, so her vocal part winds its way down an octave before coming to rest on the dominant of G minor. The grinding dissonances formed with the bass enhance the mood of total desolation.

This descent of a 4th provides the point of continuation with *Flow my tears*, written nearly a century earlier, which contains a similar descent from tonic to dominant in the vocal part (most obvious in bar 1). But Dowland transposes and manipulates his diatonic motif, whereas Purcell's chromatic bass figure remains unchanged throughout.

The **air** (another word for a song) starts at the change to triple metre, and so overlaps with the last note of the recitative. It is constructed upon a five-bar **ground bass** that is repeated ten times. This ostinato descends chromatically from G to D, followed by a three-note cadential figure. The chromatic descent from tonic to dominant taps into a long tradition in European music in which this formula signified emotions such as grief, sorrow and mourning.

The declamatory style of bars 25–29, with its use of a single pitch, silences and repetition to intensify the pathos of 'Remember me', is a technique Purcell learned from studying Italian music (we know that he copied out a madrigal similar to *Ohimè, se tanto amate*). As in Monteverdi's madrigal, the vocal part covers a huge **range** (from middle C to G a 12th above). Purcell cunningly keeps within a range of a 10th until bar 33, when Dido suddenly swoops up to top G for another, varied repetition of 'remember me' (once heard no one can forget the spine-tingling effect it makes!).

As in *Flow my tears* the vocal melodies are **asymmetric,** the first (bars 6–14, repeated in bars 16–24) being nine bars long and the second (bars 25–36, also repeated) being 11 bars long. Both also contain within them shorter asymmetric phrases. The melodic line implies imperfect cadences at the end of the first two phrases (bars 9 and 14 respectively). These vocal cadences are out of phase with the cadences at the end of each statement of the ground (bars 6, 11 and 16) and the same is true of the second melody. This skilful **overlapping** is a hallmark of Purcell's ground-bass technique.

Purcell uses a **tritone** (the expressive interval also seen in *NAM 33* and *NAM 35*) to intensify the word 'trouble' in bars 12 and 22.

Finally, in the concluding instrumental **ritornello,** the chromatic descent of the ground is dramatically extended to cover an octave in the first violin part as Dido seals her own fate with a dagger.

You should revise the information about 'My mother bids me bind my hair' on pages 114–115. The additional points here concern comparisons and contrasts with the earlier works we have studied.

We encountered the medium of solo voice and accompaniment in *NAM 33*, but Haydn's supportive piano part contains nothing like Dowland's contrapuntal lute textures. Similarly, Haydn's jolly and regularly-phrased vocal part is quite unlike the assymetric phrases of Dowland's minor-key lament.

In bars 22–24, the chromatic fall through a perfect 4th and the rests in the vocal melody (with their very odd effect in verse 2) don't so much remind us of Dido's air as show us how very different these features can sound in another context.

The strophic form bears comparison with the structures of the first and second sections of *NAM 33*, but unlike the second and fourth verses of Dowland's ayre, Haydn's second verse doesn't fit the repeated music verse very convincingly.

In summary, the contrasts between Haydn's song and the earlier vocal music we have studied are greater than the similarities. Most of the latter are confined to matters such as conjunct melodies that are common enough in many styles of vocal music.

Schubert never specified the type of voice he required for his *Lieder*. In his own lifetime these songs were certainly sung by men, but *Lieder* are now performed by both men and women. The vocal part of *Der Doppelgänger* covers a wider range (an octave and a 6th) than any range we have so far encountered. On CD3 it is sung by a tenor whose experience on the operatic stage informs every last syllable of the text with dramatic meaning. The darkness of the minor key, the anguish of the text and the short exclamatory phrases might all remind us of the excerpt from Dido and Aeneas – indeed, some *Lieder* have been described as a miniature, domestic equivalent of opera (although it is most unlikely that Schubert knew any of Purcell's music).

The syllabic setting is made up of melodic fragments that never coalesce into an extended phrase until the closing bars. The fragments are projected over a slow-moving chordal accompaniment. Schubert uses this technique to ensure that every word of Heine's terrifying poem may be heard and, by the silences between the fragments, to suggest the faltering breath of a man in shock. In these respects this song can be seen as a continuation of the aims that Monteverdi proclaimed more than two centuries earlier – but the irony of *Ohimè, se tanto amate* is obviously worlds away from the terror depicted by Heine and Schubert.

The song is through-composed, not strophic. Although there is some repetition, particularly in the subsequent use of the four-bar chord pattern heard in the introduction, Schubert differentiates the stanzas of the poem by matching the different **registers** of the voice to the mood of each of Heine's three verses.

In the first verse (bars 5–22) Schubert explores the lowest vocal register, extending from B in bar 17 to A (bar 21) a 7th higher. The

Haydn

NAM 37	CD3 Track 15
Elly Ameling (soprano)	
Jörg Demus (piano)	

Schubert

NAM 38	CD3 Track 16
Peter Schreier (tenor)	
András Schiff (piano)	

melodic fragments revolve around the **dominant pedal** of B minor in the piano part (the F♯ in every chord). Both of these features give musical expression to the image of a silent town in the depths of the night. The vocal part uses only the notes of the descending melodic scale of B minor (there is no A♯ in the melody). On a simple level this archaic modal effect represents the phrase in which the narrator informs us that his beloved has long ago left the town (bars 15–18), but it also injects a feeling of vague foreboding.

The second verse (bars 25–42) begins with the image of a man in the street looking upwards, and the singer become more agitated as foreboding gives way to fear. The vocal part leaps a perfect 4th to the upper tonic in bar 27, and the leading note of B minor (A♯) puts an end to aeolian modality in the next bar. The disjointed melody rises through the tonic chord (bars 28–31) to reach the singer's highest register, and the first climax of the song, on the first syllable of *Schmerzensgewalt* (pain). At *mir graust es* (I am terrified) the lowest register reappears. But only briefly, for the same leap to B and A♯ (*wenn ich sein Antlitz sehe* – when I see his face) leads to a searing variation of bars 29–31. This time, however the tension is maintained as the singer pushes on upwards to his highest note (used only once in the song) when he realises that it is his own face he sees (*meine eigne Gesalt*). So far the vocal part has remained rooted in B minor.

The last verse (bars 43–63) begins like the first, with a monotone on F♯ as the singer addresses his ghostly double directly. Underneath the voice part, piano chords creep up in semitones until a chord of D♯ minor is reached in bar 47. This heralds a change of key from B minor to D♯ minor, as the alternating I and V chords of this key confirm (bars 47–50), for the singer's angry *ff* accusation that the ghostly double is mocking the pain of his love.

The horrendous array of accidentals in the vocal part at this point indicate notes from the scale of D♯ harmonic minor.

The return to B minor is accomplished by just one chromatic chord (bar 51) and it leads to the second great climax in bar 52 (marked *fff*). This is the beginning of the only lyrical melody in *Der Doppelgänger* and it contains the only extended **melisma** in the song (bars 54–55). As the singer's anger changes to resignation, the only perfect cadence in the tonic key is heard in the piano (bars 55–56). The utter inevitability of the poem is finally expressed without words in the piano **postlude**.

Fauré

We dealt with this song in the first part of the chapter, where we noted several points of continuity with the songs by Dowland and Haydn. You should reread that section now.

The French *mélodie* was written for a solo singer with piano, so it provides an obvious point of continuity with both Haydn's light *canzonetta* and Schubert's dramatic *Lied*. The style and subject matter of all three songs is very different, but the chordal texture of Fauré's piano part has much in common with Schubert's piano accompaniment, even though the former is realised in pulsating quavers rather than solemn dotted minims. Fauré's use of aeolian modality links him to the past, but we have seen no precedent for its combination with luxuriant romantic harmony. Fauré's ability to capture and reflect the essence of the poetic text links him much more closely with Schubert – and even Monteverdi – than Haydn.

Pierrot Lunaire is as much about drama as it is about music – Schoenberg himself called it a **melodrama** and the first performer was an actress. It's significant that the vocal part is identified as a part for a **reciter** since Schoenberg's **Sprechstimme** is meant to be a halfway house between singing and declamatory speech. In this, the closest comparison (and it is not very close) is with recitative.

The dramatic element in this movement is seen most clearly in the reciter's role as Pierrot, the moonstruck clown who is spellbound by the flute's 'strange melodies'. The flautist does not accompany the singer, as does the pianist in our last three songs. Instead, the two melodic lines form a **two-part contrapuntal texture** in which the flute overlaps and intertwines with the voice.

The thin two-part texture allows every word to be heard. Indeed it often sounds as though the flute is trying to speak. But this is not a rational conversation since they share no common melodic material. Each is absorbed in its own form of madness. For instance, compare the manic raging of the flute in bars 5–6 with the introspective ruminations of Pierrot in the same passage.

The reciter needs to be able to cover a huge range of two octaves (compare bar 8 with bar 15). This follows a trend we have noticed over the centuries for composers to require increasingly wide ranges from their singers. Innovators such as Monteverdi and Schoenberg have often required much wider vocal ranges then any of their contemporary composers.

Schoenberg requires a singer who can observe the rhythms with absolute exactness, but glide between pitches using **portamento** (a type of *glissando*). His music is **atonal** whereas all of the previous vocal music we have studied has been tonal, modal or both. And in such music we have come to expect a large proportion of conjunct movement in vocal writing, whereas here Schoenberg often uses wide and difficult **leaps** (bars 13–19) to explore the emotional extremes of Albert Giraud's expressionist poetry.

The poem falls into three non-rhyming stanzas with a refrain (*Du nächtig todeskranker Mond*) in each. For Schoenberg this is too structured to express madness, so he tends to disregard obvious opportunities for musical repetition (one notable exception being *an Sehnsucht* and *tief erstickt* in bars 14–15) in his handling of the vocal part. Each line of the poem contains four metrical feet (for instance, *Du nächtig todeskranker Mond*), but this is again too conventional for Schoenberg's expressionist setting. Instead, he avoids any sort of melodic symmetry by writing phrases of 9, 13, 8½ and 8 beats in his setting of the first stanza (and his settings of the others stanzas are equally irregular). This, along with the unpredictable alternations of semitonal movement and angular leaps in the vocal part, and its abrupt changes of direction (as in bar 23), all serve to express the fevered visions in the mad clown's mind.

Gershwin's lovely melody is in a standard **16-bar blues** format of four four-bar phrases. It is entirely **pentatonic** apart from the C♯ that starts in bar 14 (although the last note of the pentatonic set, A, does not arrive until bar 20). This melody is characteristic of a traditional blues in its use of:

Schoenberg

NAM 40   CD3 Track 18
Yvonne Minton (reciter)
Michael Debost (flute)
Directed by Pierre Boulez

Another trend to notice is that of composers using evermore detailed performance directions in their scores. Compare *NAM 40* with *NAM 33–35*. In the three early works the only directions are the tempo suggestions added by modern editors.

On CD3 Yvonne Minton chooses to sing exact and sustained pitches with *portamenti* generally reserved for slurred notes. Try to compare this recording with one in which the singer makes more use of *portamento*. Also compare Minton's *tremolo* on each of the last five notes with other interpretations of Schoenberg's mordent signs.

The poem, which was originally written in French, is shown on page 540 of the *New Anthology* in the German version used by Schoenberg as well as in English translation.

Gershwin

NAM 41	CD3 Track 19

Leona Mitchell (soprano)
Cleveland Orchestra and Chorus
Conducted by Lorin Maazel

✦ A **slow tempo**

✦ The **minor pentatonic** (B, D, E, F♯, A)

✦ Frequent **falling 3rds** in the melody

✦ An **AA¹AB structure** (in a 12-bar blues the first four bars are repeated, or varied, only once: AAB)

✦ **Swung rhythm** (which is best understood by careful comparison of the dotted patterns in the score with the more flexible, laid-back rhythms on the recording)

The use of *portamento* in bar 21 is not clear on CD3, but you should be able to hear this effect in bar 10.

✦ **Portamento** (indicated by the wavy line between the first two notes of bar 21) which in this style produces an entirely different effect to Yvonne Minton's *portamenti* in the fourth complete bar of *Der kranke Mond*.

None of the works we have so far studied contain swung rhythms or pentatonic melodies. However, Gershwin supports his simple melody with a rich vocabulary of **added-6th chords** (bars 8–10 and 16–18) and **chromaticism** (bars 12 and 14). This may well remind us of how Fauré underpins modal melodies with tonal harmonies that create similar false relations (as in bar 7 of *NAM 39*) to the one mentioned *left*.

On beat 3 of bar 14 the clash between E♯ in the harmony and E♮ in the instrumental melody forms a false relation. But it sounds little like the false relations of early music because in this context we hear Gershwin's E♮–C♯ as the familiar falling 3rd of blues' melodies while the accompanying E♯ is the 3rd of C♯⁷ (a secondary dominant) that leads back to the F♯ major harmony of bar 15.

If we strip away Gershwin's blue notes, added notes and chromaticism, and identify just one main chord per bar, the blues chord pattern in B minor that supports the melody is revealed (it is much easier to hear on CD3 than to analyse from the score):

bars	8	9	10	11	12	13	14	15	16	17	18	19	20	21	22	23
chord	Bm	Bm	Bm	Bm	Em	Em	F♯	F♯	Bm	Bm	Bm	Bm	D	E	Bm	Bm
	I	I	I	I	IV	IV	V	V	I	I	I	I	III	IV	I	I

The four phrases are each basically four bars long, and are thus superficially similar to Haydn's periodic phrasing – even to the extent that the second phrase cadences on dominant harmony and the fourth cadences plagally to the tonic. But there is a subtle tension between text and music, as the following diagram shows:

Musical form	Text	Rhyme scheme
A	Summer time an' the livin' is easy,	A
A¹	Fish are jumpin', an' the cotton is high.	B
A	Oh yo' daddy's rich, an' yo' ma is good-lookin'	C
B	So hush, little baby, don' yo' cry.	B

Improvisation is a key element in a real blues. 'Summertime', in contrast, is a pre-composed and notated song in which a blues style has been blended with the lush harmonies and carefully planned instrumentation common in popular ballads and film music of the 1930s. At bar 40 Leona Mitchell soars to a high B, returning to the printed note with a superb portamento. This moment is planned, not improvised, and such vocal *bravura* (display of technical skill) is more typical of opera than blues singing. However, it fits the context so well because *Porgy and Bess* inhabits a world of fusion, in which Gershwin sought to reflect black American music through the medium of opera. None of the singers in works we have studied adapt the printed music in the way heard at the end of this song.

In baroque music singers often embellish vocal melodies with ornamentation, either improvised or pre-prepared (although we have seen no examples in this area of study), and musicians will often use some degree of controlled improvisation when realising chords in a continuo part, as in *NAM 36*.

The 16-bar melody is repeated (with different instrumentation) for the second verse of the song, starting at bar 25. This is the same type of **strophic form** that we encountered in Haydn's song, except that Gershwin wisely writes out the rhythmic changes that have to be made in the vocal part to accommodate the differing number of syllables in the two verses.

Without the added top B in bar 40, the **range** of the melody is just one octave, reflecting its function in the opera as a simple lullaby. Gershwin asked that only black singers should sing *Porgy and Bess* and, while Leona Mitchell fits that bill, her classical operatic training perhaps does not produce the natural blues style that the composer hoped for in this memorable lullaby.

The relationship between vocal melody and accompaniment in *Summertime* contributes to the luminous atmosphere of the song. The chords of bars 8–10 and 16–18 are clearly subservient to Clara's melody, but what makes the voice appear to float freely in the shimmering heat is the huge gap between it and the low, closely-spaced accompaniment. In verse 1 fragments of instrumental melody fill the gaps between vocal phrases. In verse 2, the gap between soloist and orchestra is filled by crooning female voices (reaching a climax in bar 41), while a solo violin decorates the homophonic accompaniment of the first verse.

NAM 41 appears to be a self-contained song, and that is how it is often performed. However, in *Porgy and Bess* the songs are not discrete items separated by spoken dialogue as they are in most musicals. Instead, the dialogue is set to music in a modern form of recitative and the music is continuous, with each item flowing into the next. Thus the introduction in *NAM 41* is a continuation from the opening chorus and the rests in bar 46 are filled by chords that crescendo into the next (much more lively) number.

Private study

1. What is (i) a hemiola, and (ii) a strophic setting?

2. Explain the difference between syllabic and melismatic vocal writing, giving an example of each.

3. How do *NAM 33* and *NAM 34* reflect the dance styles on which they are based?

4. What are the main differences in vocal writing between the recitative and the air in *NAM 36*?

5. How does the vocal writing in *NAM 38* reflect the text?

6. Explain the relationship between the solo flute and the vocal melody in *NAM 40*.

7. Define the terms *Sprechstimme* and *portamento*.

8. Which features of *Summertime* are typical of a traditional blues, and which are not?

Sample questions

In the exam there will be two questions on this topic, from which you must choose to answer **one**.

(a) Compare and contrast Weelkes' setting of the text in *NAM 34* with Monteverdi's setting of the text in *NAM 35*.

(b) Contrast the ways in which Schoenberg and Gershwin set the words and handle the voice in *NAM 40* and *NAM 41*.

(c) Comment on the handling of voice in the songs by Haydn and Fauré that you have studied.

Music for film and television

Special Focus Work for 2006 and 2007

NAM 44   CD4 Track 3
Conducted by Jerry Goldsmith

Goldsmith, Planet of the Apes: The Hunt (opening)

Before starting on this section you should work through (or revise) the information about the context and structure of this music given on pages 112–113 of the AS Guide. Make sure that you understand all of the terminology used on those pages.

The composer

Jerry Goldsmith (1929–2004) grew up in Los Angeles, California. He showed such early talent in composition that by the age of 14 he was having lessons from the Italian composer Castelnuovo-Tedesco, who was writing film scores in Hollywood at the time. Goldsmith also attended classes in film composition given by the very successful film composer, Miklos Rozsa. The influence of both composers is very evident in Goldsmith's own work.

This early study of film music prepared Goldsmith for work in radio and television during the 1950s, some of which included improvising at the keyboard for live broadcasts. His understanding of how effective music can be in complementing and enhancing the visual image led to commissions for television scores (including the music for a hugely popular 1960s' series called *Dr Kildare*) and film scores. Goldsmith went on to write the music for some 200 films, and is especially remembered for his powerful scores for thrillers and science-fiction films, including *Planet of the Apes* (1968), *Alien* (1979) and *Star Trek: The Motion Picture* (1979).

The film

Planet of the Apes was based on a French novel written in 1963. It uses the medium of science fiction to explore notions of mankind's superiority, arrogance and prejudice by reflecting these failings through the mirror of a world in which intelligent apes exercise oppressive social control over enslaved humans.

The harsh images and alien landscapes of the film are reflected in the modernist style of Goldsmith's score, some parts of which are very sparse. The title track, for instance, starts with merely a single repeated pitch and is nothing like the triumphal opening music heard in many of John Williams' scores. Some of Goldsmith's **cues** use only a small number of instruments and he reserves the full forces of his large orchestra for only the most dramatic scenes, of which 'The Hunt' is one of the most memorable. *NAM 44* consists of only the first part of the complete cue, which consists or more than five minutes' worth of continuous music in the film.

A cue is a more or less continuous passage of music designed for a particular point in the film.

The score

+ Parts marked E. H. are for English horn (cor anglais) and sound a perfect 5th lower than written

+ Clarinets in B♭ sound a tone lower than written; the bass clarinet sounds an octave plus a tone (a 9th) lower than written

+ Horns in F sound a perfect 5th lower than written

+ Trumpets in B♭ sound a tone lower than written

+ Double basses and double bassoons sound an octave lower than written; piccolos sound an octave higher than written.

Alto C clef (used by violas)

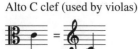

Tenor C clef (used by cellos in bars 82–88)

In 'The Hunt' Goldsmith uses the resources of a large symphony orchestra in a number of characteristic ways:

✦ **Percussion** plays an important role in developing and sustaining the drama of the chase, starting with the solo timpani notes on each downbeat of bars 1–9, followed by the entry of various tuned and untuned percussion, and culminating in the climax at bar 52, which requires four percussionists. As well as common orchestral percussion instruments (timpani, side drum, bass drum and xylophone), Goldsmith requires boo bams, timbales, friction drums and a vibra-slap (all explained in the AS Guide) – plus a bass resin drum and a conga drum.

✦ The **piano** introduces the main motif of the cue in octaves in bar 4, but when this is later developed into ostinato patterns (bars 11–22, 45–51 and 59–73) the piano is used primarily for its ability to articulate the driving semiquaver rhythms. This percussive treatment of the piano is most evident in bars 84–91, where its syncopated and doubled major 7ths cut through a variety of other simultaneous riffs (the rhythm of this ostinato was first introduced on the conga drums in bars 16–22).

✦ **Folk instruments**, such as the boo bams, friction drums, bass resin drum, Ram's horn and Tibetan horn, evoke the primitive chase that is being witnessed on screen.

✦ Conventional instruments are used to colour the orchestration with a variety of **special effects**, including wooden mutes for the horns (bar 10), felt mallets for the conga drum (bar 16) and harmonics for the violins (bars 68–73). Starting at bar 55, the trumpets are required to use plunger mutes (explained *right*) while the second and third trombones have to combine this effect with flutter-tonguing (which involves the player rolling an 'r' while producing the notes).

✦ Conventional instruments are used at the **extremities of their range**, particularly to add to the tension of bars 55–58, where bassoon, double bassoon, first trombone, cellos and double basses are all very low, horns swoop to the top of their range, and violins, flutes and piccolo rush upwards to their own highest registers.

✦ The inclusion of the **electric harp** and **electric bass clarinet** expands the range of special effects available. This kind of music technology was still very new for 1968, but it should be realised that these weren't the digital instruments we know today – they were simply acoustic instruments with pick-ups. This allowed the low notes of the harp to be processed with reverberation and a special 'buzz' effect, and the squeaks from the bass clarinet reed to be amplified, reflecting the excited chatter of the apes in the music itself (both starting at bar 52).

Another important aspect of Goldstein's orchestration is his tendency to score much of the more prominent material for wind or piano, and to use the strings for chordal accompaniments (as in bars 1–7), short links (bar 10), special effects (such as the high sustained notes above the riff in bars 11–21) and punctuating rhythmic patterns (bars 26, 30–31 and 42 onwards).

Instrumentation

Notably absent from the vast array of percussion in *NAM 44* are the triumphant crash of the cymbal and joyful tinkle of metallic percussion such as the triangle and glockenspiel. Instead, Goldsmith mainly uses a wide variety of drums and the dry wooden sound of the xylophone to reflect the fearful chase on screen.

Traditionally the piano was regarded more as a solo instrument than as part of a symphony orchestra. However, over the last 100 years many composers have included a part for the piano in their orchestral works.

A plunger mute is like the rubber suction cup on a plumber's plunger. It produces a very thin sound when the plunger is in. Alternating between closed (+) and open (o) positions creates the characteristic brass 'wah-wah' effect.

The most obvious electric instrument to use in 1968 would have been the electric guitar – perhaps Goldsmith avoided it because the guitar's association with contemporary pop music could have compromised the sound-world of a film set 2,000 years in the future and on another planet.

Structure and style

Episodic refers to music that proceeds in a succession of distinct sections.

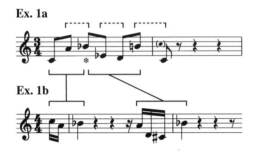

Ex. 1a

Ex. 1b

The shape of film music is usually dictated by the visual image. So, while there are often contrasts in mood and texture, points of climax, and so forth, it is rare to find musical structures such as rondo or ternary forms.

This sometimes leads to an episodic treatment that can seem 'bitty' and unconnected, but Goldsmith guards against this by manipulating and developing short **motifs** that permeate and unify the entire film score. Most notable among those in *Planet of the Apes* is the piano figure in bar 4 (transposed to the treble clef in Example 1a). It derives from the start of the twitchy main theme of the film (Example 1b) which is heard some time before the extract in the *New Anthology* begins. The transformation is achieved through:

✦ **Changes of metre and rhythm**, so that two separate motifs in Example 1b become a continuous quaver motif in Example 1a

✦ Melodically **inverting** the first interval of Example 1b (a falling minor 3rd) so that it becomes a rising major 6th in Example 1a

✦ **Transposing** the second motif in Example 1b up by a semitone so that it starts on B♭

✦ **Linking** both motifs by making the second motif start on the last note of the first motif (the B♭ marked *).

This transformation results in six different pitches of the 12-note chromatic scale being used in bar 4. Goldsmith repeats this motif in bar 9, but this time extends it to all 12 pitches, ending at the F♮ in bar 9. Just as Example 1a finished by returning to its starting note (C) in bar 5, so this extended version returns to its starting note by a further small extension (D♭–C). This final semitone is not mere padding – it reflects the semitones heard or suggested at the start of the motif (shown by dashed brackets in Example 1a) and it also looks back to the parallel- and contrary-motion semitones heard in the wind and string parts of bars 1–7. The prominent use of semitones will prove to be another a unifying idea in *NAM 44*.

The use of all 12 pitches of the chromatic scale in bars 9–10 may make you think of serialism. Goldsmith's choice and angular layout of these pitches is undoubtedly influenced by composers who used serialism, such as Berg and Stravinsky, but this is not 12-note music because it doesn't use the rigorous processes of serial technique. In fact, quite the opposite. Although *NAM 44* is both **chromatic** and **dissonant**, the style of the music is rooted in tonality. We can see this in the way that:

✦ The note C is heard as an **articulated pedal** at the start of every one of first eight bars

✦ The important piano motifs in bars 4–5 and 8–10 each begin on, and return to, C.

Goldmith uses a bar of $\frac{5}{4}$ time (bar 10) to mark the end of the first section. The piano motif from bar 4 is then transposed to start on G (the dominant, if we regard C as the tonic). At the same time it is turned into a bass **riff**, above which the right hand's offbeat semiquavers enhance the rhythmic drive. These form a double pedal on G (the dominant) and E. If you have any doubt that the

'The Hunt' is tonal at heart, despite its frequent dissonance, notice that an articulated pedal on the dominant is heard on every downbeat in bars 11–22.

Above the riff, a high sustained violin note crescendos into an offbeat semitone at the end of bar 13. This transformation of the semitone motif from a melodic to a harmonic idea is anticipated by lower strings and harp on the second beat of bar 13 (F–E). The violin crescendo is heard three times at different pitches, but the F–E anticipation remains constant each time. Now look at the tiny figure played by flutes, piccolo and xylophone in bars 13–14. Can you see how this is related? If not, look back at Example 1b. Before we move on, take note of the conga part that enters in bar 16. This increases the rhythmic tension by introducing **cross-rhythms** of two main notes per bar (effectively ♩. ♩.) against the predominant three-beat pulse (♩ ♩ ♩) of triple time.

Once again, Goldsmith uses a bar of $\frac{5}{4}$ time to mark the end of the section. At bar 23 the tonal centre moves to E♭ (there is no modulation), the piano motif transfers to electric harp and woodwind, and the trombones take over the crescendo on a sustained note (now elongated by one beat) formerly played by the violins. Notice how Goldsmith winds up the tension by adding a diminished 5th to the concluding semitone in bar 26 (G♭ in trombone 1 against C in trombone 3, while the second trombone's D♭ simultaneously supplies the semitone against C). Meanwhile, the strings play fragments of the wind parts from the start of the movement (bars 26, 30–31 and 35–37). You might also spot that the conga's cross-rhythm appears sporadically in double bass and side drum parts.

Although Goldsmith doesn't employ such tonal devices as modulation or cadences, the use of third-related tonal centres (here C, G and E♭) is not a particularly modern aspect of *NAM 44*. Such 'tertiary relationships' are common in 19th-century music.

In bar 40 the idea of a long note leading to a semitonal dissonance is turned on its head – the opening note is reduced to a quaver and the offbeat semitone becomes the part of the motif that is sustained – with powerfully dissonant results. This idea forms the impetus for the repeated semitonal dissonances in the next four bars. Notice the melodic use of falling semitones in the trumpet figures and the strident cross-rhythms between strings and wind.

After this first climactic section (marked out again by changes in metre) the tonal centre returns to C at bar 45. The piano riff returns, transposed to provide its articulated pedal on C, and the crescendo motif returns in abbreviated form in the horns, also on C.

This brief respite leads to a second climax at bar 52, in which the array of ethnic and electric instruments enter as the full horror of the apes on horseback becomes clear. At the bottom of the texture the lowest instruments repeatedly rise from E♭ to E♮ against a sustained E♭, creating the most earth-shaking semitonal dissonance of all. In bar 54 four horns in unison join the bellowing ram's horn, swooping to their highest register. And then in bar 55 Goldsmith unleashes his full orchestral resources. Adding to the elements already noted, trumpets repeatedly climb to a piercingly high dissonance (it is a semitone, of course) on which they open their plunger mutes, the third trombone growls its flutter-tongued melodic semitones, and the upper woodwind and strings pile on scales and cross-rhythms, increasing the cacophony by decorating their repeated Gs with semitones above and below.

Ex. 1b

Ex. 2a

Ex. 2b

After this brilliantly-scored climax the piano riff returns (bar 59) in almost its original version, based on G. However, there are some significant changes. Bars 11–22 were in triple metre, while now we are in quadruple metre. This results in two more quavers being added to the riff (G♯ and D♯ at the end of each bar). Why these two pitches? Because they both create semitonal dissonances against the G♮–E ostinato in the pianist's right hand.

There are also changes in scoring. The violas double the pianist's right-hand ostinato, but in a rhythm of their own, and the cellos and basses also have a three-note ostinato figure. Can you see how it relates to the first three-note motif in Example 1b?

In bars 63–65 Goldsmith transfers the crescendo on a sustained note to muted trumpets, but instead of terminating in a semitonal scrunch, it ends with an inversion of the three-note figure we noticed in bars 13–15, shown in Example 2a. (Notice that this is doubled by the highly unusual combination of three piccolos in unison, as well as xylophone). This three-note figure was originally derived from the start of Example 1b, and in this new transformation we can see that it has morphed into yet another variant of the semitonal idea that has dominated this work (F♯ below the long G♮, ending with G♯ above it, as shown in Example 2b). Even when this in turn starts changing (bars 68–69) the omnipresent semitone is heard high above in violin harmonics (these sound two octaves above the printed black notes).

A very condensed version of the long note plus semitone appears in the horn parts at bar 75, but now the urgent rhythms cease and for the first time Goldsmith uses predominately minim movement and mainly strings. They double the horns in bar 7, but sustain the terminating minor 2nd (the semitone beteen G and A♭). The ensuing passage of **two-part counterpoint** provides a brief relaxation in tension (although no respite from dissonance), designed to throw into relief the final section of the extract, which starts at bar 84. It is based on three simultaneous **ostinati**:

✦ A much more rhythmic variant of the semitone pattern, heard high in the flutes and piccolo

✦ Repeated clashes of a minor 2nd and its inversion (a major 7th) between the B♭s and As heard high in the piano and violin parts. First violins always play on the beat, against which second violins and piano have syncopated cross-rhythms (the barlines and ties make these look more complicated than they sound – the basic patterns are shown without barring in Example 3).

✦ A quaver-based figure in the lower strings – four of its five pitches form falling semitones between B♭ and A.

Ex. 3

Piano

Violin 2

Violin 1

From the end of bar 88, the string parts in this third ostinato are shadowed by bassoons in crotchets, and the violas start moving in contrary motion (shadowed in crotchets by the English horn). The repetitive impulse of the ostinato, its expansion by contrary motion, the addition of more instruments and the accompanying side-drum rolls all increase the tension as the music moves towards the next section, signalled by the change of time signature in bar 91. There the score in *NAM 44* comes to an end, but 'The Hunt' continues.

Private study

1. (i) What is the relationship between the parts for bass clarinet, first bassoon and horns in the first three notes of bar 10?

   (ii) What is the *sounding* pitch of the trumpet note in bar 63?

   (iii) What term describes the relationship between all of the string and horn notes on the first beat of bar 75?

2. What special effect do the trumpets use in bars 71–73?

3. Compare the piano part in bars 11 and 59.

4. Explain the terms riff and cross-rhythm, giving examples of each from *NAM 44*.

5. What helps establish a sense of tonality in bars 1–22 of this work, and what helps to destabilise that sense of tonality?

Remember to take account of transposing instruments when answering question 1.

Sample questions

In the exam there will be three questions on this work, from which you must choose to answer **two**.

(a) Describe how Goldsmith uses rhythm to generate a sense of tension in this extract.

(b) Trace the use of the piano motif in bar 4 of *NAM 44* throughout the extract.

(c) Comment on Goldsmith's balance of tonality and dissonance in *NAM 44*.

Continuity and change in use of instruments and texture

For examination in summer 2006 and 2007

You do not need to study this topic unless *Music for film and television* is the Area of Study that you undertook for AS Music and which you are now extending for A2.

Before starting work on this topic you need a thorough understanding of the material on *Music for film and television* in the AS Guide (pages 106–119). Remember that for A2 the topic draws on works from across the **entire** Area of Study, not just those in one of the two lists, A or B.

It is important to remember that **texture** refers primarily to the number of simultaneous parts in a passage of music and the way in which they relate. At A level you should beware of describing texture in vague terms such as 'thick', 'thin' or 'open'. Generally you will need to be prepared to use precise technical terminology.

For instance, you may need to describe a texture not only as contrapuntal but also as consisting of two-, three- or four-part counterpoint, and you may need to indicate whether the type of counterpoint is fugal, canonic or just freely imitative. Similarly, you may need to describe a texture as not just homophonic but as melody-dominated homophony ('melody and accompaniment') or homorhythmic (all parts moving in the same rhythm).

Auric

NAM 42   CD4 Track 1
Royal Ballet Sinfonia
Conducted by Kenneth Alwyn

Like the other members of *Les Six*, Georges Auric (1899–1983) has a reputation for witty music and sparkling orchestration – a style that he developed particularly through composing numerous ballet and film scores. He was also successful in writing music that had popular appeal – in fact, the song 'Where is your heart?' from his 1952 film *Moulin Rouge* was in the top 20 of the hit parade the following year.

NAM 42 is presented in short score, which doesn't give full details of the orchestration – you may well be able to add more through careful listening. It will be evident, though, that the work is scored for a medium-sized orchestra of woodwind, brass, percussion and strings.

Auric's popular touch is very evident at the start of *NAM 42* – the trilling woodwind and strings, trumpet fanfares and cascading horn scales (repeated in diminution) are film-music clichés, designed to create an exhilarating mood of anticipation – and that is precisely the effect that Auric knew they would have on the 'Ealing comedy' audiences. He uses a number of such devices in his orchestration. They would have been subliminally familiar to the many film-goers of the 1950s and serve to flag events in the fast-moving action:

✦ **Woodwind trills and grace notes** add to the musical activity in order to reflect the lively street scene (bars 9–10)

✦ A sudden change of texture from mainly **free counterpoint** to a single pitch (G) in bar 13 focuses attention on the newspaper headline, and brass enter in stark octaves on a highly dissonant F♯ to punch home its 'shocking' message

✦ Low strings and a gurgling bassoon poke fun at the politicians in bar 15 (a **monophonic texture**, despite the octaves) and are answered in the next bar by cheeky comments from different parts of the crowd – illustrated by the **antiphonal exchanges** between onbeat strings and offbeat woodwind

✦ Tubular bells announce the next headline (bar 31)

✦ A 'suspense chord' halts the action in bar 51 to signal another headline – its news of deadlock is dramatised by the well-worn combination of a **bowed tremolo** played by divided violas, and a lugubriously chromatic motif that descends low in cellos and double basses.

A celeste is a keyboard instrument in which the hammers strike metal bars. Compare this doubling of piccolo and celeste with bars 23–25, where the piccolo is doubled by a glockenspiel (an instrument with metal bars that are struck directly by the player, using beaters).

Doubling of the same melody by two or more different instruments (either in unison or one or more octaves apart) can create distinctive new timbres – it is one of the most important skills in orchestration.

Although such devices were the stock-in-trade of film music at the time, this doesn't diminish their effectiveness. But Auric's real skill comes in their integration, and in the way that he always holds the attention through rapid changes in instrumentation and texture (complemented by equally rapid changes of key). For instance, the low-pitched mock-drama of bars 52–53 quickly gives way to the most delicate of orchestral textures in which a melody for piccolo, doubled by **celeste**, is charmingly accompanied by pizzicato strings. This transparent, high-pitched texture provides a vivid contrast as well as ludicrously portraying the 'dainty' arrival of a helicopter!

Auric often uses pizzicato strings – some passages are marked in the score, but he also uses pizzicato to articulate the opening horn scales and to lighten the bass part throughout much of the extract. Textures vary too quickly to mention many more (but note the clear **homophonic** writing in bars 47–48). An important part of Auric's armoury is his use of **parallel intervals** – for instance, 3rds and 6ths in bars 1–8, consecutive 5ths and octaves in bars 5–6, and parallel triads in bars 47–48.

The full instrumentation of *NAM 43* is shown on page 374 of the *New Anthology*. This is clearly a **large symphony orchestra**, bigger than that used in *Passport to Pimlico*. In addition to the transposing instruments listed on page 128, Bernstein requires a clarinet in E♭ (a small clarinet that sounds a minor 3rd higher than written) and an alto saxophone (which sounds a major 6th lower than written). Like the piano, these instruments are not part of the regular make-up of symphony orchestras, but all three have appeared in numerous 20th-century orchestral works.

Bernstein's orchestral writing is often technically demanding, as is very evident in the opening horn solo. The top note in bar 4 (B♭, sounding a 5th lower) is a semitone above the very high A we noted in *Planet of the Apes* – and there the players have mutual support (four horns in unison) and the cover of much noise from the rest of the orchestra. Here the player is entirely alone in a **monophonic texture** that offers no supportive accompaniment. Little wonder that Bernstein cued this solo into the first trumpet part, in case it proved too high!

At bar 7 the opening theme is heard in **two-part canon** between the unusual combination of flutes (in octaves) and muted trombone. The second part of the theme then appears on muted trumpets, sounding *lontano* (distant), in a simpler two-part texture, over a pedal F in clarinets. When the clarinets move off this pedal at the end of bar 17 they play fragments of the first part of theme in very quiet, breathy sub-tone – Bernstein has returned to the monophonic texture of the opening, but now heard in bare octaves.

The sparse scoring of this opening for wind (and harp) reflects the film's theme of the lonely individual faced with a regime of corrupt practices. It contrasts strongly with the percussive *Presto barbaro* beginning in bar 20, with its depiction of the seething, dangerous atmosphere of New York's docks in the 1950s.

The Presto begins with a six-bar syncopated theme for piano and three timpani (played by one player, using hard sticks). A second set of timpani enters with this theme a tritone higher in bar 26, followed in bar 32 by three drums of different pitches which give an outline of the same theme. This produces a **fugal texture**, rather like the start of a fugue, but unusually for percussion (Bernstein treats the piano as a percussion instrument in this work). The three percussion entries come together in bar 40 to form a **riff** which then accompanies a jazz-like solo for alto saxophone. Bernstein marks this 'crudely', leaving little doubt about the brash atmosphere he wishes to create.

Bernstein tends to use his large orchestra in blocks. The riff is assigned to percussion (including piano), joined by the entire orchestra for the gloriously dissonant *tutti* in bar 78–87, where the texture is not just homophonic but **homorhythmic** (all parts have exactly the same rhythm). The main melodic material of the Presto is assigned to wind – either the jazz-like timbres of alto saxophone and muted trumpet in the quieter sections, or wind mainly in octaves in the louder sections. The strings have little independent material before bar 88 and mainly double the other parts. Bernstein is of course treating the orchestra like a huge jazz band. Only in

Bernstein

NAM 43	CD4 Track 2
New York Philharmonic	
Conducted by Leonard Bernstein	

Notice that Bernstein cues the trumpet parts for oboes, if necessary. This is because the first trumpet's top B♭ is difficult to produce at very quiet dynamic levels. If oboe tone is used for the melody, then the much easier second trumpet part must also transfer to oboe so that both parts match in timbre.

the last four pages are the strings given a role of their own, and even then it is more in the nature of a special effect, sustaining single pitches or icy dissonances against the forceful interjections of wind and percussion.

These powerful orchestral textures contrast vividly with *NAM 42*, in which Auric presents his short, tuneful motifs in a kaleidoscope of rapidly-changing instrumental colours and textures. Only in the 'suspense motif' that appears in bars 106–107 and 110–111 of *On the Waterfront* does Bernstein fall back on a device that we noted had become something of a cliché in film music, and even here he is careful to integrate it within its context.

Goldsmith

NAM 44   CD4 Track 3
Conducted by Jerry Goldsmith

We discussed the instrumentation and textures of this work in some detail in the earlier part of the chapter, which you should now revise. Goldsmith's score clearly has much more in common with Bernstein than Auric, particularly in his use of riff-based textures in which the piano plays an important role as an extension of the percussion department. Also similar to Bernstein is Goldsmith's use of a large symphony orchestra, often employed in powerful and dissonant *tutti* sections. However, for the special effects he requires, Goldmith adds to the orchestra electronically processed sounds and a range of ethnic percussion and wind instruments.

A further similarity between the two scores is a preference to allocate much of the more prominent thematic material to wind instruments or piano, and to use violins for special effects. The most notable example of the latter is Goldsmith's motif of a high sustained violin note that crescendos into an offbeat semitone above a riff, which should be compared with Bernstein's use of a broadly similar idea in bars 88–105 of *NAM 44*.

Williams

NAM 45   CD4 Track 4
City of Prague Philharmonic
Conducted by Paul Bateman

E.T. was orchestrated by Herbert W. Spencer, not by the composer (the use of a specialist orchestrator is not unusual in film music). However, John Williams would have been involved in the main decisions about timbres, textures and instrumental effects. For simplicity we have therefore referred only to John Williams in these paragraphs.

John Williams' essentially conservative style is reflected in his use of a traditional symphony orchestra – smaller than that seen in *NAM 43* or *NAM 44*, with no unusual or electric instruments and with only very modest use of percussion. Notice, for instance, how the orchestral (crash) cymbals play only two notes in the entire extract – at bar 55, for the most triumphant appearance of the flying theme, and again for its repeat eight bars later.

Unlike the previous two extracts, the warm sound of strings is to the fore throughout *NAM 45* and the music is based on a memorable melody that can serve as a motto theme for the entire film – the type of theme that audiences are likely to hum as they leave the cinema, and quite unlike the terse, motivic-based style of Bernstein, Goldsmith and even Auric.

Williams focuses on the use of straightforward material presented in a familiar context. The quaver patterns in the introduction are rhythmically much simpler than Bernstein's riff and their totally diatonic structure is far less complex than Goldsmith's ostinati.

The textures are mainly **homophonic** – homorhythmic in the eight-bar introduction, and **melody-dominated homophony** ('tune and accompaniment') in most of the remainder. The orchestration gives prominence to the melody which, on its main appearances, is presented in octaves by woodwind and most of the strings, the accompaniment for brass and piano being supportive and chordal

A varied repeat of the main tune in bar 17 includes a **countermelody** (heard in alternate bars) for flutes and bells that is then developed in the transitional section which begins in bar 25. Chugging quavers in the accompaniment also link this section with earlier material. A return of the main theme in the dominant occurs at bar 34. A second transition (bar 42) includes contrasts between string **tremolo** and **pizzicato** (bars 46–50) and leads to a grand restatement of the flying theme in the tonic (starting at bar 55), with the melody in double octaves. Notice how changes in instrumentation have helped to define the structure of the music.

When the theme is repeated Williams adds some brief **imitation** for horns (bar 63) but the repeat is curtailed by the interruption of the coda (bar 69). **Parallel chords** ascend in a quasi-imitative fashion (bars 69–73) and an altered version of the opening of the flying theme makes two final, dissonant appearances (bars 75 and 78), before bells restore order and spiral heavenwards on a broken chord of pure C major.

Barrington Pheloung's **unusual combination of instruments** (oboe, *four* horns, piano, harp and strings) forms an ensemble of chamber-music proportions, contrasting vividly with the instrumentation for symphony orchestra used in all the other works in this area of study. The texture is very sparse throughout, consisting mainly of melodic fragments in the wind or piano, heard against sustained notes played by muted strings. The strings move between single pitches (usually doubled) and two (rarely three) simultaneous pitches. The term homophony doesn't really describe such an unusual texture.

The huge contrast between this and the film scores we have studied comes about mainly because Pheloung's 'Morse' music is intended to be an adaptable and non-intrusive background for domestic viewing of television drama. The intensity of a full orchestra, which can be so impressive when heard over the sound system of a large cinema, can seem compressed and out of proportion in the living room. And so Pheloung uses minimal resources to create an ambient mood in which quiet, individual sounds register on a subconscious level, never seeking the attention demanded by the film scores of Bernstein, Goldsmith or Williams.

The work falls into three sections, **defined by instrumentation**:

✦ The first section, ending in bar 52, uses upper strings in a **low register**, piano and horns (either two in unison, or just one)

✦ The second section overlaps with the first, starting with the first entry of the oboe in bar 49 – apart from the oboe replacing the horn, there are few significant changes

✦ The third section begins at bar 98, and is differentiated by the first appearance of low strings and harp, and by the use of all four horns (in unison). Textures are thicker in this concluding section, and the melodic fragments are closer together, but at no point does Pheloung use all of his instruments together.

In the first section, much of the fragmentary material is introduced by the pianist (rarely playing more than two notes at a time) and later by the horns. These ideas are often reflected by the other

Pheloung

NAM 46	CD4 Track 5
Conducted by Barrington Pheloung	

Notice that horns are notated at *sounding* pitch in this work.

instruments. For instance, the initial intervals in the piano part (a rising 4th followed by a descending 3rd) trigger an inversion in the strings which is extended into a long sequence of slowly descending 4ths and rising 3rds: E–B–D– A–C–G (the last note in the lower parts only). Meanwhile, an extended descending 2nd in the horns (A–G, bars 12–19) is compacted and inverted by the piano and extended to form a three-note figure (D–E–A, bars 17–19). At the same time, the first violin answers the horn's falling 2nd with a rising 2nd (C–D, in bar 18). The close association of tiny intervallic cells like these can be found throughout *NAM 46*, their simplicity often disguised by the use of irregular note-lengths and parts changing in pitch level at different times.

Pheloung restricts most of his instruments to a **very narrow range** – horns never exceed a 5th, the strings are used only in their lower register, and cello, bass and harp are silent until the final section. Similarly, dynamics only once (in bar 107) rise above *mf*.

Horner

<table>
<tr><td>*NAM 47*</td><td>CD4 Track 6</td></tr>
<tr><td colspan="2">City of Prague Philharmonic
Conducted by Nic Raine</td></tr>
</table>

Titanic was designed to be a blockbuster of epic proportions and, in the long tradition of such films, the score is written for lavish resources, requiring a large symphony orchestra and choir to which are added, more unusually, parts for synthetic vocal sounds. James Horner explained why in a radio interview in December 1997:

> We wanted to find something that would emotionally tell the story, but musically would not ... bring its own baggage with it. I was very nervous about using a big orchestra because I didn't want it to be some big Hollywood 1940s sinking spectacle. I was looking for some-thing really very personal and human, which is why I chose the voice. And I used the synths to give it a slightly contemporary feeling and also a slightly timeless feeling at the same time ... To me, the big orchestra had to be used for the most spectacular things in terms of sheer size and scope, primarily the sinking. I couldn't solve those problems with synthesisers or with a more rarified approach.

Horner's orchestration in *NAM 47* involves much doubling of parts, with little use of solo timbres. For instance, in the **imitative** opening the choir is doubled by both woodwind and strings. Similarly, in bars 21–24 both horns and trombones play the same pitches as the upper strings, but in a simpler, more legato version (sometimes described as a **heterophonic texture**). As other wind instruments are added, they too double the strings – mainly at the unison. This preference for doubling is most noticeable in the part for synthe-siser, which is rarely used as an instrument in its own right. Instead it adds colour to the strings in bars 37–48 (and rhythmic accents in similar later passages) or it thickens the middle of the orchestral texture in places such as bars 28–29.

Textures familiar from our earlier film studies include:

✦ Ostinato patterns over pedals (bars 8–20)

✦ Simple two-part counterpoint and the use of a pedal point to define tonal areas (both in bars 30–36)

✦ Clear homophonic writing (bars 37–48)

✦ Occasional contrapuntal interest (horn countermelody starting in bar 90).

Horner tends to avoid brilliance in his orchestral sound, seldom making use of the upper register in strings or woodwind. For instance, when the main choral theme is transferred to the orchestra in bar 57 he writes for unison violins in their middle register and the accompaniment is simply a triplet figure hovering around middle C, played by horns and violas in unison. Compare this with the classic scoring in bars 55–68 of *NAM 45*, in which strings sing out the theme in double octaves, supported by upper woodwind. Horner's emphasis is not on brilliance, but on the weight of the low pedal D, assigned to cellos, double basses, tuba, bassoons and double bassoon, all in their lowest register.

Notice one of the great clichés of film scoring used to underpin the crescendo in bar 79 – a suspended cymbal roll (plus a glittering stroke across a bell tree) and a long upward *glissando* from the two harps. Just as effective, but similarly redolent of a film composer's catalogue of memorable devices, is the atmospheric ending. Over a tonic pedal in the strings, a solo horn makes a final reference to the main theme, echoed by flute (doubled by clarinet and dainty glockenspiel), while harps delicately arpeggiate chords of B major. Perhaps surprisingly, the extract ends on a bare 5th (B and F♯), but the sweetness of the major 3rd (D♯) lingers on in our ears.

Private study

1. Describe the texture used in bar 19 of *NAM 42*.

2. (i) In *NAM 43*, what is the *sounding* pitch of the highest horn note in bars 1–6?

   (ii) Explain what is meant by a rim shot and flutter-tonguing, giving examples of each from *NAM 43*.

   If you have difficulty answering this, reread the AS Guide (page 111).

3. Comment on the orchestral textures in bars 69–73 of *NAM 45*.

4. (i) What special effect is used by the upper strings throughout *NAM 46*?

   (ii) In *NAM 46*, how does the viola part relate to the violin parts in bars 1–13?

5. How successful is James Horner at showing the potential of the synthesiser in combination with a large orchestra in *NAM 47*?

Sample questions

In the exam there will be two questions on this topic, from which you must choose to answer **one**.

(a) How do the textures of *NAM 46* differ from those of *NAM 42*?

(b) Compare and contrast the ways in which John Williams and Leonard Bernstein use instruments in the works you have studied.

(c) What differences in instrumentation and textures are there between *NAM 44* and *NAM 47*?

Popular music and jazz

There are *three* Special Focus works, *NAM 49*, *NAM 55* and *NAM 56*, all of which must be studied if you are taking the exam in 2006 or 2007.

Most of the music in this area of study was created without the use of detailed notation. The scores in the *New Anthology* are transcriptions, made by notating the music from recordings. It is important to remember that some aspects of live performance, particularly rhythmic placement, are difficult to notate precisely and can often be written in slightly different ways.

Duke Ellington, Black and Tan Fantasy

Special Focus Work 1 for 2006 and 2007

NAM 49   CD4 Track 8
Duke Ellington and his orchestra

Before starting on this section you should work through (or revise) the information about the context and structure of this music given on pages 123–124 of the AS Guide. Make sure that you understand all of the terminology used in that section.

Structure

NAM 49 has a title that is unusually full of meaning. 'Black and Tan' refers to the venues in Harlem, such as the Cotton Club where Ellington worked, in which black and white people came together, although in a very segregated way (audiences were white, staff were black). A fantasy is a work in which the composer follows his own fancy, often departing from structural norms. But Ellington is also using the word in its everyday sense to express his own fantasy that racial integration might one day be possible. This duality of meaning is reflected in two unusual aspects of the work, both of which refer to the social commentary implied by the title:

Bars		
1–12	*Tutti*	12-bar blues (B♭ minor)
13–28	Sax	16 bars (B♭ major)
29–52	Trumpet	12-bar blues (B♭ major)
		12-bar blues (B♭ major)
53–64	Piano	12-bar blues (B♭ major)
65–75	Trombone	12-bar blues (B♭ major)
76–86	Trumpet	start of a 12-bar blues (B♭ major), interrupted after seven bars by a modulation to …
87–90	*Tutti*	Coda (B♭ minor)

+ The 12-bar blues (which originated in black America) contrasts with a 16-bar section featuring chromatic harmony – a phrase structure and harmonic style associated with European music

+ The first blues chorus is an adaptation of a popular ballad that was familiar to both black and white audiences of the day, and the last chorus is interrupted by a coda which provides a pessimistic final comment by quoting from Chopin's *funeral march*.

The last of these two quotations is as familiar to audiences today as it was in Ellington's time, but the first requires explanation. The opening 12 bars of *NAM 49* are an adaptation of the chorus of *The Holy City*, an immensely popular ballad by the white composer Stephen Adams. Ellington's lead trumpeter, Bubber Miley, recalled it as a 'spiritual' sung by his mother – which in a sense it was, because black Americans identified with the song's dream of a new Jerusalem, where there would be no more oppression. Example 1 shows the relationship between the two melodies:

Ex. 1

The Holy City (Stephen Adams)

Je - ru - sa - lem, Je - ru - sa - lem, Lift up your gates and sing, Ho - sa - na,

NAM 49

The last three bars of Adams' tune (not shown in Example 1) are more freely adapted but remain recognisable in outline. To expand the eight-bar melody to a 12-bar blues structure, the first four bars are spread over eight bars, but Adams' simple harmony needs few changes – except for one important thing. The music has been transposed to the minor mode in *NAM 49*. Perhaps this is a bleak realisation that the new Jerusalem is just a mirage? As a result of this transformation, the bright major 3rd of B♭ major (D) becomes a much more blues-like flattened 3rd (D♭) in the minor mode. Its 'blue' quality is heightened with pitch bends in bars 3 and 7, and in both cases the D♭ falls to B♭, producing the falling minor 3rd that is one of the most characteristic aspects of a blues melody.

The arrangement

Ellington uses one of the common structures in jazz, known as a **head arrangement**. This is based on a harmonised theme known as the head because it is provides the pattern of chords (known as the **changes**) that the players must keep in their heads as the basis for improvisation. The changes are then repeated by the rhythm section, while a series of soloists improvise new melodies to fit the harmonies. Each repeat of the chord pattern is known as a **chorus**. At the end there is a section for everyone (*tutti*) which may be a repeat of the theme and/or a coda.

In *NAM 49* Ellington adopts the most common of all changes, the 12-bar blues, and he uses the type of head arrangement we have described, apart from the two exceptions noted in the bullet points *opposite*. The chord changes provide the main link between the choruses (which could be regarded as a set of variations), but some of the soloists make occasional references to the melodic shapes of the theme – for instance, the fall from tonic to dominant in bar 65, and the cadential pattern in bar 75.

The head (*tutti*)
bars 1–12

The muted trumpet melody is accompanied mainly in parallel 6ths by clarinet and trombone, while the rhythm section provides four accented beats a bar, sometimes in-filled by the piano. The bass outlines the root and 5th of each chord in steady crotchets. The head is **diatonic** (apart from a passing D♮) and its minor-key mood is severe, with **narrow instrumental ranges**, mournful **pitch bends** and no display of virtuosity. The **firmly-accented pulse** negates the legato style of the melodic ballad on which the music is based.

16-bar alto sax solo
bars 13–28

A complete change of mood is achieved with a transition to the major mode, 'western' chromatic harmonies that complement the 'western' 16-bar structure, and the mellifluous tone of the saxophone. The **wide vibrato** and almost constant use of **portamento** (gliding between notes) in this solo are characteristic of saxophone playing in the early 20th century.

The difference in harmonic style is just as significant, including a chromatic **substitution chord** (G♭^{7} instead of F^7 in bars 13–14 and 21–22) and a rapid **cycle of 5ths** in bars 19–20. The solo is also rhythmically more complex than the head, particularly in its use of **cross-phrasing** (the patterns of three quavers that cross the usual divisions of beats and bar-lines in bars 17–18 and 25–26). The first eight bars of this section are given a varied repeated in bars 21–28, still with an accompaniment of chords on low reeds.

Double chorus: trumpet solo
bars 29–52

A plunger mute is like the rubber suction cup on a plumber's plunger. It produces a very thin sound when the plunger is in. Alternating between closed and open positions creates the characteristic brass 'wah-wah' effect.

The style of writing in the previous two sections would have required notated parts rather than improvisation. But from here until bar 84 Ellington makes provision for improvised solos that each act as a showcase for the talents of the principal players.

At bar 29 the blues changes return and Ellington's co-writer, lead trumpeter Bubber Miley, takes two consecutive choruses (24 bars). **Virtuosity** immediately comes to the fore with Miley's slide up to a top B♭, held for four bars. Much of the rest of the solo features Miley's rhythmic freedom as an improviser, which is thrown into relief by the stark accompaniment from the rhythm section. His melodic style is characterised by frequent blue notes and slides, and by his use of the **plunger mute** and the growling effects that are such a feature of Ellington's *jungle style*.

The **growl effect** is described by Duke Ellington's trumpet-playing son, Mercer, in the following passage. Like many jazz musicians, he refers to the trumpet as a 'horn' :

> There are three basic elements in the growl: the sound of the horn, a guttural gargling in the throat, and the actual note that is hummed. The mouth has to be shaped to make the different vowel sounds, and above the singing from the throat, manipulation of the plunger adds the wah-wah accents that give the horn a language. I should add that in the Ellington tradition a straight mute is used in the horn besides a plunger outside, and this results in more pressure. Some players use only the plunger, and then the sound is usually coarser, less piercing, and not as well articulated.

Supporting the solo, the blues changes remain mainly simple and triadic, the harmonic interest arising mainly from the interaction of the improvisation against these chords. However, sevenths are sometimes added (bars 32 and 33) and chord substitutions start to appear – for instance, ii^7 (Cm^7) instead of V in bars 37 and 49.

Piano solo
bars 52–64

A secondary dominant is a chord used as a dominant of a *chord* (other than I) rather than as the dominant of a key. In bar 54, C^7 is the dominant 7th of F, and F^7 in turn is the dominant 7th of $B♭^{(7)}$ (the chord which follows in bar 55).

Ellington's piano solo overlaps with the end of the previous section because it begins with a **pick-up** (bar 52) before the blues chorus proper starts again in bar 53. This section forms a **break** (an unaccompanied solo) and the absence of other instruments allows Ellington much greater freedom with the blues chord-pattern. Thus, chord subsitutions can become much more adventurous, including **secondary dominant chords** (C7 and F7 in bar 54), a **diminished 7th** in bar 58, and a **cycle of 5ths** (bar 59^3–64).

Duke Ellington uses a style known as **stride piano**, in which the left hand has strikingly wide leaps between bass notes and chords. The right hand is equally athletic, with more wide leaps and rapid decoration (bar 61). Between them, both hands cover a very wide range of the keyboard.

Trombone solo
bars 65–76

The rhythm section and jungle style return for Joe Nanton's solo (the band nicknamed him 'Tricky Sam' because of his dexterity in juggling both the trombone slide and plunger mute). He plays in the trombone's highest range and, with the plunger held close to the bell, produces an almost trumpet-like tone at the start. The plunger is opened for the growl in bar 67, and this is followed by the characterstic 'wah-wah' sound of the plunger being opened and closed. One of Nanton's most famous effects occurs in bars 72–73

This 'horse whinny' begins with an upward *glissando* produced by increasing lip pressure without moving the slide. It is followed by a long, descending *glissando* that incorporates ripples in pitch and that is produced by the slide.

In many head arrangements, each soloist seems to try to outdo the previous one in virtuoso technique. In this, his second solo, Miley focuses on fast lip trills and the brilliant articulation of rapidly repeated pitches. However, this chorus is brought to a pre-mature end by a surprising entry of the reeds in bar 84. A series of secondary dominants ($G^{\flat 9}$, C^7 and F^7) leads to a return of B♭ minor and the funereal reference to Chopin in the last four bars. The gloom is enhanced by a type of ending rarely heard in jazz – a massive *rallentando* over repeated **plagal cadences**.

Trumpet solo and coda bars 76–90

Private study

1. What is meant by the term 'the changes' in jazz?

2. Compare the melodic ranges used in the first chorus and coda with the melodic ranges used in the other choruses.

3. In the trombone solo, give the bar and beat numbers of the following blue notes: (i) a flat 3rd, (ii) a flat 7th.

4. Explain the terms 'subsitution chord' and 'pick-up'.

5. What do you understand is meant by the word 'virtuosity'?

6. Comment on the role played by the rhythm section in *NAM 49*.

Jimmy Cliff, You can get it if you really want

Compared with the varied textures and techniques of *NAM 49*, this happy song will not occupy us for long. Most of the important details are given on page 130 of the AS Guide, which you should read or revise now. Make sure that you understand the notes on the structure of the piece and the various terms used on that page.

Caribbean music often reveals the rich mix of influences that can be heard in *NAM 55*. The close-harmony vocals of the backing group are a legacy of 1950s doo-wop music (which remained particularly popular in Jamaica), the high trumpet riffs are a feature of music from the nearby island of Cuba and from Mexico on the American mainland, while the tight rhythmic style betrays Latin-American influences. Guitars have a subsidiary role. The lead guitar is used mainly as a rhythm instrument, its picked semiquaver patterns giving an almost calypso-like feel to the texture, while the second guitar provides background chordal support in partnership with the electric organ (an instrument often used in the Jamaican styles of ska, rocksteady and reggae).

Much of the track's character comes from the bass part. It is often low, prominent in the mix, and mostly consists of the root of each chord played in an onbeat rhythm that rarely changes. Its heavy, steady nature reflects the name given to this style of Jamaican music – rocksteady – and differentiates it from reggae in which the bass is usually syncopated and often silent on the first beat of the bar.

Special Focus Work 2 for 2006 and 2007
NAM 55   CD4 Track 13
Desmond Dekker and the Aces

The influence of reggae (which was just starting to appear around 1970) is thus not seen at all in the bass part, but it can be felt in the prominent **backbeat** of the drum part. The drums are supplemented by the fast tambourine pattern notated in bar 5, although this is so far back in the mix that it is often inaudible on CD4.

The melody focuses on a three-note stepwise descent (F–E♭–D♭, the pitches 3–2–1 in D♭ major). This appears in so many bars that it becomes almost as **riff**-like as the bass part. The lead vocal extends to other pitches, but mainly keeps to notes of the **pentatonic scale** and within a **narrow range** – the high falsetto notes in bars 25, 43 and 56 being all the more effective for their rarity. The backing vocals are similarly confined to a narrow range.

The harmony is based mainly on **two chords** (another feature that anticipates reggae). The hypnotic alternations of chords I (D♭) and IV (G♭) are occasionally supplemented with other closely related chords, most notably $V^{(7)}$ ($A\flat^{(7)}$) near the ends of the verses and refrains. The only harmonic surprise occurs in the instrumental, where the **unrelated chord** of E major appears (bar 37) followed by a descent down the **whole-tone scale** in bar 39. When the effect is repeated four bars later, the wind section descends this whole-tone scale in **parallel chords**. However, these are only moments of **chromatic** colour – the song remains in D♭ major throughout.

Van Morrison, Tupelo Honey

Special Focus Work 3 for 2006 and 2007

NAM 56   CD4 Track 14
Van Morrison

Before starting on this section you should work through (or revise) the information about the context and structure of this music given on pages 123–124 of the AS Guide. Make sure that you understand all of the terminology used in that section.

Tupelo Honey has a fairly standard verse-and-chorus form (with an introduction, an instrumental, a middle eight and a coda). It looks complicated because there are many repeats in the score and because neither of the two sections marked 'Coda' is actually a structural coda. Also, it sounds difficult to follow because there is little melodic or harmonic differentiation between sections. The following table unpacks the repeats and explains the form, but you will need to get used to following the score in the *New Anthology* while listening to the recording.

Bars		
1–4	4 bars	Introduction
5–12	8 bars	Verse 1
13–20	8 bars	Chorus
5–12	8 bars	Verse 2
13–20	8 bars	Chorus
21–36	16 bars	Instrumental
5–12	8 bars	Verse 3 (= verse 2)
13–20	8 bars	Chorus
37–44	8 bars	Middle 8, played as ‖:37–40:‖:41–44:‖:37–40:‖
5–12	8 bars	Verse 4 (= verse 1)
13–20	8 bars	Chorus
45–52	8 bars	Chorus (varied repeat)
53–56	4 bars	Coda (repeat to fade)

Van Morrison's style emerged from a complex musical background that started with a childhood in Belfast, where his mother was a singer and his father was an avid collector of jazz and blues records. He left school to tour in a rhythm and blues band, later returning home to form his own group called Them. Despite success, he left this with the intention of quitting the music business completely, disliking its commercialisation. He was persuaded to build a new career as a solo artist in America, where he developed a style that draws on the many influences of his formative years – a fusion of jazz, blues, rhythm and blues, and celtic folk music. Many of his songs, which continue to have a large following, deal with aspects of spirituality, belief and mysticism.

Van Morrison has a reputation for bucking commercial trends, and Tupelo Honey is no exception being, at almost seven minutes, very long for a 1971 pop song. Its structure is shown in the table left. The soul-influenced rhythmic freedom of this ballad at first seems very different to the rocksteady beat of *NAM 55*, but there are similarities. The vocal melody is again based on the **pentatonic scale** (probably Van Morrison's celtic influence). The harmonies are based on a repeating chord pattern, only a little more complex than Jimmy Cliff's: I–III–IV–I–(V). This gives the hypnotic quality and anchors the song to the key of B♭ major throughout – it is **entirely diatonic**, with neither modulation nor chromatic notes.

NAM 56 has an improvisatory quality, and yet the texture seems too complex for true improvisation. The reason for this can be found in the way that arrangements of this sort were developed. As Mark Jordan, the piano and organ player in this recording, explained in an article in *Rolling Stone* magazine, 22 June 1972:

> [Van Morrison] doesn't read or write music, so a lot of times you have to follow his fingers on the frets. Sometimes he'll have really dramatic lyrics but he needs to flesh out the melody. We'll throw out suggestions and he'll tell us when something's not working.

Essentially the arrangement was developed in a cooperative manner by the members of the band. Particular specialist contributions were credited on the original LP – for example, Bruce Royston was credited as the arranger of the flute part. As Van Morrison himself said, 'I need to have guys who can take an arrangement and work on it'. A result of this empirical method of working was that details of the piece often changed in live performance (just as they do in jazz), although the version refined in the studio for this recording can reasonably be regarded as definitive – commentators at the time certainly felt that live performances of *Tupelo Honey* rarely captured the sweetness and innocence of the recorded version.

The inclusion of a short flute solo at the beginning is unusual, although the flute appears in a number of other Van Morrison songs and reflects the composer's roots in Irish folk music. Here it is used to introduce a two-bar hook, played twice, variations of which permeate the song – compare it with the second-verse vocal in bars 7–8, for instance, or compare its second, third and fourth notes with the first three notes of the chorus.

The lead guitar is used as a melody instrument, largely in the upper part of its range, in much of the song. Initially this is in dialogue with the flute or voice, but from bar 21 it takes part in a complex web of counterpoint with high acoustic guitar, saxophone and bass. Note especially how the wide stereo-separation helps differentiate between the two different type of guitar sound.

There is a gradual build-up of dynamics and texture through the song, and the decoration of its one basic pattern becomes increasingly impassioned – especially in the instrumental, but also in Van Morrison's increasingly elaborate vocal decoration (culminating in top B♭s at the start of both the middle eight and the coda). The high tessitura of the vocal and guitar parts, set against a low bass and with piano in the middle, gives the song its warm, rich texture. This is enhanced by its jazz-like freedom of rhythm and hypnotically repeating chord pattern, a mellow combination that produces, in the words of the *Penguin Encyclopedia of Popular Music*, 'an almost unbearable nostalgia, transmuted into art by talent'.

The arrangement

Notice the notation Dm/A in bar 1. This is is sometimes known as a 'slash chord' and it indicates that the chord of D minor should be played with the note A in the bass.

Private study

1. Explain the terms diatonic and chromatic.

2. Write out examples of (i) a pentatonic scale starting on C and (ii) a whole-tone scale starting on C.

3. Compare the use of guitars in *NAM 55* with the way they are used in *NAM 56*.

Sample questions

In the exam there will be three questions on the three works you have studied, from which you must choose to answer **two**.

(a) Compare and contrast the style of the vocal parts in *NAM 55* with the vocal parts in *NAM 56*.

(b) Describe the influence of the blues in *NAM 49*.

(c) Show how bass-guitar parts have become more sophisticated by comparing the bass parts in *NAM 55* and *NAM 56*.

Continuity and change in harmony and melody

You do not need to study this topic unless *Popular music and jazz* is the Area of Study that you undertook for AS Music and which you are now extending for A2.

Before starting work on this topic you need a thorough understanding of the material on *Popular music and jazz* in the AS Guide (pages 120–132). Remember that for A2 the topic draws on works from across the **entire** Area of Study, not just those in one of the two lists, A or B.

West End Blues

NAM 48	CD4 Track 7

Louis Armstrong (trumpet and voice)
Jimmy Armstrong (clarinet)
Fred Robinson (trombone)
Earl Hines (piano)
Mancy Carr (banjo)
Zutty Singleton (drums)

The use of this chord, along with the way the clarinet follows the trumpet melody in 3rds in bars 7–10, strongly suggests that the opening of this chorus was pre-arranged rather than purely improvised.

West End Blues differs from the collective improvisation of the very earliest style of New Orleans jazz in the way it gives prominence to solo playing. This is a fingerprint of the Chicago-jazz style of the late 1920s and the greater use of solo work enabled players to improvise away from the underlying chord pattern, giving jazz a freedom that became increasingly important in the years ahead. Such freedom is particularly evident in the unaccompanied introduction, where Armstrong's rhythm has a cadenza-like flexibility.

In bar 6 the band enters with an augmented triad on the dominant (B♭–D–F♯). This chord is used not merely for its colourful chromatic effect but also because the F♯ is the first note of the theme, and so provides the smoothest of transitions to the opening chorus. It is only in bar 7, when the band so satisfyingly resolves this dominant discord to chord I, that it becomes clear we are to hear a blues in E♭ major, melodically based on a song by Joe Oliver.

NAM 48 uses five choruses of a standard 12-bar blues in E♭. As you can see from the changes shown in the box on page 121 of the AS Guide, the underlying harmony is mainly triadic, with occasional use of 7ths. However, the improvised melodies add a rich vocabulary of extra dissonance, including blue notes and 9ths (e.g. trumpet B♭ above A♭ major harmony in bar 11). Chord substitutions are already evident in this early work (e.g. ♭IV in bar 24).

The third chorus (starting at the up-beat to bar 31) is a duet – a dialogue between the main melody in the low clarinet and the imitative responses sung by Armstrong in his innovative scat style.

Chorus 4 (bars 43–54) is a free, virtuoso piano improvisation, with considerable elaboration of the chord pattern and only the sketchiest of references to the original melody. Can you spot how the 12-bar blues pattern has been embellished by pianist Earl Hines?

Much of the melodic variation consists of elaborating previous ideas, but chorus 5 begins with the greatest possible simplification – the first phrase is reduced to just its distinctive three opening notes. Of course this belies what is to follow – the sparkling, cadenza-like treatment of the middle phrase, and the final piano phrase which vaporises into the tiny coda, based (as was so often the case in the early blues) on a decorated plagal cadence. The plagal nature of this cadence will seem clearer if you read it as $A\flat m^7 - E\flat^6$.

The supremacy of the soloist in this Chicago-style jazz is obvious in the three central choruses, but even in the *tutti* choruses (1 and 5) notice that Armstrong's melodic gifts dominates the texture, the other frontline instruments supplying mostly sustained harmony notes, enlivened with the occasional short point of motivic interest.

We dealt with most aspects of this piece at the start of the chapter, which you should now revise.

Black and Tan Fantasy

NAM 49	CD4 Track 8
Duke Ellington and his orchestra	

There is clear continuity with *NAM 48* in Ellington's use of the 12-bar blues changes – although they appear in a minor key in the first chorus of *NAM 49*. The severe nature of this first chorus, with its mainly undecorated harmonies and narrow-range melodies, is quite unlike the style of *West End Blues*. However, later choruses show a similar use of elaborate melodic decoration and a tendency to decorate the basically triadic harmony with 7ths and chord substitutions as the piece proceeds. The most notable difference in harmonic style occurs in the 16-bar saxophone solo and Ellington's piano break, where we noted a number of chromatic chords and features such as circles of 5ths which are more associated with western popular song than blues harmony, and which go some way beyond the relatively simple chromatic variants of the piano break in *West End Blues*.

Four

Four is a head arrangement with changes based loosely on the 1940s' popular song *How High The Moon*. This forms a 32-bar harmonic pattern (much longer than the blues patterns we have studied), in which almost all chords have 7ths and many have 9ths, 11ths, 13ths and chromatic alterations. The melody line makes little use of the variation techniques seen in the two earlier works – instead there is a process of thematic substitution, in which a short motif is briefly developed, and then substituted with a new idea that fits over the same pattern.

NAM 50	CD4 Track 9
Miles Davis Quintet	

Virtuoso trumpet decoration links *Four* with *NAM 48* and *NAM 49*, but the idea of doubling the opening trumpet melody an octave lower by the tenor saxophone has no precedent in either of the earlier jazz works, both of which rely mostly on solo tone in their melodic lines. Another important difference is in the way in which chords often don't fall on down-beats but are instead syncopated, and how the bass doesn't always play harmony notes – just as the trumpet often plays away from the basic chord progression, creating a richly dissonant counterpoint with the comping of the piano. Throughout *NAM 50* the rhythm players have a largely supportive role, occasionally emerging into the limelight in order to give Miles Davis a chance to breathe.

In the first chorus Davis' skill at melodic elaboration is seen in fast runs, rapid tonguing, slides and pitch bends. These become more chromatically elaborate and rhythmically complex in the second chorus, and in bars 2.24–2.27 he spectacularly ascends through more than two octaves of the trumpet's range, capping this by starting the third chorus near the top of a third octave. In comparison, the final bars of the extract seem almost tame, with melody giving way to a simple monotone, decorated with half-valving.

I'm Leavin' You

NAM 51 consists of a short introduction, six choruses of a 12-bar blues in G, and a coda that fades out. The replacement of the singer by an instrumental in one of the middle choruses is typical of many rhythm and blues songs, and is a feature that was also adopted in early rock and roll. The basic chord sequence is:

NAM 51   CD4 Track 10
Howlin' Wolf (vocal, harmonica)
Hosea Lee Kennard (piano)
L. D. McGhee (guitar)
Hubert Sumlin (guitar)
S. P. Leary (drums)

bars	3	4	5	6	7	8	9	10	11	12	13	14
chord	$G^{(7)}$ $I^{(7)}$	G I	G I	$G^{(7)}$ $I^{(7)}$	C^9 IV^9	C^9 IV^9	G^7 I^7	G^7 I^7	D^7 V^7	C^9 IV^7	G^7 I^7	G^7 I^7

Although this is essentially the same 12-bar blues sequence used in *West End Blues*, Burnett prefers chord IV to chord V in the tenth bar of the pattern (bar 12 *above*) – a very common variant. What is perhaps more striking is the much freer use of 7ths and 9ths in the accompaniment of *NAM 51*. In *West End Blues* such dissonances tend to arise more commonly through the clashes between solo lines and harmony, rather than in the accompaniment itself.

Further dissonance arises from the use of the blues scale, which contains all three blue notes of the key (indicated by asterisks in Example 2), and the minor pentatonic scale, which is the same as the blues scale except that it has no flat 5th. These scales are freely used in the vocal melody and lead-guitar part, while the rhythm guitar and piano stick mainly to the major-key blues chords. Notice that both Howlin' Wolf and the lead guitar also freely mix major 3rds with their blue-note equivalents (e.g. B♭ and B♮ in bar 6).

Ex. 2

Blues scale on G

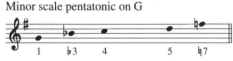

1   ♭3   4   ♭5   5   ♮7
      *   *   *

Minor scale pentatonic on G

1   ♭3   4   5   ♮7

Most of the vocal melody is based on the figure heard at the start – essentially a falling triad of G minor (D–B♭–G). In classic blues fashion this isn't transposed when the chord changes. So in bar 6 a similar G minor figure is heard over a chord of C. Compare this with bar 11 of *NAM 48*, in which Armstrong similarly stays on a tonic-minor chord of E♭ minor while the harmony moves to chord IV (A♭ major). Notice how the vocal melody transcends the four-bar units of blues harmony – the first phrase is five bars long, and is followed by three two-bar phrases, plus a rest to complete the 12-bar period. The many small differences in each verse are a clear indication that the melody is essentially improvised around a composed basic structure. The complexity of the melodic parts is underpinned by a simple bass confined to the root of each chord.

Howlin' Wolf's vocal style demonstrates the impassioned delivery of the urban blues style, and is much freer in rhythm and in its use of blue notes than contemporary rock and roll. The many small differences in the melodic line of each verse reflect the fact that the music was essentially improvised and then notated, rather than being written down and then performed.

In verse 1 the lead guitar leaves a space of three bars for the initial vocal entry, and then improvises short licks in counterpoint with Howlin' Wolf. This is a relatively independent part, unlike the mutual dialogue between vocal and clarinet melodies in the third chorus of *West End Blues*. The piano starts with the shuffle rhythm of the other accompanying instruments, but soon breaks out into passages of continuous triplets, based around the chord patterns.

The accompaniment in verses 2 and 3 offers contrast by starting with isolated chords ('stop time'). The continuous triplets in the fourth bar herald a busier texture in the rest of the chorus, with some high lead-guitar figuration from bar 19 onwards. Notice how one of the band occasionally joins in with the vocal melody at a lower octave – another indication of the essentially improvised nature of the recording.

The fourth chorus features a lead guitar solo, featuring the heavy reverberation popular at this time. The diagonal lines between notes indicate the use of *portamento* (sliding between pitches). The band keep in the background for most of this chorus, Howlin' Wolf adds some simple vocalising in the first few bars, then switches to harmonica (mouth organ) for the rest of the chorus.

After the repeat of verses 2 and 3 the coda features the same descending blues scale from the lead guitar that was heard at the end of the instrumental, followed by a play-out based on the vocal motif from bar 7, accompanied by a short guitar riff.

Rock and roll combined elements of rhythm and blues with features of country-music rockabilly style, so it should not be surprising to find similarities between this song and *NAM 51*.

The familiar chord pattern of the 12-bar blues links this song with a number of previous tracks we have studied, although the blues format is given several unusual adaptations in this song. Bars 6–29 contain two 12-bar blues sequences, but these 24 bars are divided into an eight-bar verse and 16-bar refrain, giving the song a more European feel than the more usual 12-bar sections of the blues:

Honey Don't

NAM 52	CD4 Track 11
Carl Perkins (vocal, guitar)	
James 'Buck' Perkins (rhythm guitar)	
Lloyd 'Clayton' Perkins (upright bass)	
W. S. Holland (drums)	

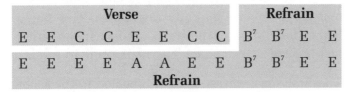

	Verse								Refrain			
Bars 6–17:	E	E	C	C	E	E	C	C	B⁷	B⁷	E	E
Bars 18–29:	E	E	E	E	A	A	E	E	B⁷	B⁷	E	E
				Refrain								

The first of these patterns substitutes chord ♭VI (C major in the key of E major) for chord IV (i.e. C replaces A in the table *above*). This gives the song more of a country-music feel, and a chord of C provides good support for the blue 3rd (G♮) of the key.

The guitar solo starting in bar 30 uses a clever contraction of the above chord scheme, cutting the first blues pattern down to eight bars and substituting B^7 for C in the eighth bar (bar 37) in order to then move straight into the second pattern:

Bars 30–37:   E   E   C   C   E   E   C   B⁷
Bars 38–49:   E   E   E   E   A   A   E   E   B⁷   B⁷   E   E

A different type of contraction occurs in the second guitar break (bars 74–83), which reduces the first blues pattern to ten bars by omitting the eighth and tenth bars of the chord sequence.

Melodic movement is similarly heavily dependent upon the underlying chord progressions, being more often triadic than stepwise. The frequent use of blue flat 3rds (G♮) and 7ths (D♮) in combination with the characteristic falling minor 3rd of the blues (there are three examples in the last four bars) leaves us in no doubt about the strong influence of the blues on early rock music.

The basic harmonic vocabulary of this song is typical of early rock and roll in its use of:

✦ Just four chords (E, A, B^7 and, more unusually in this key, C)

✦ A firm walking bass that outlines these chords, adding 7ths and passing 6ths in the process

✦ No modulation to other keys, and no melodic chromaticism (other than blue notes, and these are so much part of the blues mode that they cannot be regarded as sounding chromatic).

All of these points strongly contrast *Honey Don't* with the modern jazz style of *Four* (first recorded only two years earlier) and link it more closely with the older blues-based pieces we have studied.

Waterloo Sunset

NAM 53	CD4 Track 12
The Kinks	

Waterloo Sunset became a primary source of inspiration for the BritPop revival of the 1990s. In 1995 Damon Albarn, lead singer of Blur, recorded *Waterloo Sunset* (which he described as one of his favourite songs) as a duet with its composer. It forms the final track of the 2002 album, *The Songs of Ray Davies and the Kinks* (Praxis).

The success of this song as one of the most memorable rock ballads of the 1960s is largely due to its graceful melody, contrasting with bittersweet lyrics, and its elegant, traditional structure built around simple harmonic and melodic patterns.

Much of the melody springs from the five-note hook first sung to the words 'Dirty old river' (bars 8–9). This motif is repeated in descending sequence for 'must you keep rolling' and again, slightly varied and extended, for 'flowing into the night', completing the first four-bar vocal phrase.

The downward direction of both motif and phrase echoes the imagery of the lyrics, but right from the start there is a dichotomy between such apparent melancholy and the use of the bright key of E major at a fairly fast tempo. This contradiction is one of the reasons for the song's enduring appeal. The music denies the sad tale of loneliness in the lyrics, and seems to affirm that it is good just to gaze at the sunset – perhaps pride in self is all that matters.

The first vocal phrase is then repeated to the second line of lyrics in bars 12–15, the frequent repetitions of the hook nicely reflecting the words 'makes me feel dizzy'.

For the third phrase in bars 16–19, the hook is dropped, the lyrics suddenly become defiantly positive ('But I don't need no friends'), the melodic line heads for an aspirational top G♯ on 'need' and the first use of chromatic harmony appears in bar 18.

The last phrase of the verse starts in bar 20, and is a repeat of its first phrase, modified at the end. This completes a 16-bar structure in the pattern AABA, known as 16-bar popular song form, that rose to prominence in the music of Gershwin, Porter, Berlin and other song-writers of the 1920s and 1930s. This very traditional structure is used in each of the song's three verses.